Student Politics &
Democracy in Nepal

Nirala Series

STUDENT POLITICS & DEMOCRACY IN NEPAL

Dr. Meena Ojha is a well-known Nepalese scholar and political analyst. She was educated at Tribhuwan University where recently she received a Ph.D for her research in contemporary politics. She has received numerous awards and honors including, *Mahendra Vidya Bhushan.* She works as assistant professor at Tribhuwan University and lives in Kathmandu.

STUDENT POLITICS & DEMOCRACY in NEPAL

MEENA OJHA

Nirala

Nirala Publications
G.P.O. Box 7004
Daryaganj, New Delhi-110002
niralabooks@yahoo.co.in
niralapublications.com

First Edition 2012

ISBN-81-8250-025-7

Cover Design : S.A.A. Wasti

Printed at
H.S. Offset Printers
New Delhi-110002

Foreword

History comes into being through the interaction between historical and a historical process; but politics is deeply rooted in the past and bears fruit in the future. This interesting monograph entitled "Student Politics and Democracy in Nepal (1940-1990)" is both historical and political study by an young scholar, Dr. Meena Ojha, currently an Assistant Professor at Tribhuvan University, Kathmandu. I am extremely delighted to introduce the first fruit of Dr. Ojha's scholarship amidst the world of academics, researchers, students, teachers and the general readers. She has chosen a very exciting theme which can also be labeled as 'Current History.' Current history mingled with recent politics makes the book graphic and fascinating. In fact, the episodes are so neatly and carefully arranged that once you open the book you do not feel like closing it. She has beautifully combined three disciplines -- history, political science and journalism to form a harmonus whole. The main strength of her research lies in the fact that she has interviewed more than hundred active participants in the revolutionary drama of the student movement spanning from 1940 to 1990. Her research does not stop here for she has crosschecked the information obtained from student leaders with interviews with political leaders and intellectuals. This is further supplemented with the facts and figures provided by newspapers, constitutions, bulletins, election manifestoes, journals, magazines and documents, both official and demi-official in nature.

The author is free from any sense of pride and prejudice, which often characterizes the assessments of events so close to our own eyes. Her analysis of the complicated episodes is so clear and scientific, thus free from clouded vision that often undermines such studies. There is another feature that impressed me, namely, she does not indulge in any unwarranted theorisation. The facts which are meticulously brought out before us speak for themselves giving us as a lead to what would follow next.

Dr. Ojha writes freely with courage confidence and competence, which makes the work fruitful and rewarding. I am sure that this book will bring her much honor which she definitely deserves. To conclude I must say, Dr. Meena's study deserves a serious attention and blessings of great scholars in the arena of history and political science.

April 27, 2010

--Prem Uprety

Professor of History
Tribhuvan University

Acknowledgement

The third world is based on the democratic structure. Democracy is not an isolated subject matter itself but rather a lofty pile of outcome of the infinite struggles and sacrifices made by countless people. The rolling of time and the courses of events which keep on playing an endless role in building history also automatically play a prominent role in determining a chapter of a new epoch in the history of struggles. In the same context, the building of the chapter of democratic system became possible in the history of Nepal. Numbers of people have played a very important role in different ways in building the history of their country. Among them, the role of the educated young students has been found more striking and more effective. However, it is difficult to find evidences to prove that the roles of students can be totally positive, because, if comparative studies and researches of the student movements in countries like Burma (Myanmar), Iran and Indonesia and biased student role in Nepal itself after 1960 are analyzed, they are found mostly negative. What becomes clear is that it is not the students themselves but the political leadership that can drag the nation into crisis.

In course of learning and teaching, various questions like, "What roles of students may be there apart from study? What may be the causes of student movements"

Why do only students initiate movement and remain at the forefront? Is it necessary for them to do so or not in the particular contents? What are the causes, and results of the movements? Where and who make the plans and programmes of the movements?" always remained in my mind as matters of curiosity and subjects of studies as well as researches. I was always haunted by such burning curiosity and could not satisfy myself without doing anything less than this research. Being confined to these thoughts and perceptions, I began to study the student movements and the democratic movement of Nepal along with the world student movements, their causes and outcomes. After the study, I arrived at the conclusion that, leaving aside some exceptions, the role of young educated students in democratic movements becomes earthshaking. Hence, I decided to carry out research on the title, "Student Politics and Democracy in Nepal."

I am extremely grateful to Head of Central Department of History of the Tribhuvan University, Prof. Dr. Tulasi Ram Vaidya who gave me valuable advice, instructions, and helped me in naming the title towards the end of this research.

It is my sincere duty to express gratitude to Prof. Dr. Prem Raman Uprety, of the Central Department of History, T.U. I would like to thanks him for his valuable suggestions, ideas and good will for the completion of my task.

Democratic and student movements of Nepal is itself a very complicated subject. While writing this, I have fully tried to be without any prejudice and misjudgment. I have tried my best to get to the truth by consulting the students who participated in the movements and interviewed those who led the student movements at different times. These students remain the main sources of my research. Their names have been mentioned in the bibliography. I would like to express my gratitude to them for their help in completing this work. They told me without irritation about the sweet and bitter experiences of what their lives, of what they saw and underwent in the courses of students movements. I would also like to thank the intellectuals, specialists of the related fields and all the well wishers and comrades for their kind help.

The posters, booklets, leaflets, bulletins and several materials provided by different student organisations proved to be of great support for which I cannot help without thanking the related organisations.

I am also indebted to the families of National Department of Archaeology, National Library, Central Library of the Tribhuvan University, Keshar Library, Madan Library, Gorkhapatra Corporation, Ministry of education, Ministry of Home Affairs as well as different newspaper publications. And I express gratitude to my family members for lending me their kind and encouraging hands in this mission.

Above all, I wish to thank Yuyutsu RD Sharma for valuable advice as Editor, Nirala Series. I am also indebted to Nirala Publications, New Delhi for bringing this book out in time to make my study known to the world.

-- Meena Ojha

Contents

Chapter -V
STUDENT UNREST 1950-1990

Student Politics &
Democracy in Nepal

CHAPTER ONE

Introduction & General Background

Historic events in different countries have testified to the fact that there is no dearth of people fighting for liberation if the nation is under colonial tutelage, struggling for rule of law and democracy. The journey of human emancipation from subjugation and tyranny does not stop. The dictatorial regimes collapse and totalitarian polity and autocratic governments fall due to sacrifices of the people who are dedicated to fight till their last breath.

The development and modernization of Europe has been the result of the contribution made by educated elites and intelligentsia. The revolutionary events and changes in the world have been triggered off on account of the ideas and thoughts of the educated elites and intelligentsia. Magnacarta of the United Kingdom, American war of Independence, Bolshevik revolution, Chinese revolution, French revolution and Independence movement in India are some of the examples which can be directly attributed to the growth and development of educated elites and intelligentsia.

Educated intelligentsia is a group of people involved in writing, and reading. It is also called as one involved in acquiring education. Another group of educated intelligentsia is one that is associated in learning and teaching activities. It is the group of people that gives intellectual inputs and nourishment to the nations, and in case of need launches struggle in restoring rights of the people and nation. In fact, students who are also called a category of educated intelligentsia are dynamic section of intelligentsia who fight for rights through recourse to demands and sloganeering.

In the Third World, students are the conscious and progressive group of the society. Majoworld events have shown that students who have borne major responsibilities also become a focal point of change. After the Second World War, the nations have fought liberation movement in which the role of student has been a crucial one. Students have become a militant fighting force to overthrow colonialism and external domination so as to achieve national liberation.[1]

Student movements have achieved major successes. They constitute milestones in political changes in the world. Some of the notable successes are as follows:

In 1995, students overthrew Peron in Argentina. Students launched movement for freedom in Poland in 1956. In 1990 students resorted to agitation to protest security alliance between Japan and the USA. In 1996 students launched anti-Sukorneo agitation, French students launched struggle against De Gaulle which was successful and caught imagination of the people across Europe. Similarly in Pakistan, students waged struggle against Ayub Khan in 1969. Likewise, 1919 movement and Tinamein Square Movement of 1990 in China are said to be the highest form of student movement: Korean student movement, Bangladeshi student movement, anti Shahen Shah struggle of students in Iran are prominent of the recent times.

The student movements launched in Nepal during 1972, 1975 and 1979 have occupied prominent place in recent times. In course of student movements, hundreds of students scarified their lives for democracy, humanism and liberty. Other smaller events of struggle launched by students are of greater positive consequences.

The role of students for revolutionary causes in their respective contents has been appreciated by leaders and statesmen in significant terms. Leader of the Democratic People's Republic of Korea (DPRK) Comrade Kim-Il-Sung has thus summarized the role of youths and students- "In South

Korea students are in the forefront of struggle for change and in course of their struggle they shall emerge as the potential agent of revolutionary change." In fact, students have played key role towards social reforms, liberation and socialist transformation of the society.[2]

The history of movements of Nepali students can be traced from the time when religious platforms were used for student movements. Students engaged in religious studies or receiving lessons from religious discourses demanded that there should be no discriminations and inequalities and they should be guaranteed the right to receive education. The dispute between teacher and students in this context is sufficient. Many ups and downs have been witnessed following that. Though education may be based on religion, in the changing context the teachers-learning environment should be adapted to modern changes.

In the medieval society of Nepal, there were a great number of political intrigues and conflicts; opportunity and education was not widespread. The unification of Nepal was carried out during the 19th century. The post-unification period saw the rise of court intrigues and manouvering. The family rule of the Ranas was established by Jung Bahadur Rana. The Rana rule shut all possibilities for the spread and development of mass-education. It adopted the policy of intervention in the field of education. During the greater part of Rana rule people led a life of slavery and bondage. During the Rana family rule, there were some reform minded rulers like Dev Shumshere. He was the leading Rana ruler who had an inclination to serve the people by introducing reforms in the field of education. In 1901 A.D. restriction was clamped on the propagation of education. As a consequence, Dev Shumshere was ousted and exiled from the country. This event evinced an interest in the people to search for an acquisition of knowledge secretly. But they were not in a position to express their interest in education and hunger for knowledge. Slowly people started to hate the Rana's oppressive rule. The contempt of the Rana rule in the heart of the Nepalese people ignited the sparks of revolt. In fact it was a century ago that the rebellion gathered in the mind of people against the Rana autocracy. In 1901 A.D. Dev Shumshere had started the publication of "Gorkhapatra" and established some schools. This initiative dawned upon in the mind of people a feeling of rebellion and resistance against the oppressive rule. The second important event in this context was the publication of *Makai Ko Kheti* written by Krishna Lal Adhikari. This book also sowed the seed of revolt against the Rana Rule. The third is the *Jayatu Sanskritam* movement that gave significant contribution in the fight against the oppressive rule of the Ranas.[3]

Though the political environment for education development and modernization of the Nepalese society was not conducted at that time,[4] Nepalese youths and students marched ahead. They were greatly inspired by the independence struggle of the neighbouring country, India. The World Wars created and spread the wave of changes across the world. The non-cooperation movement launched in India against the British rulers perpetrated deep inside Nepal. *Subba* Devi Prasad Sapkota, *Khardar* Krishna Prasad Koirala, Surya Bikrama Gywali, Dharanidhar Koirala and Thakur Chandan Singh started to speak and write against the Ranas from Varanasi. Similarly students studying in Calcutta including Tulsi Man Singh and his friends met Annie Beseant and associated themselves with the Theosophical Society. They also created students' organization. The news that students studying in India formed organizations seeped inside Nepal. This had some effect inside the country. It also gave rise to the spread of mass consciousness.[5] The organized movement launched on behalf of students against the oppressive rule was started in Nepal 50 years ago.[6] However it was not the sudden development; students had a direct and indirect role in the movement against the Ranas. Even before that students had constituted a focal energetic group associated with the publication of "Sarada magazine" and the formation of the *Praja Parishad*. Students also ignited sparks of protest against the Ranas through different media including the use of literacy tools. Students were also at the forefront of the strike at Biratnagar Jute Mills led by Manmohan Adhikari. Moreover, they formed Nepali *Chhatra Sangathan* and also performed major role in the establishment of the Nepal Congress.

1.1 Introduction to Student Movement

Students are the important agents to usher the world to new era. They are the carriers of knowledge and consciousness. Students mobilize opinion and intellectual resource against social injustice and exploitation. Generally, students are not satisfied with the social, economic, religious, political and educational policy of the state. They begin to raise protest against such policies and programmes. They also take interest in the international events.[7] In fact, student unrest is the general occurrence in the developing and less developed countries. Students are the most active and energetic components of the society.[8] Students are active in bringing about changes in the society. Students voice opposition against the corruptions in existing political system. The basic character of the students is to put forth-reasonable demands and launch movement for the realization of the demands. They also exert pressure upon the responsible authority for the realization of their demands.[9]

Generally, students demand for a timely appointment of teachers, an equipped library, arrangement of magazines and journals in the library, well equipped laboratory, sports facilities, scholarship, hostel facilities, accommodation and so on. If the authority concerned is not attentive to the students' demands and interests, political parties take advantage of the disappointments pervading among students and use them as their tools to achieve their political goal. Political parties lend support to students in furthering their interests.[10]

Students are considered as the organized and dynamic class of people everywhere in the world. They share common traits and role. In developing society, they shoulder roles and responsibilities. First they engage themselves in studies and secondly they undertake tasks relating to politics. In fact, this is the demand of the situation prevailing in the developing and less developed societies. Though other segments of the people in societies take part, they cannot spare time and energy in contributing to the political movement. They have family responsibilities too. They cannot march ahead fearlessly as do the students from their own part. Students possess youthful energy and vigour. Students are free from social and domestic bondage. They can easily have access to information relating to global development and current world affairs. They can argue and debate for and against an issue and come to a conclusion. They are active and dynamic, and there are many instances to show that they have performed a key role in toppling the regime.[11] They are very sensitive to the situations evolving inside and outside the country. They raise reasonable demands to improve the situation in the country.[12]

1.1.1 Nature and Definition of Students

As defined in the "Comprehensive Nepali Dictionary", students are those who continuously engage in the pursuit of Studies.[13] The word student includes all those who are engaged in acquiring education. But, in practical life, this word denotes those who are formally registered to study in school, colleges or campus, university in the respective level or below that level.[14] Student movement should therefore be studied as the movement launched by the students formally engaged in the pursuit of learning in university pressing for the fulfilment of their educational and academic demands. But sometimes students involve in activities that are non-academic or remain beyond the purview of educational domain. They take interest in public or national problems such as violation of democracy and human rights and suppression perpetrated by the state agencies. However, the ultimate goal of the movements that do not fall under the academic category is not related to academic pursuits but as they are launched by students they can be said as being the student movement. Student movements have played, important and effective role in different contexts. For example, the student movement of 1979 A.D. forced the then Panchayat authorities to declare for the national referendum.[15] 'Vidya' means learning and 'Arthi' means engaged in the pursuit or obtaining. 'Vidhyarthi' in Nepali thus means those engaged in acquiring learning or knowledge. Student movement is a struggle of students meant for the fulfilment of academic needs and interests. But in the world today, students do not limit themselves to their interests only and take interest in the nation's issues and problems. They are also engaged in other aspects as well. In fact, this is due to their consciousness that they contribute to the issues of the national context. Students perform the role as the youths are supposed to do for their nation. This is the nature of students.[16] Those, who engage in acquiring or learning are students. Those, who are formally and continuously engaged in studying or acquiring knowledge, are students.[17] Student movement is that movement that is meant to fulfil educational interests, offer resistance to social injustice and contribute to the defence of the Nepali nationality. This is the outcome of student's nature.[18] Those, who are contributing to the development of knowledge and have a definite view on the life and world, are students.[19] Those, who study in educational institutions, are the students.[20] Student movement is that movement that is launched by student in case their demands relating to educational development are not fulfilled.[21] In general comprehensive term, we are all students. In practical term those engaged in the pursuit of formal learning are defined as students and student movement denotes movement launched by students, no matter whether the issues may relate to national or global context.[22]

Those regularly studying in the educational institutions are students. Students should fight in defence of their rights and interests. But when national interest is in danger students should not remain as mute spectators and they should launch agitation.[23] Those, who acquire knowledge, are all students in general time. But in special term, those studying in schools and college launch student movement in defence of their academic interests and physical facilities. Students are easily impressed by the immediate environment and context. Those, who engage in study in the formal educational institutions are students.[24] Those continuously studying in the educational institutions are students. There are several examples to show that students endowed with political awareness and consciousness take leadership of movement when nationality is in crisis.[25] Students mean learners and acquirers of education. In fact those who learn from the society and gain experiences from their own activities are students. But those who are admitted in schools and colleges to acquire learning are students.[26] Education helps refine the character of a person. Conscious group of people who are aware of natural and international events and help others know about national and international contexts are students. The word student therefore carries comprehensive meaning.[27] Students are defined as those who acquire learning in whatever occupation they are engaged.[28] Those who acquire learning are students.[29] Besides engaging themselves in acquiring education, the process of understanding about the environment and social surrounding, students must try to be ideal citizens.

1.1.2 Types of Student Unrest

Youths have inexhaustible enthusiasm and energy. This force is the backbone of the nation and students are future pillars of the nation. Students are free from economic, social and political fetters. They may find the prevailing situation in their respective situation quite opposite of what they see, perceive, and understand. They understand the reality of life from the books, school, college, parents and the prevailing environment. They question the prevailing values to distinguish right from wrong, myth from reality. They do not care for their life and take part in the revolutionary activities if they find the situation not up to their taste.

The form and content of student unrest varies from place to place. However, the following can be summarized as the major contributing factors to students' unrest and disappointments-

(a) Child like innocent nature:

Students are potent and organized force. They are the source of new leadership and social support. No other class or group can be as potent and explosive as the students can be[30] students by their very nature are curious and inquisitive to learn new things. Nothing is impossible in their perception and thinking. They are keen to remove the hindrances and obstacles. They undertake attempts relentlessly. As a result, they resort to rebellion.[31]

(b) Ignorance, illiteracy and poverty:

Students by their very nature prefer to be free and prosperous. They find ignorance, illiteracy and poverty as main hindrance in achieving their goal.[32] They resort to the road of protest to overcome this obstacle.

(c) Effect of Hindu caste hierarchy:

The Hindu mythology, religious and social tradition are based on caste hierarchic order. This led to the creation of division and inequality in the society. It also created discriminations among people. The Brahmins, the upper caste people, exercised the exclusive privilege to read and acquire an understanding on the *Vedic* knowledge, to do daily ablution rituals and read religious scriptures. They went to Haridwar or Benaras to obtain Sanskrit education. Some even got an opportunity to have English education. Their fellow students had also the right to learn Sanskrit and gain knowledge of it. But the Brahamans felt that the domain of Sanskrit education is their exclusive privilege.[33]

(d) Justice and peace lovingness:

Generally students favour justice. They express what they see, perceive and experience. Students everywhere want to use the planks of justice. However, they understand about the reality in their later stage of life. They express their discontent in the form of struggle when they are not happy with the prevailing situation.[34]

(e) Imaginary World:

Students have their own imaginary world. They long to live in a world that is free from fears, hindrances and handicaps. But they find it difficult to get it in their family and local surrounding. They, therefore resort to the path of rebellion to achieve their goal.[35]

(f) Equality:

Students have the faculty to perceive and think about the discriminations and disparities in the society. Students advocate for equality. When they find that the society is full of disparities and inequities and dissatisfactions, they agitate to remove these distortions and social evils. Since students are the educated lot in the society, they take a lead in establishing egalitarian environment in the society.

(g) Age factor:

Quite a big number of people may know and understand about the situation prevailing in their respective contexts, but they may not be able to spare time for it. Students are the ones who have sufficient time to address to these national concerns. They can solve the problems facing the nation. Age factor is crucial as the students are fearless hardworking and free from the social bondage. They can offer resistance to the situation that is not in their favour or liking.

Thus, students are at the forefront as the basic and potential groups of the country. They have dauntless energy and enthusiasm. They do not bend backward and they are ready to face difficult situation. Adults do not have the energy that is found in the students. They have imaginary world in their mind, different from the real world. They seek to distinguish right from wrong. When they feel that they are divorced off the real situation, they take recourse to the revolutionary path.[36] Students are the vanguard of the social change. So they are the advocates of change. However, sometimes, they may take to wrong path.

1.1.3 Demands on the Student Movement

There may be several reasons of the student movement. Different events and causes create discontent and despair among the students. The reasons of the discontent may be academic, domestic or global developments. On the basis of these factors, demands are framed and students slowly march towards agitation. In many developing countries resistance against colonialism and imperialism provided basis for students to frame demands and jump into a movement, In Nepal, opposition against the Rana regime provided agenda for movement. There is no denying the fact the Nepalese Student Movement was influenced by the struggle for independence in India. Students studying in India participated in the movement launched against British imperialism. This event made them conscious of their rights and inspired them to work in creating new environment in the country. This helped them focus their attention on the developments inside the country. When needed, they became prepared to press for demands concerning their rights. Demands are both of academic and non-academic nature. It is found that their demands were focused on the fulfilment of their educational and professional interests. The demands included availability of teachers in time, arrangement of facilities like library, laboratory, sports, hostel, fooding, and incorporation of the subjects like political science, geography, economic history civics in consonance with the changing global context[37] (Demands of the 'Jayatu Sanskritam Movement' 1947 A.D.). Provisions of equal remuneration for all teachers, and examination taking facility, establishment of colleges and universities in the country, freeing education from the government interference, concessional school fee, subsidized transportation facilities for students, adequate provision of road, bridge, bus and other means of transportation were some of the demands put forward at that time. If the concerned agencies failed to pay heed to these demands in time, students go astray and political parties tend to impart their influence in the student activities.[38]

The demands of the academic character confine within the educational institutions. When these demands are not resolved of fulfilled, the dimension of demands goes beyond the educational institutions. National and international demands are added to the educational demands. Students express their resentment over educational problems. Later, political issues are added due to the influence of political parties. Political causes can be both national and international.[39] Some demands are based on the international events such as the US intervention is Indo-China, Indian annexation of Sikkim, Soviet intervention in Afghanistan. Assassination of Pakistan's Prime Minister Zulfikar Ali Bhutto and so on. Similarly in the national issues were the end of the Rana regime, India's encroachment in Susta, protest against the Treaty of 1950 with India, opposition of National Guidance Act, opposition of the Partyless Panchayat Polity and protest against the New Education Plan of 1971 A.D. Other demands included the restoration of multiparty democracy, price hike, and abolition of some of the Draconian acts.[40]

In many countries, student movements are directed against the government policy. In the countries where there is no democracy, the first and foremost demand is the establishment of democracy. The students, however, do not directly demand for the establishment of the multiparty democracy. They conceal their political interests in the garb of academic demands. They commit to academic demands fearing that the government can be repressive against them; though the intrinsic urge of their movement is to carry the message for the establishment of democracy. In 1989, when the Chinese students launched movement against the totalitarian communists, their demands were not semi-political.[41]

References

1 Gobardhan Rana, *Prajatantrik Andoloan ma Nepal Bidhyarthi Sangha* (The Nepal Students' Federation in the Democratic Movement), (Kathmandu: Nepal Students' Federation, Western Zones Co-ordination Committee, 1994), p. 1.

2 *Larko Bulletin*, Bulletin No. 2, (Kathmandu: Nepal Krantikari Vidyarthi Sang, Nepal Revolutionary Students Federation), p. 8.

3 Ramchandra Paudel, "Jayatu Sanskritam Andolan Aitihasik Paripachya", (Jayatu Sanskritam Movement Historical), *Gorkhapatra Daily*, 2054, Marga 30 (1997, Dec., 15, Monday), p. 4., see also Prem R. Uprety, *Political Awakening in Nepal: The Search for a New Identity* (New Delhi: Common Wealth Published, 1992), pp. 25-30.

4 Prem R. Uprety, *Political Awakening in Nepal: The Search for a New Identity*, (New Delhi: Common Wealth Published, 1992), pp. 25-30.

5 Bhim Bahadur Pandey, *Tes Bakhat ko Nepal* (The Then Nepal), Vol. I, II & III, (Lalitpur: Research Center for Nepal and Asian Studies, 2039 B.S. (1982), p. 12.

6 *Ibid*.

7 Soorya Lal Amatya, Jagadish Agrawal & Kirshna P. Pradhan, *A Study of Student-Problem in Tribhuvan University*, (Kirtipur: TU, Rector's Office, Research Division, 1980), p. 1.

8 From an interview with Tirtha Ratna Bajracharya on 1998/10/2, Kathmandu.

9 Amatya, Agrawal & Pradhan, f.n. No. 7.

10 From an interview with Yadu Nath Khanal on 1998/7/2, Kathmandu.

11 From an interview with B.C. Malla on 1996/4/15, Kathmandu.

12 From an interview with Kashi Raj Upadhaya on 1997/2/5, Kathmandu.

13 *Nepali Comprehensive Dictionary*, (Kathmandu: Royal Nepal Academy, 1983 A.D.), p. 1220.

14 From Interview with Bhuvan Lal Pradhan on 1997/3/7, Kathmandu.

15 *Ibid*.

16 From interview with Ganesh Ballav Pradhan on 1997/3/15, Kathmandu.

17 From on interview with Shambhu Ram Shrestha on 1998/9/2, Kathmandu.
18 From an interview with Diwakar Bikram Rana on 1998/9/7, Kathmandu.
19 From an interview with Mahesh Kumar Upadhya on 1998/9/15, Kathmandu.
20 From an interview with Yagya Prasad Acharya on 1997/11/6, Lalitpur.
21 From an interview with Bipin Koirala on 1997/4/10, Kathmandu.
22 From an interview with Prithu Charan Baidya on 1996/2/19, Bhaktapur.
23 From an interview with Niranjan Thapa on 1996/2/20, Kathmandu.
24 From an interview with Prem Suwal on 1996/2/22, Bhaktapur.
25 From an interview with Bala Bahadur K.C. on 1997/7/25, Kathmandu.
26 From an interview with Bishnu Bahadur Manandhar on 1997/7/28, Kathmandu.
27 From an interview with Shiva Prasad Bhattarai on 1997/7/11, Kathmandu.
28 From an interview with Dilli Raman Regmi on 1997/7/20, Kathmandu.
29 From an interview with Hikmat Singh Bhandari on 1997/5/2, Kathmandu.
30 Rana, f.n. No. 1, p. 2.
31 From the interview with Kamal Raj Regmi on 1997/5/10, Kathmandu.
32 *Ibid.*
33 *Ibid.*
34 From interview with Tirth Ratna Bajracharya on 1998/10/21, Kathmandu.
35 *Ibid.*
36 From interview with Sharan Bikram Malla on 1996/1/19, Kathmandu.
37 From interview with Shree Bhadra Sharma on 1996/1/25, Kathmandu.
38 Amatya, Agrawal & Pradhan, f.n. No. 7, p. 2.
39 *Ibid*, p. 4.
40 *Ibid.*
41 Rana, f.n. No. 1, p. 7.

CHAPTER ONE

Political Awakening of the Nepali Students (1900-1936)

2.1 Introduction

Student movements in Nepal were launched with a view to fight social distortions. Students not only agitated over educational issues, their movement is also connected to issues relating to political, social and economic development.[1] They make demands concerning society and launch struggle in a relentless way. The students in general want to establish an egalitarian society, especially in the developing society, they possess the doctrinal knowledge, they are not able to gain practical knowledge. Their frustration and discontent grow.[2] The Ranas held the policy not to let the democratic winds penetrate inside the country. Nepalese people got an opportunity to know about democratic activities. Nepalese youths thus became very conscious and aware of their democratic rights.[3]

Madhav Raj Joshi brilliantly interpreted the aphorism of *Veda* in a scholastic manner. He opposed the practice of idol worship when the matter was raised. Only Har Dayal Singh, a Punjabi scholar, an observant, supported him. He was charged of dishonouring and disrespecting Pashupati and beaten ruthlessly. He was taken round of the city and sent to prison. He was made an out caste. His sons were disqualified from studying in Durbar High School. This event inspired youths to conduct anti-Rana agitation and meet the commitment to bring Rana rule to an end.[4] In 1919 A.D. Amar Raj, the eldest son of Madhav Raj, organized *Satyacharan Malami Guthi* with a view to push social reform. Chandra Shumshere arrested the members of the *Guthi* and sent them to exile. The Nepalese youths who were conscious of the importance of education, thus continued opposition of the Rana misrule.

In 1940, *Subba* Krishnalal Adhikari of the *Kaushal Adda* wrote a book called, *Makai Ko Kheti* and made a satirical expression on the depressed condition of the Nepalese people.[5] Those who consented to publish the book were also dismissed from the official employment and sent to prison. They were *Raj Guru* Durganath Adhikari, Upendra Bahadur Basnet, Chudamani, Rana Bahadur. Altogether 10-11 persons were sacked in this case and sent to jail. Writer Krishna Lal died of Tuberculosis (TB) in 1923.[6] In 1929 over 45 people drafted a petition to His Highness Rana Prime Minister for permission to establish a library. That was not tolerated by the Ranas. Those associated with this Yogbir Kansakar, *Sahu* Hari Krishna Shrestha, Dharma Raj Thapaliya and Laxmi Narayan Josi were arrested and sent to prison. Baikuntha Lal Lakoul, Laxmi Prasad Devkota, Krishna Prasad Khatiwada etc. were fined Rs. 100 each and released.[7] In 1931 an organization called *Prachanda Gorkha* was established on the advice of Captain Khanda Man Singh Basnet, Ranganath Sharma, Umesh Bikram Shah to annihilate official 'Ranas' through bomb attack. The Ranas suppressed their attempt cruelly and ruthlessly. Associates in this organization were tortured. Khanda Man and Maina Bahadur died in prison. This event helped in the spreading the anti-Rana feelings among the people.[8] In 1936, *Praja Parishad* came into existence. It was completely a political initiative. It aimed at the abolition of Rana regime and to establish constitutional monarchy in the country. They brought Ronio cyclo-style machine and printed pamphlets against the Ranas and distributed them. This motivated the people to oppose the Ranas. In 1940 *Praja Parishad* was attacked by cruel Ranas. And those associated with it were cruelly suppressed. Some were sentenced to dealth while others were given life imprisonment. This event ignited the anti-Rana feeling among the people.

No one can refute the role of the Nepalese students to

establish democratic polity with sovereignty vested in the people. In the five decade long democratic struggle, students played a key role on different capacities. Nepalese students upheld independence, territorial integrity and sovereignty of Nepal and contributed immensely to the democratic movement.

2.2 Reasons for New Resurgence and Consciousness

2.2.1 Family Conspiracy of the Rana Rule

Before the Ranas, politics was limited to court conspiracy. The members of the Royal family were not satisfied with the activities of Jung Bahadur Rana. It was established by conspiracy of Prince Upendra Bikram, Jaya Bahadur Kunwar, Kar Bir Khatri. They had made a plot to assassinate Jung Bahadur on Feb. 17, 1851.[9] But Bom Bahadur leaked the secret and the plot failed. However, it is not yet clear whether it was the conspiracy hatched in real terms or a making of Jung Bahadur Rana to sideline Upendra. However, this event sowed the seed of conspiracy among the Ranas. The rule relations to agnate succession by Jung Bahadur was the basis for conspiracy. Conspiracy was growing among the Ranas. The murder of Ranodip in 1942 B.S. by Bir Shumshere and his brothers is an event to testify it. This transferred power from Jung to Shumshere brothers.

2.2.2 Democratic Leanings of Dev Shumshere

Dev Shumshere has a special place as a democratic and liberal minded ruler of Nepal.[10] He had made a great plan to achieve an overall development of the country. He had expressed his wish to develop Nepal comparable to Japan within ten years. He planned to establish parliamentary democracy under the leadership of the King. He opened several schools and started the publication of "Gorkhapatra."[11] He was in favour of restoring power of His Majesty. Fearing that this move will harm the interest of the Ranas, Chandra Shumshere was critical of Dev Shumsher's opening of schools and printing of newspaper like *Gorkhapatra* which transmitted new feelings and encouragement to youth. But the ruthless and tyrannical Ranas did not tolerate it. Dev Shumshere's brother Chandra Shumshere was suspicious and opposed to democratic concessions and reforms in the country. Chandra Shumshere made a plot for the downfall of Dev Shumshere,[12] who was later exiled to India. Gehendra Shumshere and Durga Shumshere were sent to Dhankuta. Dev Shumshere committed himself to philanthropic and reformist ideas till his end. The rule of Dev Shumshere was very short. But his period is very significant for the democratic development of the country. His period gave a substantive encouragement to the people to engage in the anti-Rana struggle. Students in the country and in India contributed a lot for the movement against the Rana rules.[13]

2.2.3 Absolutist/Autocratic Tendencies of Chandra Shumshere

Chandra Shumshere was the first Rana Prime Minister who had passed Matriculation. He was more loyal to British than to his predecessors because of the influence of English education. As he was not only educated and but also ruled for 29 years, he was able to meet his individual and successor's interests. During his rule, the period struggle against the British rule was gaining momentum in India.[14] Conscious and educated Nepalese youths were aware of this new development. They had made their views open against the Ranas through different outlets. Amidst this situation too, Chandra Shumshere ruled the country in a ruthless and despotic way. He was very cruel in suppressing the rising aspirations of the people. He did not let the developments in the neighbouring country India and outside have any influence in the unchanging the context of the country. His period is the 'dark period' in the history of Nepal.[15] Chandra Shumshere was definitely aware of the ongoing development in the world.

2.2.4 Role of Newspapers and Magazines

Newspapers and magazines are the forceful mediums to present the image of world activities. Newspapers and magazines play a role to inform the public about various developments and movements. The British Indian newspapers brought about a revolutionary change in the psyche of the Nepalese people. Keeping in mind, that Nepal would realize the importance and demand of the newspapers and that it would utilize them, the democratic minded Rana Prime Minister Dev Shumshere had initiated the history of newspapers in Nepal by publishing *Gorkhapatra* in 1901.

Another Nepalese to co-operate to this job was Jaya Prithvi Bahadur Singh, whose contribution and inspiration helped Dev Shumshere to have inscribed his name in history as a democratic ruler. Jaya Prithvi Bahadur Singh worked for the *Gorkhapatra* and made efforts to make it people oriented and developed it in a democratic way. This can be proved if we make a study of the *Gorkhapatra* of the time.

We find that he had pointed the injustices, oppression and absence of order caused under the Rana regime through the medium of *Gorkhapatra*. No one could have dared do this at that time.

It is possible that he had been sacked after working in *Gorkhapatra* for 15 years due to his reformist attitude. It also shows how great and effective can the role of the newspapers and magazines be.[16] Likewise, the great leader of Nepali Congress B.P. Koirala once said, "Politics was a prevailing atmosphere at our home. All adults in the house used to study newspapers and magazines considerably and they used to make strong arguments on news from within the country and abroad."[17] The Rana rulers were very careful and took adequate measures to suppress the trend of revolutionary activities which took place in neighbouring India or elsewhere. But newspapers carrying articles and news which arouse people's consciousness could enter the country in one way or the other, and they were read by the people with great curiosity.

In this way articles to make the people conscious of their rights were published in newspapers and magazines. They played a dual role of making the people aware on one hand and alarmed the Rana rulers on the other.[18]

The literary and industrial magazines "Sharada" and "Udyog" and the political magazine "Yugbani" published by Nepali student groups in India also contributed to the democratic movement of Nepal. In fact, the students had made these newspapers and magazines a medium to express their dissatisfaction with the autocratic Rana regime, poverty and illiteracy. Nobody will disagree with the view that the people took inspiration to start agitation from these magazines.

2.2.5 Contribution of Humanist Jaya Prithvi Bahadur Singh

The avant-garde humanist for world peace was Raja Jaya Prithvi Bahadur Singh. After differences erupted with the Rana regime, he constructed Jaya Prithvi Bhawan at Bajhang Chhabisa where he opened the *Satyabadi* School and gave his brothers the responsibility to open school. Chandra Shumshere conspired to keep Jaya Prithvi away from public contact, therefore he appointed him as chief of the *Bharadari Adda* in 1908. Whoever got his proximity became honest, nationalistic and efficient civil servant.

As a result, Nepalese people whether they were at home or abroad got the inspiration to unite against the Rana regime. Most of them were from the community of educated people or students like Jaya Prithvi Bahadur.

Thus the first Nepali to make a clarion call for democracy in Nepal was Raja Jaya Prithvi Bahadur Singh. The phases of people's awareness set a systematic pace from his very programmes.

His role in the educational development of Nepal has been important. His presence in Nepalese democratic movement became a driving force and will remain memorable forever.

2.2.6 Activities of the Government and Public Schools

Jung Bahadur Rana had realized during his European tour that education is the primary basis for development and that education gives liveliness. When he returned to Nepal from Europe, educational institutions in Nepal were non-existent. Therefore, as he returned from Europe, he established the 'Durbar School' in 1983 to educate the boys of the Rana palaces.[19]

The literary percentage at that time was even less than one percent, not to talk of the educated ones. In 1900, arrangements were made for the general public to get education from this school. Though the Durbar High School was opened by the Rana rulers for the Ranas themselves to study and to be run by themselves, it spread the rays of modern education among the people quietly and consistently for decades, as the country's first educational institution and also as the country's first educational institution and a monument of the nation's long and hard struggle for the development of its own educational infrastructure.[20]

At that time, education was almost non-existent even among the rulers. There was no awareness among parents to educate their children. For the general public, education was a luxury.[21] To run a school in Nepal was a strange subject. The Durbar High School was established in such an atmosphere. In brief, we can say that this school has made an incomparable and exemplary contribution in various spheres of national upliftment and development through the students who were the products of this school since the beginning to this day. Besides this, most of the patriots who were ready to sacrifice for the establishment of democracy were students of this school. The revolutionary democratic fighters who struggled to overthrow the Rana regime were products of this school. It can be agreed that there was some influence of the time, but the contribution of the school cannot be neglected.[22] The students of Durbar High School began to know the events around the world during their study. New waves of awareness were created among the people. The Indian freedom movement made the Nepali students excited and courageous. The students knew the image of the autocratic Rana regime and made plans to express through various media their grievances against the regime.

The *Teen Dhara Pathshala* (School) in Kathmandu (currently Sanskrit hostel) also had an important role in bringing about awareness and revival in Nepal. After the historical 1885 incident of Nepal, power came to Bir Shumshere and his 17 brothers. This school was established in April 1887 under special initiative and supervision of Bir Shumshere. Teaching and learning here was traditional religious education through the medium of Sanskrit language only. The glamour of teaching and learning English soon had its influence on the teaching and learning of Sanskrit. Likewise, the students here got an opportunity to think about their own rights because of the Indian independence movement and the world events. The students who were enlightened with the changing times wanted to have their curriculum modernized.

The students who came from various parts of the kingdom mingled together at the school. They used to hold discussions together and secretly participated in events of conspiring against the Rana regime. They were not spared from being influenced from the nationwide tide of awareness against the Ranas. As they saw the awareness among the English learning students, they too longed to bring about improvements in their studies.[23]

They launched an agitation by putting forth demands against the Rana regime. The then government never heeded them, instead it hindered them by resorting to *Lathicharge* and beating them in their processions. The students found no other alternative to agitation. They took refuge at the *Bagmati Ghat* at Tripureswor by abandoning the *Pakshala* (hostel) and the *Pathshala* (school).[24] They named their movement as 'Jayatu Sanskritam' and carried it ahead. A strange atmosphere had been created in the capital when the 'Jayatu Sanskritam' movement was underway.

The people already had the impression that the Rana government is anti-people. And, now, it was evident that they were also anti-Sanskrit or anti-religious. This movement made the Rana rulers think seriously. Therefore, they assumed that the government would fulfil their demands within six months. The students detained were also released. They stopped their agitation and remained in the *Pakshala* (hostel).[25] Thus the students of *Teendhara Pakshala* Sanskrit hostel fought against the Rana rulers for their demand that modern subjects be included in the traditional Sanskrit curriculum. They proved that no reforms can be made without overthrowing the Rana regime.[26] Thus they participated in the struggle to bring about democracy in Nepal.

The *Jayatu Sanskritam* movement has proved that it is difficult for a national event or change to be successful unless the students take part or run such movements.

Similarly, it has been a matter of pride among Nepali students that the *Jayatu Sankritam* movement itself laid the foundations of Nepalese student movement and democratic culture. In this way, the *Teendhara Sankrit Pakshala* was successful in finding a principal role in developing high degree of people's awareness and democratic culture in Nepal.

As for the activities of the schools, the role of the *Satyabadi Pathashala* established by *Raja* Jaya Prithvi Bahadur Singh is also noteworthy. Jaya Prithvi Bahadur Singh, who was himself aware of the national context, international events and was educated in modernity had a clear idea that Nepal needs to spread and develop education and that it can be more effective in people's level. In 1906, he opened the *Satyabadi* School at Naxal Durbar, he himself became the headmaster and taught after printing books from the hand press that was brought from Calcutta. He worked for the raising of Nepalese people's awareness on humanism and human development.

As discord grew with the then government, he built the *Jaya Prithvi Bhawan* at Bajhang *Chhabisa* and opened the *Satyabadi* School in that building and gave the responsibility to run the school to his younger brothers there by igniting the light of education in such a remote area like the far west.[27]

This was the first among public schools to run classes up to tenth grade in Nepal and was second only to government run Durbar School in Kathmandu. This school was established around 1931.[28]

There was a new attraction in the teaching of *Adarsha* School which was lacking in the Durbar School in Kathmandu. Both girls and boys learned together. The school anniversary was celebrated once a year as well as the birthday of Prime Minister Juddha Shumshere with much fanfare.

The activities and carefree atmosphere nowhere to be found in other parts of the country was heart touching. This school also contributed considerably to the democratic movement of Nepal.

During the rule of Juddha Shumshere, Nepal was being influenced by the awareness increasing in India. At that time, many national colleges had been established with the inspiration from Mahatma Gandhi in India. In a move to copy it, some enthusiastic youths opened the *Mahabir* School in 1935 on Shivaratri festival day. This was probably the second public school opened in the kingdom.[29] Fatte Bahadur Singh and Chiniyalal Singh had run this school in their own home at Khilhatole and had not acquired consent from the Rana government. Till this date the youths of the capital were under the waves of mental awakening. To open a public school and to spread education was a great work. The youths of the time were being aware that political and social reforms were possible only after people become educated.

The *Mahabir* School was established with two goals, to develop education and to have discussion on politics.[30] This school had a good impression on the people's mentality and the number of students grew day by day. One after another the upper level classes were opened. The Rana government's attention was drawn towards the increasing awareness among people.

In 1940 most of its teachers were arrested in the valley and the school was closed.[31] However, people's awareness at that time was multiplied day and night. The timely activities of the awakened youths began to increase in education sector as in other sectors. Besides the Durbar School, the Juddhodaya Public School and Padmodaya School were also fully run by the government.[32]

Among the schools opened at that time in Kathmandu, the *Shanti Nikunja* School has a special place. Similarly, at the Nepal *Padmajyoti Pathshala* (School) at the house of Diwakar Bhaju at Nayakantala, and at the school in Naghal Bheda Singh, Amir Bahadur Rajbhandari, Astamangal Bajracharya, Nandalal Joshi, Bhuwanlal Joshi and Kesharlal were teaching many students. The *Shanti Nikunja* School came into being after merging all the students from all the three groups. As current pro-people activities were held besides teaching in this school, the Police Incharge, of the Police Station Chandra Bahadur Thapa, used to call this school *Kranti Kunja*.[33] Being influenced from this school, some enthusiast youths of Bhaktapur opened a co-education school *Shantibhakta Bidhyalaya*.

Similarly, the Nepal *Jayotsna Bidyalaya* was also established for the *Harijan* students in Kathmandu. Thus the trend of opening schools continued among educated youths. The *Tripadma Niketan* and *Adarsha Kanya Niketan* in Patan, and the schools opened in and around Banepa have turned today's shape as *Ajad* Secondary School. Likewise, the schools opened all over the kingdom and educational institutions created for the purpose of awareness have their own importance and specialty. So they which can be a subject of more historical research.

The Trichandra College and the Durbar College encouraged of these schools in creating awareness as a solid form which will be duly mentioned in later chapters on students movement and student organizations.

2.2.7 Influence of Economic, Social and Religious Organizations

Education creates economic, social and religious awareness and spreads it further. The Renaissance of Europe is one lively example, and the *Arya Samaj* of *Raja* Rammohan Raya in India and the social, religious and economic activities are regarded as very important in the context of Nepal. As a result of these events, Nepali youths had secretly opened economic, social and religious organizations and created people's awakening. Most of them were led by students. These efforts were greatly aided by the theosophical beliefs of Swami Dayananda Saraswoti, Swami Vivekananda, Ram Krishna Paramhansa, Anne Besant, Gandhi's non-violence and application of goods of indigenous industries. Under their influence Nepali educated youths opened institutions such as *Arya Samaj*, publicity of spinning wheel, the Nepali civil rights committee, the *Satyacharan Malami Guthi* (trust), the *Adamobari Mat*, and the *Buddha Dharma Uddhar Sangh* and they organized opportunities for earning through industry oriented works and the act of developing anti-Rana opinions in the political field. These works had a positive role in the people's awakening in Nepal.

2.2.8 The First Open Demonstration of Public Opinion Against the Rana Regime

The educated Nepali community was thoughtful on how to create people's gatherings, rouse anti-Rana awareness and how to organize them against the Rana regime. On the other hand, the arrogance of the Rana family had reached its climax. They looked at the people as their slaves and gave priority to their own luxury and entertainment. In the meantime, they decided to hold a football match between the Rana rulers and the people.

In 1934/35 a plan was made to develop the game of football in the same systematic way as the sports council does it today, under the initiative of Major General Nara Shumshere. The Jawalakhel Football Club (J.F.C.) A and B teams, Nepal Football Club (N.F.C.), the education department and Mahabir Thamel etc., a total of six teams, took part in the tournament immediately. Football had already become popular at that time.[34]

From the start of 1934, students from the Trichandra College, Durbar School, and Patan School gathered at Lainchaur to select players according to their playing skills, in playing football. After long tests, Najarman Singh Pradhan, Major General Arjun Shumshere JB Rana, Ram Narayan Shukla, Gopaldas Vaidya, Krishna Prasad Shrestha, Surya Prakash Shumshere JB Rana, Bhim Bahadur Pande were selected from the Trichandra College, Rajendra Bahadur Shah, Shumshere Gurung and Govinda Man Singh from the Durbar School, Keshar Man and Gopalman Shrestha from Patan School, Bijuli Man Singh Pradhan from School Goswara to take part in the tournament. Thus the team of education department was formed and the people were much attracted to hear that football will be played in a new style. The football tournament began in 1934 at Patan Tundikhel with much celebration. Six or seven teams big or small were ready to play. Most of the teams were made up of Ranas and their sycophants, but the education department team had a few Ranas and the rest were from among students of school-colleges and were the sons of general public and therefore naturally they attracted the sympathy of the people.

The people began to encourage education department team as it defeated one team after another.[35] This team defeated J.F.C. 'B' and was to play with the J.F.C. 'A' in the final. Gradually this football tournament brought a political twist. There are several instances as to how soon the people are agitated from an ordinary thing. On April 4, 1979 when former prime minister of Pakistan Zulfikar Ali Bhutto was hanged and the student movement in Kathmandu led to the announcement of referendum on May 24, 1979 as the students were barred from protesting, the winning and losing in the football game instilled on unprecedented fighting spirit among the students and people against the Rana regime.[36] In this tournament the J.F.C. 'A' team defeated the education department team by one goal. Thus the anti-Rana public opinion had surfaced for the first time in an open manner.[37]

2.2.9 Need of the Political Organization Realized

In fact, the educated Nepali youths used to discuss comparatively about Nepal's historical events, world's democratic events, first and second world wars and the Indian independence movement and talked to each other what decisions to take in the context of Nepal. Some of these students had gained theoretical and practical knowledge by being directly involved in the Indian independence movement. Most of the students were of the opinion that the Rana government lacked the elementary human behaviour. From various incidents, they came to the conclusion that the rule of the Ranas should come to an end for which political organization should be active. Thus, most of the Nepalese educated community realized the need of a political organization. So, the *Arya Samaj* and *Prachanda Gorkha* came to fulfil the need.

2.2.10 Efforts Made by Nepalese Intellectuals and Students for Showing Importance and Necessity of Modern Education

In those days teaching and learning of Nepalese history and geography was prohibited in schools and college. The glorious history of Nepal, kings, prime minister, courtiers, people and their historical contributions remained in darkness during the whole Rana period. So both the teachers and students were ignorant of history and geography. If the teachers had known anything, they would show themselves to have known nothing about these subjects. Only text books could be found in books shops. It was terrifying to keep political books at home. The Rana government would keep a hostile watch on anybody who would collect books, read and give them others to read. The Rana authorities had the concept of giving modern English education only to the sons of higher class Ranas but it was also limited in number based on requirement. So, the then Rana Prime Minister Chandra Shumshere after inaugurating the Trichndra College in 1918 had regretted, saying that he had struck his own leg with an axe.[38]

In such a terrific situation, some courageous youths and intellectuals used to collect different books and give them to others to read secretly. Surya Bahadur Bhardwaj was himself an active living library. He used to give revolutionary books to several persons and urged them to read.[39] A person called Biharilal, who used to live on the upper floor of a shopkeeper's house just behind the police post at Dillibazar, had dedicated his life in reading, collecting and distributing different books as if he were himself a library, from about 1923. He would secretly distribute books to several persons walking himself door to door. His unselfish service was really a great one. He would visit door to door to collect the previously distributed books and give the new ones according to the readers' interest. Such services increased the new knowledge and modern thoughts among the youths. They would be known as anti-Rana activists. The young students wanted to read books of modern subjects and began to express dissatisfaction with the Rana Rule.[40] Research and study about such a high minded noble person like Bhiarilal has yet to be done. The then conscious intellectuals had a supportive view to the youths that they should be allowed to read or study modern books and newspapers. They had opened libraries and schools in several places and organized the youths. A decision was made to establish a library in the house of Prem Bahadur Kanshakar. Its name, in short, was kept NPP, and its name in full was

Nepal Pradipta Pustakalaya. The Martyred Dasharath Chand at his last meeting with Ganesh Man Singh and Govinda Prasad in Singha Darbar School building some days before he was executed had said NPP is our life, so long NNP remains we remain.[41] The students used to express their dissatisfaction through NPP because *Praja Parisad* had already gone underground.

The attack on *Praja Parisad* created a new wave of awakening and sentiment among the students and intellectuals in the capital. They began to express dissatisfaction through different media. Among the intellectuals of the capital, Gopal Prasad Rimal was a wise and nationalist person. He made an effort to make the Rana authority, including Prime Minister Mohan Shumshere, keeping consultation with his previous class mates Mrigendra Shumshere, Vijaya Shumshere, etc. that the new age had come, India had already got independence, and in such a situation it would be good to give permission to open political organizations. But receiving negative response from Mohan Shumshere, he conducted a programme of public praying to Pashupatinath to make the people participate and awaken them. The lines of the prayer were as follows:

> *I serve the nation, grant me strength every one may get pleasure and well being from me.*
>
> *The other lines of the prayer could not be found.*[42] *Gopal Prasad Rimal led a public Prayer Program at Pashupatinath every morning and at Shovabhagabati in the evening with a view to arouse anti-sentiment and activate the people against the Rana government. The number of people at the prayer spot multiplied day by day. On the 7th day tens of thousands people assembled at the prayer. Then there began lecture program after the prayer, and the slogan, 'Jaya Nepal' also was chanted.*[43]

The prayer-song of Shovabhagabati was as follows:

The time has come, this is an opportunity,
Now look round opening the eyes wide,
Removing the darkness from the heart,

shed brilliant light on it.
You who can see the Innermost.
How I can name you a blind,
You who can hear voice of the heart
How I can say you are deaf.
What a miserable plight ours is,
Pray, you look only once
O ! Goddess Durga, the Mother of the universe,
hear our appeal, the prayers,
May the nation improve, we hope,
Mend the mind of all
we are the Nepalese, Nepal is ours,
let this feeling arise in all.

Later on, a very beautiful song written by Gopal Prasad Rimal about the emblem of sun and moon one finds marked on the Nepalese flag also was sung after the prayer. This song and the chanting of 'Jay Jay' began to awaken and excite the people's mind and thought. The song follows:

The red flag marked with the sun and moon and the military symbol of ours, burning like the lively blood, the pride of ours never did it but bow, stood firm like the Himalayas, and never did our military symbol fall behind none. When it came to exist, many attacks came on it, Two imperialist attacks were defeated, but our pride did not taste defeat. So long as the sun and moon remain in the sky, our blood remains red of ours own. Those who are living in this world are the sants like course.

The military symbol of ours is the shelter of all. Some days after the prayer was begun, Chandra Bahadur, the Police Officer and Prem Raj Sharma, the editor of "Gorkhapatra" also took part in the prayer at Shovabhagabati one evening to find out the mystery of such activities. At the end of the prayer and lecture program, they said to the mass including Gopal Prasad Rimal: "A very great change is being made by the Maharaja, but you are interfering the noble wish of the Maharaja by pretending to hold prayer programme."

Gopal Prasad Rimal coming forward replied "If the Maharaja bring such great changes, we are praying the goddess for blessing us with the might to take part in the changes in this Hindu country." Saying this, he showed his chest opening the shirt, this action brought a great excitement among the people there. Looking such a situation at the prayer both the government officers slipped away. Next day Gopal Prasad Rimal, Krishna Prasad Rimal, Daman Raj, Tirtha Raj Tuladhar, Pushpalal, and Jayandra Bahadur Thapaliya were arrested from their homes, and kept under custody at Mohan Shumshere's barrack.[44]

These events were of 1946. The students used to express their dissatisfaction and resentment through such programmes. Indeed, its success was massive participation of the students. During the same period, *Shivaratri* festival also approached. They formed a volunteer service committee for the pilgrims who would come to Kathmandu from different part of Nepal and India. Many groups of students and youths at different places like Birganj, Siraha, Rautahat, Janakpur, including Kathmandu formed volunteer service committees and helped the pilgrims.[45] Similarly, they established tent-service camps for the pilgrims at Thankot, Kalmochan, Bankali, Ranipokhari, and other places. Many teachers and students had taken active part in this programme. Such activities of the volunteer service committees and youths could not be tolerable for the Rana government, so the then Police Chief Chandra Bahadur Thapa with a group of policemen interfered the service programme. They looted the goods and dispersed the youths. This action provoked the students further. The volunteers who were bundled in the police van chanted the following slogans for the first time at the center of the capital city. The slogans were:

Long live Revolution !
Long live volunteers !
Long live Padmashamsher !

Similarly some youths had also formed a volunteer organization for the service to the pilgrims who would come to Pashupatinath on the occasion of Shivaratri and Bala

Chaturdasi in 1937. This was a new thing for the then Nepalese society. The volunteers had a uniform and caps of *Khaki Kotica* color. After the festival had finished, the volunteers were called to the police station, asked questions and fined. So this volunteer organization could not progress as desired.[46] Most of the members of this organization were educated youths. The students got an encouragement and enthusiasm from this organization. The students would express their dissatisfactions if they found any fault with the school and campus administration. This would be taken as a headache by the Rana government. The students would be charged with different crimes and punished. They were deprived of education, had to suffer for the rest of their lives. Such events are worth mentioning in the history of Nepal's student movement.

2.2.11 Spontaneous Sentiments Expressed Against the Rana Government by the Nepalese Student Community

The establishment of Darbar High School had caused a stir among the people, especially the youth. They would frequently go to different cities of India for different tasks and business. They would learn new facts about politics, government, independence, war, justice and democracy.

They also learnt that education was the major prerequisite for change and democracy. So they began to seek right to get educated at any cost. But the Rana government held the orthodox view that education would weaken the foundation of their regime. No one was allowed to open a school. The students of Darbar School and later, the students of Trichandra College, Sanskrit School and public schools got the opportunity to peep into the evil mind of the Rana regime. They began to oppose the restrictions imposed on people in different sectors.

During the terrifying days of Rana autocratic rule, no one could venture to stand straight. Whatever the students expressed anger against the Rana atrocity, they were instantly punished.

2.3 Origin of the First Step

Realising that education remains the basis of modernization in the world, Chandra Shumshere, the Rana Prime Minister who himself had taken English education in Calcutta, India opened the Trichandra College in the capital and inaugurated it with pomp and show to spread his own reputation in the international arena. He understood the consequence of setting up the college. So, his government adopted a policy of interference, even in the teaching/learning regulation. But due to the revolutionary nature of the students, protest against the government's policy began to come out. The policy of the Rana government to keep the educated mass as slaves provoked the students. Disgruntled expressions towards the Rana regime began to rise from educational institutions, especially Trichandra College. For instance, the heroic leadership of Dilliraman Regmi, Ramhari Sharma, Dasharath Chanda, Gangalal Shrestha, Jeebaraj Shastri, as mentioned in the previous chapter, is no less important in the democratic history of Nepal. There is also no dispute that the Trichandra College was under restrictions and strict control of the Rana regime over education. Being conscious as well as influenced by the modern democratic environment, the students of Trichandra College proceeded to break restrictions through different ways from the very beginning. Most of the college/teachers were also not in favour to support the government's interference in the teaching and learning sector. Gurudayal Singh, an Indian citizen and a teacher at Darbar High School was expatriated as punishment for supporting the news of Madhavaraj. He went from Kathmandu but he was not seen to reach India.[47] The anger expressed by Amarbabu, a teacher of Trichandra College, against the Rana regime, as mentioned in the previous chapter, also helps a lot to know about the system of the Rana regime. The oppressive actions of Rana authorities such as expulsion of teachers and severe punishment to students, depriving them of education was due to provocative rebellious sentiment in both the teachers and students. In the course of protesting Raina's unjust and tyrannical actions, many incidents took place in Trichandra College. However, two of them described below in detail, played a vital role and occupy an important place in the educational history of Nepal.

2.3.1 Bhava Dev Incident

When the foundation of modern education started, the Rana government had a plan to limit modern education within the predominant Rana family circles and give education as required for the official works. The Rana Prime Minister Chandra Shumshere, after the inauguration of the Trichandra College in 1922, had also expressed regret for founding the college. In those days, except the textbooks no other reading materials could be found in the book stalls. Keeping political books or materials was an act of terror. The government would keep a hostile watch on those who would collect books, read them and teach others or give books to others to read. In such an imprisoned situation, both the teachers and students were furious. They could learn various news of national and international events through different means and media of their own. The teachers knew such news would remain muffled but the students would seek ways to express their dissatisfaction. But the government always found ways to suppress information in various ways.

The education system did not provide any opportunity to the people to learn new things and gain new knowledge. This paralyzed the enthusiastic and high-spirited youth. There was no suitable environment for teaching and learning activities and no opportunity for all those who wanted to get education. Those who managed to get education could not learn freely and the teachers could not teach frankly in that hostile environment. There were restrictions on every side. The teachers' act of teaching in classes, interacting with the students, debating or discussing with faculty members was considered a serious crime and they were given severe punishment. But the students could not tolerate injustice.

We can find several evidences to prove this. The student movements have succeeded in bringing about revolutionary changes in different parts of the world and have occupied a glorious place in the world's history. The role of students in the democratic movement of Nepal also has taken an important place in the democratic history of Nepal. Organized student movement and expression of students' dissatisfaction originated from Trichandra College. Their discontent and irritation make the government more oppressive.

A Trichandra College student named Bhavadev Panta used to speak against college environment, even against the government policies with his friends openly expressing his dissatisfactions. Most of the students used to keep contact with him, hear him and agree with his views. They would enthusiastically take part in the bold and revolutionary activities of Bhavadev Panta in the college. He spoke freely speak against the Rana regime and in the presence of the Rana students in the college. He even openly spoke of toppling the Rana government. Often he would put question to the teachers and claim the rules and regulations of the college were in contravention to the rights and interests of the students. Such bold expressions and views of his had implanted courage and confidence into his fellow students.[48]

Due to the courage and revolutionary spirit of Bhavadev Panta, there began to appear miraculous changes in the Nepalese politics. At that time, other revolutionary students like Gangalal, Dasharath Chand, Ramhari Sharma, Jeevaraj Sharma were also studying in the same college. Bhavadev Panta can be taken to be one of the major factors to inspire Tanka Prasad Acharya's ideas for an instant movement against autocratic Rana system.[49] On the other hand, Gangalal had raised voice against the government from inside the college and given open challenges to the Ranas. For such revolutionary spirit in him, Bhavadev Panta was one of the sources of inspiration.[50] So, Bhavadev, whose inspiration made the Nepalese students organize themselves and launch movements and push them towards putting demands for democracy and finally bring about a fundamental change in the Nepalese politics, can be called the first leader of the student movement. His name will remain immortal in the history of Nepalese student movement in the times to come.

2.3.2 Chalise Incident

The then Prime Minister Chandra Shumshere had established Trichandra College only to show his vainglory. The Rana government did not need dissemination, arrangement and promotion of education. So the autocratic Rana rules were in favour of patronizing and dictating the education sector on their own interest and willingness. But international political activities, environment and new events of neighbouring countries influenced the Nepalese students, especially the students of Trichandra College to be at the forefront. The Trichandra College students understood and assessed that the punishment which the director general of the department of education gave to Bhavadev under the instruction of government was a mean and condemnable act.

This action spread agitation among students. Many of them began to openly raise voices against the Rana government, demanding modernization and promotion of the education sector. They began to keep contact with the other students in India who were suggesting an end to the Rana government by making the education system as the primary issue. The students used to spread anti-government feelings through any form or any medium that might be either during the time of study or in the literary competition or any discussion among them. Despite a strict watch on the students' activities, the government could not get smell of many of them. The government authorities would torment the student for even a trifle matter. In such ongoing context, the next heart-rending incident called Chaleese Incident occurred at Trichandra College. Laxminanda Chalise, a brilliant son of the poet Chakrapani Chalise, was studying in

Trichandra College. He was very talented.

Perchance, the copy reached to Major Colonel Bal Krishna Shumshere J.B.R. While checking the essay he found the blames put on the Rana families and he was so frightened that the matter was reported to Prime Minister Juddha Shumshere J.B.R. If the Ranas were in trouble, the others in and around the palace would be ruined. There is a saying: "either sword or the palace" would be hanging on the everyone's lip of the courtiers.[51] Chalise's essay was again discussed at the government level. Instead of high respect to the Rana family, a student had stained the powerful Ranas in the essay which enraged the Ranas and they finally decided to give a hard punishment of imprisonment to him, charging him of a crime against the state. When he was being taken to the prison, Laxminandan Chalise, bidding good bye, to his friends with the challenging words to the Ranas. "Friends! life is nothing, I fulfilled my duty and you too shall not stray from your duties".[52]

It was a warning to the Ranas who wanted to imprison people's wisdom, knowledge and ideas. In the hellish prison, Chalise suffered from tuberculosis. Soon after he was released; and he died. The Rana authorities expelled his father, Chakrapani Chalise, charging him of being unable to keep his own son under control. The event is known as Chalise Incident.

The event left the students with a deep hatred and contempt of Balkrishna Shama for sometime.[53] This Chalise Incident shall remain as a major point of talks among the Nepalese students. The government widely propagated this incident as a warning, so that the students might be afraid of repeating such things against the Rana regime. Despite such occasional bitter events, and undesirable situation, teaching and learning activities continued in Trichandra College. There was no groupism among the students, because there existed a very friendly relations among them.[54] But as a consequence of Chalise Incident, there grew secret political activities among the students. They began to create a challenging environment for the government by expressing dissatisfaction with the college facilities, library facilities and by demanding for opening Service-Unions and so on. In the same context, a street rally chanting slogans led by the students of Trichandra College in 1947 remains a brilliant example of protest. The Chalise Incident had implanted fresh awareness among the students.

Laxminandan Chalise was also a successful writer. He had an ability to denounce the then injustice, separation, and the autocratic tendency through writings. His essay which had terrorized the Rana regime has been already mentioned above. His writings have been published in different magazines and newspapers including *Gorkhapatra* and *Sharada*.

Soon the students came to the conclusion that miserable condition of the nation should be ended as soon as possible and the first attack should be made on the Rana regime. The aforementioned two incidents that took place in Trichandra College had emboldened the students with fresh confidence.

As a result, Tanka Prasad Acharya got an idea of *Praja Parishad* and organized it under his own leadership. Most of the members of this organization were students. This organization had been like a main student organization. All the members used to fulfil their duties properly. Among them, Bal Bahadur Pandey's role can be taken as an important one. He had got the membership of *Praja Parishad* at the time when he was a student of Darbar School. He was a son of Gurupurohit (Priest) Indraraj Pandey. Despite being a member of an elite family, Bala Bahadur Pandey was critical of the government policies.[55]

After the Cyclostyle-machine for printing leaflets was brought to *Praja Parishad* and there was the need of more members. Bala Bahadur Pandey, Keshavraj Karki, Chitra B. Khatri and many others were given membership of *Praja*

Parishad at a time.[56] Later on, Bala Bahadur Pandey kept the cyclo-style machine secretly at his home at Maligaun from where the leaflets were used to be printed.[57] Ramhari Sharma, Govinda Prasad Upadhyaya and Bal Bahadur Pandey were involved in the leaflet campaign in the Kathmandu city in 1940 during the Machhendranath Bhoto festival at Jawalakhel. They were arrested the same year and taken to Singha Darbar and three months later on the 6th of February, they were sentenced to life imprisonment with property confiscation, along with their other comrades.[58] After 12 or 13 months, Bala Bahadur began to show a nature of mental disorder. He began to sit silent. Later, he began to behave like a madman and finally died in 1942. Bala Bahadur Pandey had joined *Praja Parished* with a pledge to demolish the Rana regime and the pamphlets dispersed for the first time against the Rana regime in 1940 were printed at his home. This pamphaleting became like a "time bomb" hung on the neck of the Rana rulers[59] and shocked their blood-strained regime. Bala Bahadur Pandey, a true revolutionary, never bowed before the oppressive Rana rulers and did never beg pardon but rather lost his consciousness, suffered a lot and finally got martyrdom, leaving a deep impression on the other students.[60]

All these events became a source of inspiration to the remaining students. The 1940 episode awakened the young students in the country. On the other hand, Ganesh Man Singh escaping from Bhadragol prison in 1944 reached India and gave the Nepalese youth leaders and students every detail information about the new political development in Nepal. Indeed, these events made the Nepalese living in India realize the need of a strong as well as resolute struggle against the Rana regime. It aslo made them believe that the base of the struggle should be politics.

As a result of it, "Nepali Rastriya Congress" was founded in India. The students living in India also decided to conduct a student movement against the Rana regime. They held discussion about the establishment of "Students Union" representing all the Nepalese students but it could not get a broad shape. Gradually, the students studying in India began to realize the necessity of organized programmes. This will be discussed in the following chapters.

References

1 Soorya Lal Amatya, Jagadish Agrawal & Krishna P. Pradhan, *A Study of Student Problem in Tribhuvan University,* (Kirtipur: T.U., Rector Office, Research Division, 1980), p. 1.
2 *Ibid*, p. 8.
3 From an interview with Ramhari Sharma on 1996/2/10, Kathmandu.
4 From an interview with Dr. D.R. Regmi on 1997/7/20, Kathmandu.
5 Govinda Prasad Upadhyaya, *Nepal ko Prajatantrik Itihas- Sandarva* (Context of Democratic History in Nepal), (Kathmandu: Ratna Pustak Bhandar, 2054 (1997), p. 21.
6 *Ibid.*
7 Balchandra Sharma, *Nepal ko Aitihansik Ruprekha* (An Outline of the History of Nepal), (Banaras: Madav Prasad Sharma, 1969), p. 409.
8 *Ibid.*
9 Padma Jung, *Life of Jung Bahadur,* (Kathmandu: Ratna Pustak Bhandar, 1971), pp. 156-178.
10 Sharma, f.n. No. 7, p. 45.
11 *Ibid.*
12 *Ibid.*
13 Interview with Bhuvan Lal Pradhan on 1997/3/7, Kathmandu.
14 Sharma, f.n. No. 7, p. 355.
15 Rajesh Gautam, *Nepal ko Prajantantrik Andolan ma Nepal Prajaparishada ko Bhumika* (The Role of Nepal Praja Parishad in the Nepalese Democratic Movement), (Banarash: Sri Krishna Printing Press, 2046 B.S. (1990), p. 18.
16 *Ibid.*, p. 25.
17 *Ibid.*, p. 17.
18 Bhuwan Lal Pradhan, *Nepal ko Jana Kranit 2007 B.S.* (People's Revolution of Nepal 1950), (Kathmandu: Rumuॣ Prakashan, 2047 B.S. (1990), pp. 68-69.
19 *Ibid.*, p. 10.
20 Bhuwan Lal Pradhan, *Durbar School: Samchhipta Jhalak,* (Mirror of Durbar High School), (Kathmandu: Durbar High School, Ranipokhari, 1997), p. 1.
21 *Ibid.*, p. 2.

22 *Ibid.*
23 *Ibid.*
24 *Ibid.*
25 *Ibid.*, pp. 306-07.
26 Upadhyaya, f.n. No. 5, p. 180.
27 Min Bahadur Singh 'Baganji', "Jaya Prithvi Bahadur Singh ko Parichaya" (Introduction of Jaya Prithvi Bahadur Singh), *The Humanistic*, (Kathmandu: Humanistic and King Jaya Prithvi Bahadur Singh, Research Division, 1998), p. 4.
28 Upadhyaya, f.n. No. 5, p. 92.
29 Gautam, f.n. No. 15, p. 49.
30 *Ibid.*
31 Pradhan, f.n. 18, p. 84.
32 *Ibid.*, p. 258.
33 Pradhan, f.n. No. 20, p. 259.
34 Bhim Bahadur Pande, *Tes Bakhat ko Nepal, Pahilo, Dosro ra Tesro Bhag*, (The then Nepal Vol. 1, 2 and 3), (Kathmandu: Research Centre for Nepal and Asia Studies, 2039 (1982), p. 67.
35 *Ibid*, p. 69.
36 *Ibid*, p. 71.
37 *Ibid*, p. 72.
38 Pande, f.n. 34, pp. 208-08.
39 Upadhyaya, f.n. 5, p. 117.
40 *Ibid.*
41 *Ibid.*
42 *Ibid.*
43 *Ibid.*
44 *Ibid.*, p. 120.
45 *Ibid.*, p. 119.
46 *Ibid.*, pp. 84-85.
47 Pradhan, f.n. No. 20, p. 43.
48 From an interview with Ramahari Sharma on 1996/2/10, Kathmandu.
49 From an interview with Chandra Shekhar on 1996/4/10, Lalitpur.
50 From an interview with Dibakar Bhaju on 1997/7/10, Kathmandu.
51 Pande, f.n. No. 34, part I, p. 204.
52 *Shahid ko Gatha* (Martyr's Sacrifices), (Kathmandu: Madan Asrit Pratisthan, 2052 (1995), p. 27.
53 Pande, f.n. No. 34, part I, p. 204.
54 *Ibid.*
55 Upadhyaya, f.n. No. 5, p. 91.
56 *Ibid.*
57 *Ibid.*
58 *Ibid.*
59 Martyer, f.n. No. 52, p. 28.
60 Upadhyaya, f.n. No. 5, p. 92.

CHAPTER THREE

Role of Students in the Democratic Movement (1940-1950)

3.1 Introduction

The Nepalese Student Union of the Banaras Hindu University and the other Nepalese living in Banaras began to concentrate their mind to form political organizations. Some time later, B.P. Koirala published an appeal in several Indian newspapers including "Searchlight" calling for foundation of any political party to take necessary steps for the establishment of democratic system in Nepal.[1]

3.2 The Foundation of "Nepali *Rastriya* (National) Congress"

The end of the Second World War, the democratic waves sweeping through the world and the independent India movement filled the Nepalese living in India with a new inspiration and encouragement. Politically conscious and active youth, especially students in Nepal, were well informed about such events through different means and media. Moreover, the 1940 incident made the Nepalese realize the need of political organization and political movement; its credit goes to Ganeshman Singh who escaped from the *Bhadragol* prison in 1944, reached Banaras suffering a lot of troubles and met the educated Nepalese like B.P. Koirala, Dilliraman Regmi and others. He told them every detail about political events taking place in Nepal and also presented the plight of the Nepalese at the students gathering, which prompted them to center their mind towards the formation of political organization. B.P. Koirala published an appeal in different newspapers calling for establishment of a political party to do necessary works for bringing about democracy in Nepal.[2] Ganeshman Singh had suffered much in prison. After escape, he reached India and did his best to bring democracy in Nepal.[3] In fact, the source of fuel for the foundation of Nepali Rastriya Congress (Nepalese National Congress) was Ganeshman Singh.

After the end of the World War II, numerous changes appeared in the international political scenario. In the general election of England, the Conservative Party was defeated by Labour Party which had promised in its election manifesto to grant independence to India if the party won the elections. The Labour Party government very wisely adopted the policy to grant independence to India. General Amnesty was declared for all the political prisoners of India. The Labour Government of England made an arrangement to hand over the central council of Ministers of India to the official representatives of the 'Indian National Congress' and the 'Muslim League' from 16th June 1947. The two leaders of the 'Social Party' of India Rammonahar Lohia and Jaya Prakash Narayan, with the intention to experiment their socialist political programme in Nepal suggested to the Nepalese youth B.P. Koirala who was one of their party members to organize a political party of the Nepalese living in India.[4]

Later, on October 31, 1945, a political organization was formed at the residence of Devi Prasad Sapkota at Teliyabang, Banaras. It was named "All India Nepalese National Congress".[5] A grand conference of the representatives of the political workers from outside and inside the country was held at Bhawanipur, Calcutta on January 25th, 26th, 1947 for preparation of the manifesto of the delegates form different parts. It was the most important conference in which attempts were made to bring democracy in Nepal. In the conference, the following things were mentioned:

Places of Nepal and Nepalese Dwellings	Delegate's Name
Kathmandu	Surya Bahadur Bhardawaj Ganesh Man Singh Sundar Raj Chalise
Birganj (Representing All Terai)	Bir Sundarlal Shrestha
Mohattary	Saroj Prasad Koirala Narendra Regmi
Dang	Bharat Mani Sharma
Darjeeling	Devabrata (D.B. Pariyar) Lakpa Tshiring Sherpa
Nepalgunj	Jageswor Mishra
Nepalese Student Union, Banars	Iswori Baral Govinda Prasad Lohani Kashiraj Upadhayaya Viswobandu Thapa
Banaras	Gopal Prasad Bhattarai Krishna Prasad Bhattarai
Saptari	Rudra Prasad Giri
Far-east	Narendra Kumar Pradhan Mahananda Sapkota[1]

Apart form these delegates, a large number of the Nepalese living in or working or studying in different parts of India including B.P. Koirala, Dilliraman Regmi, D.N. Pradhan and Dhanaman Singh Pariyar also were present.[1] Several Indian leaders had sent messages wishing the conference a grand success. This conference officially endorsed the name of the party as "Nepali Rastriya Congress" which was founded sometime ago in Banaras and called it "Nepali Rastriya Congress". Following the 'Calcutta Conference' a wave of organization of party units in the homeland and aboard had speeded up. In this way, the political objectives and popularity of "Nepali Rastriya Congress" grew day by day.[2]

Before officially naming this political party as "Nepali Rastriya Congress" the conference of the delegates representating all the parts and sectors of the kingdom of Nepal was the first conference of the first political party founded in foreign country. The educated and enthusiastic youth living in and out of the country were the participants in the conference.[3] Of course, it would not be an exaggeration to say that the foundation of Nepali Rastriya Congress was the outcome of the necessity, devotion, effort and enthusiasm of the Nepalese students. This political party was to give special emphasis on upholding the ideals and objectives of *Praja Parisad*. This fact has been mentioned in the programme-report of the inaugural ceremony of Nepali Rastiya Congress Ganesh Man Singh proposed the name of Tanka Prasad Acharya, who was in prison in Kathmandu, for the post of chairman of 'Nepali Rastriya Congress'; all the attendants unanimously supported the proposal and B.P. Koirala was made acting chair-person to administer the programme.[4] Besides "To give Nepalese support for the entire-freedom of India," Nepali Rastriya Congress in its objective made a decision giving importance to uphold the objective of *Praja Parisad* "to establish a government responsible to the people under the constitutional leadership of His Majesty the King in the kingdom of Nepal".[5] In this way, "Nepali Rastriya Congress" was established by the "Praja Prarisad" organized and piloted by students. So, the establishment of Nepali Rastriya Congress and its works have clarified the fact that any movement and organization would become successful if they are equipped with good political culture.

3.3 *Jayatu Sanskritam* (Long Live Sanskrit)

Jayatu Sanskritam is one of the most talked about subjects in the democratic history of modern Nepal. It has a multi-dimensional importance. Most importantly, it symbolizes the first ever students movement based on purely academic demands. Just as the students of other countries have played a pioneering role in many revolutionary changes and development, so have the Nepalese students played a leading role in charting out the way for the continuity of the movement. It has not only helped create the history of student movement in the country, it has also succeeded in establishing their leading role in the movement. Many political parties and student unions have been set up under the existing political structure. While studying, writing or making research of their history, the students refer to *Jayatu Sanskritam* and its movement. These movement enhanced the glory of *Jayatu Sanskritam*. This incident had given vent to the dormant feeling of opposition of the Nepalese people to the Rana government. This movement provided inspiration to the student to launch struggles by a potent means. That is why there was a substantial role of the students in the Revolution of 1950. It is vindicated by the fact that the student mass is equally ready to participate in the movements even now.

In this context, Shree Tin Bir Shamsher had established Sanskrit Hostel in May 1887. There were altogether 210 seats combining 200 specified seats and 10 excess seats.[6] There was a provision for providing traditional education on *The Ramayana, The Mahabharata,* Vedas and other Hindu religious scriptures and the students were provided food from a common mess. It is said that Bir Shamsher had made a provision from official level to impart education to Brahmins in order to exculpate himself from sins. The students were to be educated in old culture, carefully preventing them from coming under the influence of modernity. But it was not possible. The medium of education was Sanskrit. The students had to go to Banaras each year in order to appear in their examinations to obtain the degrees of *Madhyama, Shastri* and *Acharya*.e.[7] Despite strict control, many active, eager and curious students came to know the situation prevailing outside their school. Coming as they did from different parts of the country, the students came to know many things during their journeys to and from school. The events taking place in the country and the Independence Struggle of India helped students to acquire rich experience on actual situation. These very events might have agitated the students of this school.

The students of the *Tin Dhara Pakshala* (Sanskrit Hostel at present) could not remain untouched by the nationwide awakening that had started since 1886. In view of the awakening in the then English schools, they expressed their desire to bring about reform in their studies also. Bishwanath Upadhyaya of Mahankal has stated the following on an event that had taken place in 1887.

> *"This incident occurred on 1887... Some students of the Sanskrit Chhatrabas, Ghantaghar, Kathmandu including myself happened to fall in the bad book of Shree Tin Juddha Shamsher, the then Prime Minister. .....The students of the school secretly discussed people's awakening in India while Mahila Guruju Hem Raj spied on the activities of the students of the hostel day in and day out poisoning the ears of the Prime Minister. On the basis of the report of the Guruju, Juddha Shamsher ordered Ram Prasad Banstola of Sitapail, Purna Prasad Dhungel of Katunje, Bhaktapur, Jagannath Timilsena of Gorkha and I, Bishwonath Neupane of Baudha Mahankal, Kathmandu to stay confined in their own village for thirteen months."*[8]

This event serves as a burning example of the government's attitude towards the students. The government itself had divided the students, creating inferiority towards each other. The basement rooms of the Durbar High School were used as study rooms for the hostel. The students and teachers of the Durbar High School just upstairs looked smarter and while they discussed geography, history, political science and current affairs, the students of the Chhatrabas were at a loss.[9] The students of Tin Dhara Chhatrabas were not far away from political events taking place since 1940. The saga of the martyrs and political prisoners had aroused in their minds a sense of service towards their nation. They felt electrified and whispered about martyrs when they reached the place of their martyrdom while going to Shobha Bhagawati or Shiphal on their way to Pashupatinath or Teku. They were inspired by a sense of sacrifice for the ideal and felt desperate not knowing what to do.[10]

The students of *Tin Dhara Pakshala* could not remain untouched by the nation-wide awakening sweeping the country since 1943. These students also became eager to bring about a reform in their studies drawing inspiration form the awakening among the students of English schools.[11] The students of the Sanskrit school had to go to Banaras to appear in their exams. There, they came to know about the activities of Indian Independence Movement and the history of Indian leaders like Mahatma Gandhi, Jawaharlal Nehru, *Pundit* Malawiya etc. They were impressed by the free atmosphere of India, and coming back home, became worried and desperate to free their motherland from the evil rule of the Ranas.[12] Similarly, there was a sharp contrast even in the way of life and social status of the English and Sanskrit teachers. The starting pay scale of an M.A. teacher of that period would be some where between Rs. 300 and Rs. 508. Whereas, a Sanskrit teacher with a degree of Acharya which is equivalent to M.A. had to manage with a meager salary Rs. 50 per month. A person studying English could get job in administrative service. But those studying Sanskrit became religious preachers or priests. In this way, the Sanskrit education was devalued in the only Hindu religious kingdom of the world.[13] As a result, a number of questions such as why the Sanskrit students can't study modern subjects, why there is a difference between English and Sanskrit education, whether Sanskrit education cannot be imparted in a modern way were raised. In this way, both the teachers and students realized the need of modern knowledge in order to keep abreast of the modern age. They thought that the discrepancy existing between English and Sanskrit education can be removed if subjects like modern history, geography, political science and elementary science were introduced in the Sanskrit education also.[14]

Jayatu Sankritam is the first and decisive movement launched by Nepalese students inside the country putting forward academic demands. In a situation when no one could even speak or write against the Rana rulers, the students of the Sanskrit school courageously and fearlessly reached Padma Shamsher's palace located in Bishalnagar after various stages of procession and demonstration launched in sympathy with the Nepalese people. The students did not receive any support from political parties nor any financial assistance was forthcoming to them though they were already conscious of a need to fight for a change. Even in this situation, the students met their needs by asking alms and pawning their watches and risked hostel accommodation and scholarship provided to them by the Ranas. These students finally brought the autocratic rulers to their knees. They had to honour the demands and spirit of the students. This should be considered as one of the important achievements of that time. It took time for the fulfilment of their demands, but culminated in the victory of the student strength.

The most important aspect of this movement was to establish the fact that it is necessary for the students to become conscious and that political party must be organized for the development of the country. It also constitutes the first stage of democratic political culture. For further vindication of the fact, the researcher deems it relevant to quote the statements of pioneering leaders of the movements, Sribhadra Sharma and Kamal Raj Regmi: "We were present at the time of the founding of the Nepali Congress. We also met with other student leaders staying in India. We listened to the speeches of B.P. Koirala, which made us politically conscious. When we returned to Kathmandu, we had come under political influence."[15] Thus *Jayatu Sanskritam* movement was a political movement. The incidents of 1890 were not the sole causes of the movement. There were many other causes also.

In 1885 Bir Shamsher overthrew the rule of the Jung family and brought the reign of power within the Shamsher family. In 1881 he established the hostel. But he imposed a strict control on education system instead of letting it to be run freely. As a result, the students became dissatisfied with the way of the government.[16]

Nothing can be created in isolation without external influence. There were many shortcomings and discrepancies in Sanskrit education. The most important was that there were discriminations in English and Sanskrit education imparted in the same building. The students had very well understood the discriminatory attitude of the government. After their contact with Indian leaders, they began to question this discrimination in education and began to discuss as to why this could not be removed. They come to the conclusion that the course of studies for Sanskrit education should be at par with the syllabus for English education. They considered it necessary to launch a movement to achieve this. *Jayatu Sanskritam* was its consequence.[17]

According to government restriction, only the sons of Brahmins could receive Sanskrit education. It is usual in a Brahmin family to recite the Vedas, perform *Upanayana,* receive holy mantras and to perform religious service and other rites. The sons of Brahmins also went away from home to Haridwar and Banaras for study. As they had outside exposure, they thought that they should not confine themselves only to Sanskrit education and jumped into the movement demanding modern education and culture.[18]

The only and the first Sanskrit school was the sole place where the students coming from different villages and with different ideas could stay together in an organized way. The gathering of the students, exchange of ideas, discussion on national and international events, their curiosity about the progress of the Second World War and the biographies of the world leaders raised their consciousness. All this resulted in *Jayatu Sanskritam.*[19]

> *We also become deeply impressed by the event of 1940, and the Satyagraha launched by the students of the Trichandra College and other schools. As we had to go to Banaras and stay there for a couple of months to appear in our exams, we were able to watch the events of the Indian Independence Movement. The industrial revolution and modern development of the world made us highly conscious.20*

> *Before meal each day, the students were required to say 'Long live Shree Tin Maharaj!' This gave the meal a taste of servitude. While saying long live, some students even said 'Down with' in a subdued voice. Towards 1946 the students of the school were treated to a religious film called Bhakta Mehata. In the film there was a hymn called Bhajo Govindam. While singing the hymn, one of the characters of the film, a dumb person, miraculously broke into speech. We were greatly impressed by it and reached to the conclusion that kept some pre-historic ashes bringing it all the way from Bajrayogini. All the students began to apply the holy ashes on their forehead and sing Radhe Govinda Bhajo every evening ending their religious song with Bolo Bajra Biharilalki Jay. The informers of the Government heard it as Bolo Jawaharlalki Jay and informed it to the palace. Th students became enraged when the government banned the singing of the hymn. We then decided to march ahead in struggle writing our pledges with our blood.[21] In discussion, we raised the issue of devaluation of Sanskrit. Director of Sanskrit school Guru Hem Raj and Pundit Somnath Sigdel cautioned us against our anti-government activities. But the rest of the Pundits were in the favour the students.[22]*

Jayatu Sanskrit movement was not started in the spur of a moment. Nor was it started due to revenge, deviation and dissent. National and international events, extreme neglect to Sanskrit education and the suppressive and undemocratic activities of the Ranas were responsible for the outbreak of this movement.[23] Though the teaching and learning of Sanskrit took place in the country at that time, the students had to go to Banaras to appear in their exam. According to a record available in the Balmiki Campus, Nepalese students had started to go to Banaras to appear in the exam as early as 1940/41. In this process they got the opportunity to get acquainted with the Indian independence movement. On the other hand, political parties were carrying on anti-Rana political activities, albeit clandestinely, since 1936.[24] There seems to have been a ten year long background for *Jayatu Sanskritam* movement even among the students. Since 1937/38, the students had started to feel bad about the exploitation, injustice, tyranny and family autocracy of the Ranas. According to Gopal Sharma Regmi (now living in Nepalgunj), 11 students of the Sanskrit school had smeared soil on the statue of Juddha Shamsher and had placed a hat of a crockery pot on his head one night in the month of December 1938. Those involved in this event were, Bhanu Acharya (Baluwatar), Shiv Prasad Kafle (Baluatar), Hari Prasad Paneru (Chandol), Devi Dutta Kharel (Handigaun), Durmukh Paudel (Chuchhepati), Hiranyagarva Sigdel (Lamjung), Bekha Shivdayal Lamichhe (Puthan) and Gopal Sharma Regmi.[25] According to Regmi, some students of the Sanskrit school had closely watched the execution of the martyrs in 1940. When the Ranas put one of the martyrs before the firing squad at Shobha Bhagawati, Regmi and some other students secretly watched the event from behind a nearby hillock.[26] This event greatly enraged the students and a sense of fear, terror and revolt was engendered among the people. The event of 1940 became the talk of the town.

One of the reasons of the movement is the fear and inferiority complex emanating from the widespread suppression, injustice and tyranny meted out by the Rana rulers. There were sporadic protests by the students. But they were mercilessly suppressed as a lesson for others. This provoked anti-government sentiment among the students instead of being subdued. The students of this school had become anti-Ranas since 1934. The episode of 1940 made them more angry.[27] The incidents continued one after another to take place in the Tin Dhara Pathshala to harass the Rana rulers. One day a piece of bone was found in the food prepared for the Brahmin students. The students refused to eat and asked for another food. The employees refused to make new food and informed the matter to Guru Hemraj, who called all the students at the Putali Bagaincha in Singh Durbar and reported the incident to Juddha Shamsher. Juddha Khanal (Tanahun), Tikaram (Dang) and two others whose names remain unknown were to be exiled.[28] These students could not protest immediately, but they bore a deep sense of revolt. "When we went to Banaras to appear in our exam, we came back deeply impressed by various stages of Indian Independence Movement, the teacher-student relationship, a free atmosphere for studies and the Hindu-Muslim riots that took place in India then.[29] While in India, we students also participated in the Convention of the Nepali Rastriya Congress held in Calcutta on January 26, 1947. We heard speeches and held talks with B.P. Koirala and other Indian leaders on the situation in Nepal. What the leaders discussed there was about Nepal and was compatible with the actual situation here. This raised our consciousness and attracted our attention to politics. We students, who were present there decided to move ahead politically after returning home.[30] When we went to Banaras to appear in our exam for the second time, the workers' movement had already taken place. We discussed the movement there. We were staying at Mangala Gauri Dharmashala where we discussed and decided on launching political movement after returning to Kathmandu. We decided to raise the question of reforming Sanskrit education. We made our friends take oath of secrecy and decided to serve a 15 day ultimatum to the government to fulfill our demands. When the government did not pay any attention to our demands, we started the movement from 15th June, 1947. The movement acquired dynamism and intensity owing to the policy of the Rana government.[31] The workers of Biratnagar Jute Mill defied the Rana government by starting a strike. In this connection, B.P. Koirala and other leaders were arrested by the Ranas. B.P. Koirala was brought to Kathmandu and was detained there. We students of the Sanskrit school knew this and were enraged. Because of the central location of the Sanskrit school, the students came to know the activities of the Rana rulers.[32] We were somehow hearing the stories about the rise of the Ranas, stories about Sri Tins, the arbitrariness of Chandra Shamsher, *Makai Parva, Shuktisindhu Parva* etc. It will therefore be incorrect to say that *Jayatu Sanskritam* movement was related only to the demands for the introduction of subjects like Geography, History and political science in the syllabus. There should be no hesitation to say that this movement was politically motivated and was led by politicians.[33]

Towards 1947, Nepal was isolated from the rest of the world. But it could not remain aloof from the course of events of the Second World War. As information about the World War was more readily available in India than in Nepal, Nepalese students reaching there for exams knew about the incidents of war. According to Kamal Raj Regmi, the Gurus of the Sanskrit school assembled in mid day recess and discussed the war. They referred to Hitler, Churchill and Stalin as first, second and the third uncle.[34] The Sanskrit students closely watched, heard and experienced the Indian Independence movement. From their contact with newspapers, processions and speeches, it was but natural for them to be conscious about their duties. In 1946, our examination was postponed after a couple of papers owing to Hindu-Muslim riots. Though the Indian government had assured us to hold the exam of the remaining papers in Nepal, it could not take place due to the indiscretion of head Guru and Mahila Guru. The students demanded reimbursement of Rs. 100 which they had spent in India but Guru Hemraj provided only Rs. 15 which was insufficient to meet the expenses. This made the student indignant.[35] *Jayatu Sanskritam* movement was a cumulative effect of various national and international causes. The ex-student of that school, Purna Prasad Brahman was the motive force behind the movement. He was the first initiator and the vanguard of the movement. He was a talent who showed a great knack in study, political organisation and composing poetry. He started organising students as soon as he became enlightened and was expelled form the hostel three times. As early as 1943, Brahman had laid a strong foundation for *Jayatu Sanskritam* movement which started form the 1st of Asar. He came to our hostel form outside and inspired us actively.[36] Purna Prasad Brahman had became very dissatisfied from the degradation of and discrimination to Sanskrit education. He did not like the attitude of the government. He expressed his dissatisfaction in a round-about way even when he was a student in the school. He was expelled from the hostel on a number of times. In order to protest the degradation and devaluation of Sanskrit, he even refused to take the degree of Acharya which the school had conferred to him in 1942.[37] The initiator of the *Jayatu Sanskritan* movement was thus the ex-student of the Sanskrit school and he had gone through various troubles to draw an organised plan of the movement. His contribution will always find a mention in the history of students movement as a source of inspiration. *Pundit* Muralidhar of Kalimati is also found to have played a significant role in explaining the importance of Sanskrit language and raising people's consciousness. His main vocation was to narrate the *Puranas* and take part in discourses. His style of narrating the *Puranas* was different from the traditional style of other *Pundits*. He related the episodes of the *Puranas* with the reality of the contemporary Nepalese society and explained each and every point lucidly through examples and analogy. His recitation did not contain only religious teaching, it contained many things which explained social, economic and political situation of the country, the independence struggle of the Indian Congress, Gandhi's personality and his theory of non- violence, *Satyagraha*, civil disobedience movement, hunger strike, boycott of foreign goods and the policy of division and suppression being pursued by the British in India.[38] He used to say that servitude and liberation were obtained through one's own effort. He then stressed in *Karma* or action and organization. He indirectly inferred that the Nepalese people should take initiative to bring about a timely change in their country also.[39] The *Nagarik Adhikar Samiti* arranged a *Purana* to be narrated by *Pandit* Muralidhar during the whole period of *Chaturmas* of the year 1938, and he held his audience spellbound. People interpreted the explanation according to their own outlook. This *Purana* created quite a sensation among the people. *Pundit* Murlaidhar, who urged the Nepalese people to organize against the Rana rulers will remain immortal in the history of Nepal. It is necessary to undertake an in-depth study on his personality. According to Purna Prasad Brahman, *Pundit* Muralidhar was a great scholar and was well versed in Sanskrit. He was not only successful in explaining the importance of Sanskrit language to the Nepalese people, he was also successful in raising their political consciousness. We were deeply impressed by him. After listening to his discourse, we became convinced that the Sanskrit education should be reformed and modernized to achieve real freedom. *Pundit* Muralidhar's style of thinking must also be considered as one of the motive forces of *Jayatu Sanskritam* movement.[40] These various national and international factors had motivated the students of the school to go into action.

3.4 The Beginning of the Sanskrit Student Movement and the Arrest of the Students

The students of this school went to Banaras in November 1946 to appear in their exams. The outbreak of the Hindu-Muslim riot affected the exam. As Sharma point to out when we had finished seven papers out of fourteen papers, the riot badly affected the area and the exam was postponed for an indefinite period of time. When we contacted the authorities, they told us that arrangement could be made to take the exams. in Nepal if the Nepalese government requested the Indian authorities. When we gave a written petition upon our return, the government not only showed indifference, it also deducted some amount from out exam allowances. It provoked us and we launched a strike after organizing all the students of the school.[41] Before the strike, we informed the authorities that we would go on strike from 1st to 15th of June, 1947 if our demands were not met within a week. As the government paid no heed to these demands, we had to go on strike.[42]

The postponed examination was to be taken after some time. It could not take place in Nepal owing to the indifference of the Nepalese government. But the government provided the students only Rs. 25 to cover the expense of their journey to and stay in Banaras. Despite their protest and demand to increase the amount, the government did not pay any heed to their problems. The students went to Banaras and appeared in their exams with a heavy heart.[43] Most of the students had stayed at Mangla Gauri Dharmashala, which was near to the office of the Nepali Congress. It became easier for the students to listen to speeches of its leaders and come into contact with them. The speeches of the leaders of the Nepali Rastriya Congress made the students happy and excited. The students pledged to organize a movement after coming back to Nepal. They decided to raise the issue of reforming Sanskrit education.[44] Incorporating these feelings and ideas, an appeal entitled 'demand and spirit' was registered each to Sri Tin Maharaja and four commanding generals and the chief of the Sanskrit school Mahila Guru in the month of May, 1947. They made it clear that, if the 'demands and spirit' of the students were not met until the last of June 15, they would boycott, their classes as the first stage of the *Satyagraha* and if need be, the second stage of struggle could also be contemplated.[45]

The students' demands boiled down to the following three things:

(1) The usual 210 seats should be maintained in the hostel.

(2) The syllabus of the school must include Geography, History and Political Science.

(3) Arrangement should be made to hold examinations in Nepal and a university be opened in Nepal.[46]

After returning to Kathmandu in May, 1947, a copy of 'demand and spirit' was submitted to educational director. We had expected response within a week. We sent reminders. But there was no response. Finally we served an ultimatum for June 15, 1947 to go on strike. There was still no response. The demands of the ultimatum were as follows:[47]

(1) Subjects like Geography, History, Economics and political Science be introduced in the syllabus with appropriate reform in Sanskrit education.

(2) New teachers be appointed for the teaching of these subjects.

(3) Arrangement be made to hold all the examinations up to Madhyama in Nepal.

(4) Sanskrit University be opened in Nepal.

According to Sribhadra Sharma, a demand for the resignation of the director of the Sanskrit school was also included later. According to Hemnath Devkota, the opening of school in rural areas for ordinary people was also included in the demand.[48]

The students waited for two months for the fulfilment of their demands. But when the authorities did not pay any heed to these demands, the students led a procession from Lainchaur to Bishalnagar where the palace of Padma Shumshere was located.[49] When there was no response to their demands until the last of Jestha, the students loudly rang the bell of the Narayan temple in the evening. The message of the bell was to inform that there was an urgency and all the students are requested to assemble for consultation. In the Rana period, all the landlords were required to assemble in Tundikhel if there was a bugle call from the top of Dharahara.[50] Hearing the sound of the bell, all the students assembled at the crossroads. Student leaders made a fiery speech on the importance of 'demand and spirit' and the indifference shown to it by the Ranas. They also obtained words for the solidarity and support for the boycott of classes to be observed from the June 15. In this way, all the students made up their minds for struggle.[51] The movement started on the appointed day; classes were boycotted at the Sanskri school.[52] The incident of the previous day had already reached the ears of Guru Hemraj. At 9.30 next morning, he went to the school gate with a contingent of police and sermonized the students who had gathered there that it was mean to boycott classes. *Brahmanyaya cha dehiya chhudram kamaya nabyate* (Brhamins should not do what low class people are expected to do), he said with an air of an erudite.[53] Students were ready to court arrest. No one listened to the Guru. He ordered the police to arrest the students and walked away towards Durbar School.[54] The students boycotted the classes at the *Sanskrit Pradhan Pathshala* and picketed the gate. Soon after, the picketers were arrested. Another group came to replace them. The police arrested them also. Altogether 23 persons were arrested including another group of six persons. All of them were taken of Hanumadhoka in handcuffs. Later six more students were arrested making the total number of the arrested reach 29.[55] The arrested students were released later the same night after forcing them to sign a letter of expulsion from the hostel and rustication from all the government schools. The 29 persons expelled on the 1st to 15th June, 1947 are as follows: Narayan Bhakta Khanal (West No. 3), Ram Prasad Sapkota (Panauti), Umanath Devkota (Gorkha), Bhakit Raj Panthi (Palpa), Yadunath Adhikari (Pokhara), Ambika Prasad Ghimire (West No. 3), Kashinath Gotam (Palpa), Sribhadra Khanal (West No. 3), Kamal Raj Regmi (Palpa), Balaram Acharya (Kebalpur), Lawaraj Ghimire (West No. 3), Hari Prasad Devkota (Gorkha), Ram Prasad Neupane (Ramechhap), Hari Prasad Paudel (West No. 2), Tikaram Paudel (West No. 3), Devi Prasad Paudel (Kewalpur), Jiwanath Arjel (Dhading), Sri Prasad Gotame (Chainpur), Ek Dev Gnyawali (Ridi), Kul Prasad Bhandari (Eastern Nepal), Khaganath Nepal (Palpa), Rajeshwor Devkota (Gorkha), Giriraj Gnyawali (Ridi), Chetananth

Regmi (Raktakali), Achutraj Regmi (Palpa), Bholanath Parajuli (Pokhara), Satya Dev Acharya (West No. 3).[56] Next day all the students went to Guheshwori and recited the Chandi. They came to Naxal via Pasupatinath. On the one hand, there was a concern for the future of the movement, we were feeling the pinch of hunger and thirst on the other. Other courageous youths also joined the student procession. One Harihar Adhikari of Mandikhatar pawned his watch. With the money they ate some snacks and marched towards Bishalnagar palace. According to Harihar Adhikari, this movement was a struggle for democracy and its characteristic was that it had won the sympathy of all the people of the country. There were innumerable youths like me who were attracted by the movement.[57] Police contingent under Captain Chandra Bahadur intercepted the procession at various places. Students arrived at the main gate of the Bishalnagar place from different ways. The Maharaja wanted to meet only the representatives of the students. But the students insisted to meet the Maharaja together. After some time all the students were given audience by Padma Shumshere.[58]

Looking at the group of student, Padma Shumshere said with tearful eyes:

> *I always recite the Gita before lunch. Go to Tindhara Pathshala and help yourselves. Brother Mohan Shumsher is a good man. Go and talk to him. Sanskrit is a dead language. It cannot be compared to English. We have created a Guthi (trust) to support you. If you go on strike, it will defame us and our government. Go to the Pathshala and stay there.*[59]

The students came back disappointed hearing what the Maharaja had said. They decided to make an issue out of the remark made by the Maharaja of a Hindu Kingdom that the Sanskrit was a dead language. The students decided to burn all the works in Sanskrit language saying that they should not keep the 'corpse' of a dead language. This strange and sensational news spread quickly. It hurt the sentiment of all the people when they heard that the Maharaja had said about

Sanskrit language, a great reservoir of knowledge, a dead language.[60] Everybody began to denounce the rottenness of the Rana rule. Every one started to support the movement launched by the students of Sanskrit. The Maharaja sent for the student leaders and clarified that he had not said that Sanskrit was a dead language. "I have just come after performing religious service. I have not said so. It is a universal language. What I had said was that some ignorant scoundrels consider it to be a dead language." When the Maharaja explained his remarks calling the students before him, their threat to burn the works of Sanskrit language died down.[61]

The students were now compelled to launch an agitation for the importance and equality of Sanskrit education. The students decided to go round the city and ask for alms in a group of ten, leave hostel and stay in *Dharmashalas*, ask for alms at day time and explain to sympathetic people the mean treatment meted out to Sanskrit language by the government, attracting them towards their movement. This programme became immensely successful. The students left the hostel and started to take shelter in the sheds of *Bagmati ghats*.[62] The sky rending slogan they sang then was:

Long live Sanskrit, Long live religion!
Long live Sanskrit, Long live the King!
Long live Sanskrit, Long live the land!
Long live Sanskrit, Long live the World![63]

Early morning, they went around door to door in Kathmandu and Lalitpur asking alms in a piece of cloth marked *Jayatu Sanskritam*. People generously gave them whatever they had. A strange scenario was created.[64] In the meantime even the students studying English in Darbar High School joined the movement. Participation from a wide section of students made the movement more effective. On the eighth day a group of students started *Bhagawat* recitation at the

Dharmashala. They also started to attack the Rana rulers by innuendoes carefully interspersing stories and anecdotes with the *Bhagawat* recitation.[65] After ten days of the *Jayatu Sanskritam* movement, a strange situation was created in Kathmandu. It substantiated the people's impression that the Ranas were not only anti-people, they were anti-Sanskrit and anti-God. As the movement did not show any sign of abetting and in view of the possibility of Nepal Rastriya Congress making an issue out of it in launching anti-government propaganda in a foreign country, the Ranas thought it wise to put an end to the movement.[66] After the conclusion of the week-long recitation, four of the leading students, Kamal Raj Regmi, Kashinath Gautam, Gokarnaraj Shastri, and Achutraj Regmi went to Mohan Shamsher taking along some Prasad (offering) for him. He urged the students to go to the hostel and resume studies. In reply, the students said that they would go back if their demands were met. After taking detailed information on their "demand and spirit", Mohan Shamsher said: "O.K. go to the hostel. I will fulfill your demands." When the four leaders[67] returned with the news, the students consulted with one another and decided to shift their quarters to *Tindhara Pathshala* again. As the Ranas promised to fulfill the demands within six months, the students started to live in the hostel as usual.[68] In the meantime, Kashinath Gautam, Kamalraj Regmi, and Sribhadra Sharma met Indian scholar Sri Prakash who was living in Tripureshwor after coming to Kathmandu on the invitation of Padma Shamsher to help him draft *Baidhanik Kanun* (constitutional law). During their meeting, the student leaders apprised him of the movement launched by the Sanskrit students.[69] The first two demands were fulfiled in Mansir. But the last demand that a Sanskrit university be opened here and that arrangement be made to discontinue the practice of going to Benaras to appear in the examination, was not fulfilled. The non fulfilment of the third demand was a matter of a great distress for the students. The students therefore started the movement again. The government also refused to budge. The government then exiled five students,

Ganga Prasad Gautam (Futuk, Ilam), Padma Shankar Adhikari (East No. 2), Sadananda Shapkota (East No. 2), Tara Sharma (Pokhara), Giriraj Gnyawali (Thorga, Ridi) on Mansir 7, 8, 9, They were ordered not to come within the valley.[70] The students could not keep silent over the harsh punishment of exile to their fellow students. By the start of November, the students again started to talk about the movement. They decided to boycott the forthcoming exams which were going to be held form December. As the student leaders were confined within the hostel premises, the movement, however, could not be effective.[71] Finally another lot of 38 students were expelled from the hostel and chased out of the valley. They were: Kashinath Gautam, Sribhadra Sharma, Ek Dev Gnyali, Dilliram Timilsina, Rajeshwor Devkota, Hari Prasad Devkota, Hemraj Neupane, Buddhi Prakash Acharya, Damodar Gautam, Ishwory Prasad Acharya, Ram Prasad Bhurtel, Tirtharaj Gautam, Chhabiraman Banskota, Prem Narayan Banskota, Gokarnaraj Shastri, Gyanhari Paudel, Khaganath Nepal, Balarram Acharya, Rudra Prasad Banskota, Khubiram Acharya, Bhadranath Adhikari, Hari Prasad Pokhrel, Keshari Prasad Pokhrel, Devi Prasad Paudel, Ram Prasad Sharma, Tikaram Paudel, Krishna Prasad Pokherl, Fanindra Ghimire, Devraj Sharma, Suresh Shrama, Sadananda Sharma, Ganga Parsad Sharma Gautam, Padmashankar Adhikari, Taranath Ghimire and Giriraj Gyawali.[72] Four persons, Kamalraj Regmi, Kulmani Devkota, Ambika Prasad Ghimire and Narayan Prasad Khanal had been already exiled to Banaras even before the edict of the Ranas. The combined number of the exiled students appears to be 42. According to information available now, those exiled by the Rana regime gathered in Butwal reaching there via Kaski, Lamjung, Tanahun, Palpa and other places. They shouted the slogan of *Jayatu Sanskritam* in Butawal. Purna Prasad Brahman called upon them for the revolution through his poem. The students then went to Benaras and engaged themselves in the fight for democracy.[73] An excerpt of the poem by Purna Prasad Brahman:

Mother Nepal languishes with her hair of forests unkempt
With eyes full tears, she holds her children tight
If there is any brave man among you, come
Knock down the enemy to pay her debt of milk.
If any one stands in the way, split apart
His trunk and head, of if he speaks vile words
Twist his snout out of shape, and if
break it, forget the whole world
until the enemy drops dead.[74]

Though the students were politically motivated, they kept their political demands under surface and fought purely on academic demands. Political parties also received the help from them as their help was as necessary as those of the other sections of the society. In all cases, students start their movement demanding academic reform and equality. Later, they add their demands and politicize their movement in accordance with the necessity and the situation. *Jayatu Sanskritam* movement was no exception. When the students reached Banaras, they affiliated themselves with either B.P. faction or Regmi faction whichever they liked.[75] On the way, the students informed the masses about the movement and reached Benaras igniting the torch of the revolution. Later, these very students provided leadership in different war fronts of 1950 revolution. *Jayatu Sanskritam* was a heroic and historical movement in which the Ranas were challenged from the hostel run by the trust set up by the Ranas themselves.[76]

Jayatu Sanskritam movement was the second movement taking place in the capital after one and a half months of the *Satyagraha*. The Ranas had suppressed the *Satyagraha* dubbing it as "revolt by the Newars." This time the Brahmins also stood in revolt and proved them utterly wrong.[77] Thus the students of *Tindhara Pathshala* fought against the Rana rulers for the 'demands and spirit' which meant inclusion of modern subjects like history, geography, political science and elementary science in their syllabus. They brought a wave of enlightenment in the valley and the western hills.[78] They mustered the support and sympathy of all. They vindicated that there can be no reform without overthrowing the Ranas. In this way they became participants in the struggle for achieving democracy. *Jayatu Sanskritam* movement became an unforgettable movement in Nepal.[79] The students participating in the movement proved that the Sanskrit scholars do not like only to be priests or teachers of schools after study. They proved that they wanted to make themselves as conscious, able and democratic citizens of the country and to pursue or even be the champions of an ideal path in the nation and the world acquiring both the modern and traditional learnings.[80] The spirit, consciousness, wisdom and will of students have brought about a lot of changes in the world. Even in Nepal, it will be no exaggeration to say that the student mass has made a great contribution in the revolution started by Nepal *Praja Parishd* with a view to bring about democracy under the constitutional leadership of the king. When they reached Benaras, they dedicated themselves for the nation by organising themselves in the Nepali Rastriya Congress, which is only another form of the *Praja Parishad*.[81] In 1947, the students of the *Sanskrit Pathshala* had submitted very minor demand in the form of 'demand and spirit'. As the government did not pay necessary attention, the students became agitated. As the river taken lightly are sometimes dangerous, the movement swept away the Ranas. This incident proved to be a milestone for democratic Nepal. The students were not afraid of the government, police and the jail. Instead, they continued to keep to the path of the struggle. Various comments and remarks made by different people have emphasized its important and pioneering role. Here are some of the comments made on *Jayatu Sanskritam* movement from different sides:

(1) There are various causes of the fall of the Ranas in 1950. *Jayatu Sanskritam* movement was one of them. Though this movement was initially started to bring about timely reform in the Sanskrit education, it was directly linked with the existence of Nepal and the Nepalese. The harsh punishment which the Ranas meted out to

the participants of the movement with a view to abort it, makes it clear that this movement had a political overtone. The historians have recorded the success scored by this movement in 1947 as the first student's movement in golden letter.[82]

(2) *Jayatu Sanskritam* movement had emerged as the embryo of academic development and democratic movement in 1947. Since then, the student has been organising various activities in national interest and has scored quite a success.[83]

(3) *Jayatu Sanskritam* movement has occupied a prominent place even in the Revolution of 1950. It is therefore, our sacred duty to pay our respect to the vanguard personalities of the movement.[84]

(4) In fact, *Jayatu Sanskritam* movement had simultaneously taken forward both the political and academic struggles, which has been accepted in history. Political aspect of the movement has now become universally accepted whereas its academic aspects have fallen in the background.[85]

(5) While inaugurating the monument built in front of the *Tindhara Pathshala* on the occasion of the centenary of *Jayatu Sanskritam* movement, Former Prime Minister, and the Chief guest of the function, Surya Bahadur Thapa said, "*Jayatu Sanskritam* movement, which sounded the bugle call for the movement to introduce timely reform in the Sanskrit education to make it at par with the global standard of education, was second great historical event after the incident of 1940m in which many revolutionaries attained martyrdom.[86]

(6) *Jayatu Sanskritam* movement also happens to be the first and the most effective movement of the Nepalese students.[87]

(7) *Jayatu Sanskritam* movement is one of such saga which is inscribed in historical records. No one can erase the role the movement played fifty years ago to take the country to modernity.[88]

(8) In fact *Jayatu Sanskritam* became the base line for the 'renaissance' of education and consciousness. This

movement continues to move on mixing into the mainstream of the democratic movement of Nepal. [89]

(9) The *Jayatu Sanskritam* movement was a great revolution which brought about deep changes in political, academic, social and cultural aspects of the Nepalese society. In fact, it was a revolution in itself. Going against the practice of the Sanskrit education to look to the past for the solution of contemporary problems, this movement gave the inspiration to seek solution to these problems in the light of the present and the future.[90]

(10) *Jayatu Sanskritam* movement marks the beginning of the student movement in Nepal. This movement has it sown significance in Nepalese politics.[91]

(11) The *Jayatu Sanskritam*, movement, gave a momentum to the students' movement. Political movements in the country, the fresh air of democracy blew over the country which was being ruled by a system based on divine theory and considered as insurmountable as the Himalayas.[92]

(12) The student movement was started in 1947 by the students studying Sanskrit raising various professional demands. However, it acquired political form later.[93]

(13) I feel that the *Jayatu Sanskritam*, movement taking place in 1947, has now been accepted by all as the first organized student movement of Nepal. Every historian writing the history of 1950 Revolution has mentioned the importance and characteristics of this movement.[94]

(14) *Jayatu Sanskritam* movement marks the first historical student movement of Nepal. Its demands were pure and unpolluted. Only students had participated in it. *Jayatu Sanskritam* was concentrated mainly on students' academic demands rather than politics.[95]

(15) *Jayatu Sanskritam* movement was the embodiment of Nepalese student movement.[96]

(16) The torch of revolt which the students of *Saskrit Pathshala* lighted must be appreciated by all. *Jayatu Sanskritam* was a movement which overthrew the Rana autocracy.[97]

(17) After the incident connected with *Praja Parishad, Jayatu Sanskritam* constitutes an indestructible foundation of the movement for democracy and liberal society. Another important aspect of the movement is that most of its leaders have ever since continued to activate themselves in the socio-political change of the country.[98]

(18) The students of Tindhara Sanskrit School directly participated in the revolution for the first time by organizing famous movement called *Jayatu Sanskritam*.[99]

(19) The Nepalese students started a movement putting forward some demands in 1947. This movement is known as the *Jayatu Sanskritam* in the history of student movement. This was the first historical student movement.[100]

(20) *Jayatu Sanskritam* was the first student movement bearing a special significance in the history of democratic movement of the country. The Sanskrit students not only got their demands fulfilled through a struggle against a wrong academic policy of the government, they also initiated a process of spreading consciousness about political rights. As *Jayatu Sanskritam* constitutes the first ray of democratic movement, it occupies a prominent place in Nepal's history.[101]

(21) *Jayatu Sanskritam* constitutes an epoch making event among the Nepalese students.[102]

(22) The *Jayatu Sanskritam* movement of 1947 brought about a new turn in Nepalese history. It provided a new orientation to the Nepalese democratic movement by launching a struggle for reforms in the Sanskrit education. The active role played by the participants of the *Jayatu Sanskritam* movement in the 1950 revolution emphasizes the universal significance of the movement.[103]

(23) *Jayatu Sanskritam* is the first historical student movement ever launched by the Nepalese students within the country. We, the Nepalese students, took to street with slogan from 1947 demanding for civil rights. It has a distinct importance. It was participated in by general

> people, civil servants and teachers. *Jayatu Sanskritam* however symbolises the sacrifice, unity and perseverance of the Nepalese students. It was not a trivial matter. Each and every student of the *Jayatu Sanskritam* movement has been recorded in the Nepalese history as being greater than the heroes of the World Wars.[104]

The above remarks and comments make it clear that the *Jayatu Sanskritam* movement starting from 1st to 15th June, 1947 was a significant movement in its own right. This movement is considered as timely and necessary. It has left a distinct impression in the history of Nepalese students movement. This movement which had taken place inside Nepal and in Nepalese context, was able to shake the very foundation of the existing political system. The Rana regime had to succumb to the demands of the students. It enhanced the democratic consciousness in the country. It created a sense of urgency among the students scattered to different places of the country and India to do something for the country. As the first open movement of the students, *Jayatu Sanskritam* movement had exposed the policies of the Rana regime. This movement had enjoyed the support from the B and C class Ranas also from the very beginning. The students were also able to get the sympathy from some of the enlightened Ranas belonging to Class A. All the people realized the bravery and courage of the students who have defeated many powerful dictators of the world. The Nepalese students got spontaneous support, sympathy and suggestions from the people. It became necessary for the student organizations to expand rapidly. The ultimate goal of these movements was to overthrow the autocratic Rana regime and establish democracy in the country. *Jayatu Sanskritam* movement made it clear that students are the sole force to acquire and propagate information about contemporary situation. This movement also proved that students could act as the means of expansion and consolidation of organizations for an armed revolution. As a result, student organizations began to be set up inside and outside of the country. Credit goes to *Jayatu Sanskritam* movement for this achievement.

In the meantime, a students' organization called Nepal Students' Association also came into existence. Surendra Raj Sharma, Astmangal Bajracharaya, Yamuna Lal Maskey were elected president, secretary and joint-secretary respectively. The members of the executive committee included Gajasundar Pradhan, Goraksha Bahadur Nhuchhe Pradhan Pushkarnath Sharma, Bashudev Risal, Balaram Pyakurel, Chetnarayan Shrestha etc. Most active students of that time were: Krishana Man Shrstha, Jiwanlal Satyal, his sisters and grandson of Devendra Shrestha. These people provided a great help in both the academic and other forms of Struggle.[105]

Yet another student organization called All Nepal Students' federation was also formed at that time. Its active members were: Janakman Shrestha, Prachandraj Singh Suwal, Bashudev Prasad Dhungana, Prem Narisngh Rana, Laxmi Bahadur Halwai, Makhul Shah, Arabindnath Rimal, Sri Prasad Sharma and Baburaju Shrestha etc.[106] Some students belonging to these two unions were also arrested at that time. In the Kathmandu valley, the originally peaceful movement took a violent turn owing to a massive government crackdown on the agitators.[107]

The presence of the Nepalese King in India as a refugee became not only a matter of discussion in Delhi's diplomatic circle, it also became a matter of interest to them. The British diplomats were trying to muster international support in favour of Gyanendra Bikram Shah whom the Ranas had recently crowned king.[108] That's why, the British Deputy High Commissioner in Delhi, Frank Roberts and roving Ambassador for Far East, Ester Denning were scheduled to visit Nepal. The Indian government informed this to the Indian Embassy in Kathmandu. The first secretary of the Indian Embassy in Kathmandu S.K. Sinha thought it proper to promptly inform this to the Nepalese people. In the meantime he met with B.L. Sharma, Makbul Shah, Ekaramudding and some other two or three students.[109] The Nepalese people knew the intent of the visit of the British diplomats. They, therefore, moved from one locality to another calling them to gather at the Gauchar airport at noon next day. On the fourth of November, 1950, people began to pour into the airport from early morning.[110] The number of students was predominant. As soon as the plane landed, the mass marched forward shouting slogans in English. "British Mission go back! We want democracy! We want King Tribhuwan."[111] The police *Lathicharged* and fired at the crowd. The crowd of the people began to disperse. This provoked the people present there. The students put up a significant protest and made a show of strength.[112] The members of the British Mission were allowed passage only after thy assured that they would report whatever they had seen in Kathmandu.[113] During the stay of the British Mission, a procession of the students had gone to Lainchaur to hand in a protest letter to the British Embassy.[114] If the anti-government demonstration went on in Kathmandu valley, the armed struggle was intensified in the districts. The main participants of the movement were the youths and the students. Meanwhile, Bhogendra Man Singh, a ten-class student of the Padmodaya High School died a martyr. Many others were injured. Meanwhile, a dialogue was also going in Delhi between King Tribhuwan, the Nepali Congress and the Ranas under the auspices of Indian Prime Minister Jawaharlal Nehru.[115]

The Ranas on the other hand were scheming to suppress the people's movement. They began to flash *Khukri* in open air like Tundikhel and made unpopular speeches. As they carried naked *Khukris* menacingly, they were known as "*Khukri Dal*" among the people.[116] In this frightening situation, people began to protect themselves by organizing vigilant groups in their localities. Due to these precautionary measures of the people, the *Khukri Dal* could not easily attack the people in the localities.[117] No one can deny the courage and heroism of the Nepalese youths and students who played vanguard roles in various fronts of peaceful and violent struggles in various parts of the country.

After a prolonged negotiation, a tripartite agreement was signed between King Tribhuwan, the Nepali Congress and the Ranas. His Majesty King Tribhuwan returned to Kathmandu with his family and announced the fall of 104 year long rule of the Ranas and the establishment of democratic system under his leadership. The credit for this success goes to the courage of the Nepalese people and the able leadership of the educated youth and the students.

References

1 Bhuwan Lal Pradhan, *Nepal ko Jana Kranti 2007* (People's Revolution of Nepal 1950), (Kathmandu: Rumu Prakashan, 2047 (1990), pp. 176-77.

2 *Ibid.*

3 Govinda Prasad Upadhyaya, *Nepal ko Prajatantrik Itihas Sandarva* (Context of Democratic History in Nepal), (Kathmandu: Ratna Pustak Bhandar, 2054 (1997), p. 99.

4 *Ibid.*, p. 122.

5 Pradhan, f.n. No. 1, p. 212.

6 *Ibid.*, pp. 213-14.

7 *Ibid.*

8 *Ibid.*, p. 217.

9 Rajesh Gautam, *Kranti pachi ko Das Barsa* (Ten-years After the Revolution), 2nd ed., (Kathmandu: Ratna Pustak Bhandar, 2043 (1986), p. 263.

10 *Ibid.*, pp. 264-65.

11 *Ibid.*

12 Pradhan, f.n. No. 1, p. 304.

13 Upadhyaya, f.n. No. 3, p. 175.

14 Pradhan, f.n. No. 1, p. 303-04.

15 *Ibid.*, p. 304.

16 Upadhyaya, f.n. No. 3, p. 175.

17 Pradhan, f.n. No. 1, p. 303.

18 Upadhyaya, f.n. No. 3, p. 175.

19 *Ibid.*, p. 176.

20 *Ibid.*
21 From an interview with Sribhadra Sharma and Kamal Raj Regmi on 1998/3/7, Kathmandu.
22 From an interview with Yadunath on 1998/7/2, Kathmandu.
23 From an interview with Rajeshwor Devkota on 1998/3/10, Kathmandu.
24 *Ibid.*
25 *Ibid.*
26 *Ibid.*
27 *Ibid.*
28 *Ibid.*
29 Nabaraj Kattel, "Jayatu Sanskritam Andolan 2004," (Jayatu Sanskritam Movement 1947), *Arunodaya* (Nepali literary quarterly), (Kathmandu: Chatra Karya Samiti, Sanskrit Chhatrabas, 1997), p. 11.
30 *Ibid.*
31 *Ibid.*
32 *Ibid.*
33 Interview with Sribhadra Shamsher on 1996/1/25, Kathmandu.
34 *Ibid.*
35 *Ibid.*
36 *Ibid.*
37 *Ibid.*
38 Kattel, f.n. No. 29, p.12.
39 *Ibid.*
40 *Ibid.*
41 *Ibid.*
42 Sribhadra Sharma, *Jauatu Sranskritam Andolan ek Samjhana* (A Memoir on Jauatu Sanskritam Movement), (Kathmandu: Sribhadra Sharma, 1997), p. 29.
43 From the interview with Nawaraj Kattel on 1997/3/15, Kathmandu.
44 Pradhan, f.n. No. 1, pp. 87-88.
45 *Ibid.*
46 From an interview with Nawaraj Kattel on 1997/3/15, Kathmandu.
47 From an interview with Sribhadra Sharma on 1996/1/25, Kathmdnu.
48 *Ibid.*
49 Kattel, f.n. No. 29, p. 12.
50 *Ibid.*
51 Upadhyaya, f.n. No. 3, p. 176.
52 Pradhan, f.n. No. 1, p. 305.
53 Kettel, f.n. No. 29, p. 13.
54 *Ibid.*, p. 15.

55 Pradhan, f.n. No. 1, p. 305.
56 Upadhyaya, f.n. No. 3, pp. 176-77.
57 *Ibid.*, p. 177.
58 Kettel, f.n. No. 29, p. 13.
59 Upadhyaya, f.n. No. 3.
60 *Ibid.*
61 Kattel, f.n. 29, p. 13.
62 *Ibid.*
63 From an interview with Harihar Adhikari on 1997/3/5, Kathmandu.
64 Upadhyaya, f.n. No. 3, pp. 177-78.
65 *Ibid.*, p. 178.
66 *Ibid.*
67 Upadhyaya, f.n. No. 3, p. 178.
68 Pradhan, f.n. No. 1, p. 306.
69 Kattel, f.n. No. 29, p.11.
70 Pradhan, f.n. No.1, p. 306.
71 Upadhayaya, f.n. No. 3, pp. 306-07.
72 Pradhan, f.n. No.1, p. 306-07.
73 Upadhayaya, f.n. No. 3, p. 307.
74 Pradhan, f.n. No. 1, p. 307.
75 Upadhayaya, f.n. No. 3.
76 Pradhan, f.n. No. 1, p. 14.
77 Kattel, f.n. No. 29, p. 14.
78 *Ibid.*
79 *Ibid.*
80 *Ibid.*
81 From an interview with Kamalraj on 1997/5/10.
82 Kattel, f.n. No. 29.
83 Pradhan, f.n. No. 1, p. 305.
84 Upadhyaya, f.n. No. 3, p. 180.
85 *Ibid.*
86 *Ibid.*
87 *Ibid.*
88 Kattel, f.n. No. 29, p. 72.
89 *Ibid.*, p. 76.
90 *Ibid.*, p. 82.
91 *Ibid.*, p. 61.
92 *Ibid.*, p. 45.
93 *Ibid.*, p. 11.
94 *Ibid.*, p. 8.
95 *Ibid.*
96 *Ibid.*, p. 2.
97 From an interview with B.C. Malla on 1996/4/15, Kathmadndu.
98 *Ibid.*

99 From an interview with Ganesh Ballav Pradhan on 1997/2/10, Kathmandu.

100 From an interview with Sribhadra Sharma on 1996/1/25, Kathmandu.

101 From an interview with Shumbhuram Shrestha on 1996/1/25, Kathmandu.

102 From an interview with Nutan Thapaliya on 1996/1/17, Kathmandu.

103 From an interview with Mukunda Bahadur Shrestha on 1998/9/4, Lalitpur.

104 *Jayatu Sanskritam Movement, 1947,* programme and introductory brochure, (Kathmandu: Golden Jubilee Function Preparatory Committee, 1997), p. 2.

105 *Bidyarthi Bulletin,* (Bicharpradhan Biannual) Vol. 25, No. 1, editor and publisher: Publicity Department, (Kathmandu: Nepal Krantikari Bidyarthi Samiti, 1995), p. 2.

106 Nepalese Student Movement and a Brief History of ANNFSU (Sixth), (Kathmandu: Thirteenth Central Committee of the ANNFSU (Sixth), 1996), p. 4.

107 Gobardhan Rana, *Prajatantrik Andolan ma Nepal Biddhyarthi Sangha* (The Nepal Students' Federation in the Democratic Movement), (Kathmandu: Nepal Students' Federation Western Zones Coordination Committee, 1994), p. 14.

108 From an interview with Shran Bikram Malla on 1997/1/9, Kathmandu.

109 From an interview with Bashudev Tripathi on 1996/8/15, Kathmandu.

110 From an interview with Shahana Pradhan on 1998/7/2, Kathmandu.

111 Pradhan, f.n. No. 1, p. 462.

112 *Ibid.*

113 *Ibid.*, p. 463.

114 *Ibid.*

115 *Ibid.*, p. 464.

116 *Ibid.*, p. 465.

117 *Ibid.*, p. 467.

118 *Ibid.*

119 *Ibid.*, p. 474.

120 *Ibid.*

121 *Ibid.*, p. 483.

122 *Ibid.*

123 *Ibid.*, p. 483-84.

CHAPTER FOUR

Organizational Structure of the Students & their Loyalties

4.1 Introduction

The world events and the students who were lucky enough to study in a foreign country brought a kind of awakening among the Nepalese people. Despite strict control of the Rana government, the Nepalese people had clearly understood that a free atmosphere must be created within the country but the then government was the major obstruction to achieve this. Thinking that the only way to overcome the shortcomings in the country was academic development, the Nepalese youths were trying to do everything possible to acquire education.[1] Not that the Ranas had not understood this. They established the Durbar High School in the capital when Junga Bahadur came back from Britain with a realization that education was the only way for the development of the country. Similarly, Chandra Shumshere had also established Trichandra College. It makes it clear that even the then government had realized the need of education. But this created a kind of restlessness and curiosity among the ordinary people. The youths were especially pricked by this discrimination and a feeling why they should not be allowed to study arose in their minds.[2] The students studying in India had seen for themselves that if the academic and other issues were raised through the students' associations, most of the national problems could be solved. They used to discuss these ideas with their Nepalese counterparts during their visit to their country. The students studying inside Nepal did, in fact, try to form unions, but it was next to impossible owing to the suppression of the then government.[3] In the beginning, the Nepalese students worked with the Indian students' unions. For example, Man Mohan Adhikari was involved in the Indian Student Federation in the capacity of its secretary.[4] As other people get affiliated to different convictions, students also naturally long for their own unions. It is considered important for the development of political culture.[5]

Students and politics are synonymous words. One cannot be separated from the other. In the absence of any one of them, the nation loses its spine. Students are one of the means to make politics strong and powerful.[6]

Generally speaking students are influenced by leftist left of the center and rightist ideologies. Of the three categories there are other two concepts, radical and conventional. The Radicalists are inclined towards revolt, whereas the conventionalists try to get their academic and political demands fulfilled through legal and traditional means.[7] Both of them are found tc have carried out their programmes through students' union. When there is a debate, the extremists are more drawn towards politics than socialists and the rightists.[8] The slogans of the students of developing countries of Asia, Africa and Latin America are more vocal and full of message. The slogans or strikes of the students of developed countries have sometimes a sweeping impact. But such events continuously take place in developing countries. In developed countries, it may be possible to provide all the facilities immediately. But this is not possible in developing countries. Hence the students become restless in the hope of improving their conditions in the future. They also become rebellious due to the widening gap between the rich and the poor. They often visualize an ideal society of equality.[9] Student movements in developing countries are more violent and provocative than in developed countries.

Though different socialists have defined the students movements of the developing countries in different terms, it is generally known as the "revolution of rising expectation".[10] In those countries students take democracy as the basis of everything. The fighters of democracy are often suppressed by the nation, politics and culture. These societies look down upon the new generation as an undisciplined lot. Even the social situation is responsible for making the student mass agitated.[11] Universally speaking, the students have similar political attitude worldwide. But in the contemporary politics, prior to 1990s, we find only two major political theories; one-party system and multi-party system democracy. There are some differences between the two. Some states, which have recently assumed statehood, have propounded a novel political system. But they have not succeeded to acquire strong support from the student mass.[12] If a government is ruled in an automatic way, student associations are established in their support. We can take *Rastrabadi Swatantra Bidyarthi Mandal* as an example.[13] In such a situation, the government provokes and incites the students. It pushes the students to the path of struggle. It creates rift between the right and left students. It organizes its own students' union and pampers it with all sorts of supports and facilities setting it against the left and right students' organizations. It provokes the students to open a united front and refuse recognition to the government.[14] In such situations, the students get rebellious. However, there are several other reasons, which provoke them into agitation.[15] The animosity among students, student-teacher relationship, atmosphere of the classrooms and time and situation also constitute factors leading to movements. Generally speaking, the background of the world students' movement is found to have been created on these basis.[16]

Like other Asian countries, the students movements of Nepal have attained political overtones. Students' unions are formed out of political needs and opposition politics provides supports to them from different angles. In a country like Nepal where the history of higher education is not so long, the politicization of academic institutions should be considered a natural phenomenon.[17] It, in fact, helps in setting up students' unions, amending constitution, repealing various laws and choosing political systems.[18] As organizations are necessary for the safeguard of professional right, the need of the students' union was felt from the period of the Rana rule. In the beginning, students studying in India had focused their attention on forming student unions as it was not possible to do so in the country. Banaras and Calcutta were the main areas of Nepalese students' activities in India. Nepalese students in Patna, Delhi, Bombay, Allahabad and Lucknow also participated in the students activities in Banaras and Calcutta. The process of organization of the students had started about that time. The Nepalese students in Banaras had set up *Nepali Sangh* and *Chhatra Sangh* around 1945 and those in Calcutta *Himachal Bidyarthi Sangh*.[19] In October 1946, B.P. Koirala issued an appeal through Indian newspapers evoking political consciousness among the people.[20] In this process, a convention of the Nepalese students was held in Banaras on October 31, 1946 and All India Nepali *Rastriya Congress* was formed. Students studying in Patna, Darjeeling and Banaras held another conference at Bhawanipur, Calcutta on January 25, 1947. That very year, the Nepali students studying in Banaras University formed *Kashi Bishwabidyalaya* Nepali *Chhatra Snagh*. The Nepali Congress gave recognition to this organization. This association also participated in the Jogwani conference of the Nepali Congress on April 9-10, 1947. The students were also included in its executive committee. Nepali Congress had organized a mass meeting to call for a people's movement after the suppression by the government of the Workers' strike in Biratnagar. The students even boycotted their examinations to participate in it. The students of the *Kashi Bishwabidyalaya* had participated in the people's revolution of 1950 on behalf of the *Chhatra Sangh*.[21] In the meantime, Sanskrit Students' Association, Nepal National Students' Federation, Nepal *Chhatra Sangh* and *Nepal Students Union* were formed inside the country. All India Nepalese Students' Association was formed in India. This organization had a progressive leanings.[22] The *Jayatu Sanskritam* movement is symbolic of the relationship between political parties and the students' unions. The Nepalese students who went to Banaras to appear in their examinations returned deeply impressed by the activities of the *Nepali Rastriya Congress*. This provided momentum to the democratic movement of Nepal.

Various students' organizations had reminded the Nepalese government by raising demands about academic reforms, development and other national and international issues. In the election of 1959, the students had provided all kinds of help to the political parties and had tried to strengthen political culture. A democratic government had been formed in the election. The Royal step of December 1960 dissolved this government and a ban was imposed on political parties, organizations and association. Even the students' unions were banned. Democratic politics of Nepal began to be carried out clandestinely. Political leaders could not function openly. A situation was created in which even the voice of the political parties had to be articulated by the students.[23]

4.2 Role of Students' Union Before 1950

Every step taken by the Nepalese students for the cultivation of political culture is very important. The difficult situation in which the Nepalese students worked is vindicated by the struggle they carried out from home and abroad. Students have played a vanguard role in all the phases of democratic struggle. Political organizations like the *Praja Parisad* could be established out of the student activists.[24] The incident of 1940 made the Nepalese intelligentsia enlightened and revengeful with the government. Students studying in Nepalese colleges were confined to clandestine discussion of the political situation. Those studying in India proceeded towards opening an organization and reforming the condition of the country by overthrowing the Rana regime.[25] *Nepali Rastriya Congress* was established following the establishment of Banaras Students' Union. Even the Nepalese political culture was evolved only after the establishment of the students' union.[26] The students studying in India were deeply impressed by the situation of India and the activities of the Indian students. The Indian students used to shout slogans against the British rule even in the premises of the academic institutes. That impressed the Nepalese students. The Nepalese students were also impressed by the organization of the Indian students.[27] The Independence movement of India is found to have inspired the Nepalese students to think of their country and perform substantial work in the direction of setting up of an organization.[28] There was only one college with about 50/60 students in Nepal. Therefore, the formation of students' union was out of question. The Ranas were self centered and thought only of their family interest. It ultimately harmed the Rana regime. The lack of education in the country encouraged the Ranas to become reactionaries and autocratic in the management of state affairs.[29]

4.3 Nepalese Student's Union Banaras, 1946

The Nepalese students' union was opened in India as it was not possible to open it inside the country. One Tulsi Man Singh and some of his friends who had gone to Calcutta for study became the disciples of Anni Besent and opened a students' union which was critical about the Ranas.[30] This was the earliest form of the Nepalese student's' union. The British handed over the state to the Indian people's representatives. The central government of India had come to the hands of the Indians by June 16, 1946.[31] Some years ago, the students of the Banaras Hindu University had established *Kashi Hindu Bishwabidyalaya* Nepalese Students' Union under the inspiration of the Indian people's movement. Krishna Prasad Bhattarai, Lilanareshwor Baral (Ishwor Baral), Bharat Mani Sharma, Kashiraj Sharma and others had played an active part in its establishment. Those holding progressive ideas in the union had provided an active support to the *Ratriya Congress*.[32] In 1939, Nepali Association was established at Dudhabinayak in Kashi at the initiative of some enthusiastic Nepali students studying there. In the beginning its goal was pure, social service. But soon, political speeches began to take place. As the majority of its members were the students of the Kashi Hindu University from Nepal, the political situation of Nepal and the exploitation of the Ranas began to be the topic of discussion in its meetings. In course of time, the students studying in Banaras Hindu University opened *Nepal Chhatra Sangh* in July 1946.[33]

We Nepalese students studying in *Kashi Chhatra Sangh* have established an organization called *Nepali Chhatra Sangh*. The objectives of the association are as follows:

(1) To improve the Nepalese language and literature.

(2) To request the university authorities to remove inconveniences of the Nepalese students studying or willing to study in the university.

(3) To maintain the dignity of the Nepalese Students in the programmes of other Indian students.

(4) Try to remove misconceptions about Nepal and the Nepalese among outsiders.

(5) To raise a sense of cooperation, service and social responsibility among the Nepalese students.

According to historian Bhuwan Lal Pradhan, the students studying in Banaras Hindu University opened Nepali *Chhata Sangh*. Those who were active in the organization were, Bhishwanath Mishra, (President, an Indian professor), Krishna Prasad Bhattarai (vice-president), Kashiraj Upadhyaya, Ratna Badadur Parthiv, Maniraj Bhandari, Lila Nareshwor Baral, Ishwori Baral, Bishwo Bandhu Thapa, Bharatmani Sharma, Rohini Raj Satyal, Sher Bahadur Shahi, Bishwonath Upadhyaya, Vishnu Bahadur, Gopal Prasad Bhattarai, Bashudev Chandra Malla, Siddhi Shah, Madhabi Shah, Kumari Bhuwan Shah, Rajendra Prasad Npeali, Yog Prasad Upadhyaya (Shilong), Hari Prasad Bhandari etc. Bisheshwor Prasad Koirala and Dharanidhar Koirala also participated in programmes organized by this association. Symposiums used to be organized frequently under the auspices of the union. There used to be Hindu-Muslim riots in those days and it was not free from danger to gather a large number of people at one place. Even the government had put ban on the open air gatherings. As a result the gatherings of the students were often held at the house of Sri Prakash Gupta, one of the leaders of *Bharatia Rastriya Congress.* Some times, Indian socialist leaders Ram Manohar Lohia was also invited to deliver speech in the programmes organized by the union.

There were unions of other Indian students also. They used to celebrate different functions. The Nepalese students also began to consider celebrating Nepal Day. One of the meetings of the union was organized in the Bridal Bahaman situated within the premises of the university. There was a presence of Indian students and the Nepalese as well as other well-wishers outside of the university. This meeting decided to celebrate Nepal Day and prepare a draft constitution of the union. It also decided to hold some more similar rallies in this connection.

It was required to obtain permission to hold gatherings owing to frequent riots and disturbances. It took 15 days to obtain the required permission. The next meeting was convened at the *Nepali Dharmashala* in Dudhabinayak. There was a greater chance of riot owing to the large presence of the Indians. A great caution was exercised in organizing the meeting. Invited guests were conducted to their respective places by the volunteers. Dr. Lohiya was also present in the gathering. Learning about the gathering, Ganesh Man Singh also somehow reached there. When he was trying to enter the *Dharmashala,* volunteers asked him about his identity. He was the same Ganesh Man Singh who had been awarded life sentence by the Ranas for his involvement in the *Praja Parishad* and had somehow reached India by escaping from jail. He was allowed to go to the venue only after he gave his real identity. B.P. Koirala also reached there.

Apart from the work of the union, some people were also allowed to speak.. Ganesh Man Singh was one of them. In his speech he informed that a party called *Praja Parishad* had been clandestinely working in Nepal since 1936. He also told the mass that party had clandestinely scattered pamphlets to inform the people of its objectives. He informed the mass of the martyrdom and spoke highly of Tanka Prasad Acharya who he said was the chairman of that party. Ganeshman also said that he had escaped from jail in 1944 and was living in India since. This incident drew the attention of the students studying in Banaras Hindu University and other Nepalese in Indian to the need of political organization. Some days later, B.P. Koirala issued a statement in "Search Light" stressing the need of a political organization for the establishment of democracy in Nepal.[34]

In this way the unionist activities of the *Chhatra Sangh* had made an active contribution towards the establishment of *Nepali Rastriya Congress.* Various representatives of the students acquiring higher education in different parts of India had participated in the meeting playing a significant role in the establishment of democracy in Nepal. They were- Bharat Mani Sharma, Ishor Baral, Govinda Prasad Lohani, Kashiraj Upadhyaya, Bishwo Bandhu Thapa, Krishna Prasad Bhattarai, Gopal Prasad Bhattarai, Rudra Prasad Giri, etc.[35]

As Bishwa Bandhu Thapa pointed out while studying in Kashi University, the students used to be impressed by many incidents taking place in India. "We used to even deeply feel for our country when we thought about the situation of our country. We wondered why we Nepalese students could not be like the Indian students. Moreover, we had B.P. Koirala who constantly advised us that we would not cultivate political culture through unions unless the autocratic regime of Nepal would be overthrown. He used to instill us with courage. These and other various factors had contributed to the formation of Nepal *Chhatra Sangh.*"[36]

The Government of Nepal used to choose the head for the Nepali Department of Kashi Hindu University. At the time of the establishment of the *Chhatra Union,* Totra Raj Pandey had been the head of the Nepali department. According to the university regulation, he became the chairman of the *Chhatra Union*.[37] The union had to function according to the mandate of the government. Whatever the Nepalese students could perform through this union would be significant in the democratic movement of Nepal.[38]

As Bishwa Bandhu Thapa pointed out while studying in India they had a patriotic feeling, they became conscious of their identity, and aspired for freedom and wanted to speak out. They used to listen to the speeches of the Indian leaders. "B.P. Koirala also inspired us to open a union by unifying all the Nepalese students studying in India. Students from Darjeeling to Pilivit came there for study. We were also impressed by the fact that patriotic leader like Madan Mohan Malaviya was the founder of the Kashi Hindu University and that there was greater freedom in this university than elsewhere. Nepal *Chhatra Sangh* was established for the welfare of the student community"[39]

Age and education brings in knowledge. These very students had been active in the formation of a party like the Nepali Congress. Students get attracted towards nationalism and it is they who have been the source of political parties worldwide.[40] There is no doubt that the establishment of Nepal Students' Union had started from Banaras.[41] In the words of Man Mohan Adhikari, "I am proud to say that the *Chhatra Sangh* of the Kashi Hindu University had played a great role in the history of Nepal. I was a student of the university and was one of the members of the union. It is true that it helped in crating atmosphere for the establishment of the student organization."[42] The *Chhatra Sangh,* which was initially established for students' welfare, began to focus itself on political culture and made an immense contribution to the introduction of democracy in Nepal. There was an equal participation of all the students studying there.[43]

Nepal *Chhatra Sangh* is found to have done an important work towards forming students' union, founding the Nepali Congress and cultivating democratic culture in Nepal. When the students evolved political conviction, some of them became democratic while others chose to be progressive. More student unions were formed. That became possible only because of political conviction. The real fight for democracy started only after the formation of Nepal *Chhatra Sangh*. The students were true soldiers of the struggle in real terms.[44]

4.4 Himanchal Students' Union, Calcutta

The result of the Second World War had begun to appear in the international arena. The Nepalese students who had gone to Calcutta to study were impressed by the environment prevailing there. The atmosphere helped spread democratic culture in Asia and Africa as a new political trend. While studying there, the Nepalese students had an exposure to modernity and they became impressed by the political culture in India. In Nepal one could not even speak against the government. But in India one could criticize the government, open unions and participate in programmes held there frequently. This made the students going there from Nepal realize the importance of the unions.[45] B.P. was released from Hazaribagh Jail in 1945. As Keshar Jung Rayamajhi asserts, "We students in Calcutta discussed the events. There used to be one or the other in Banaras also. We students had access to news.[46] Students in Calcutta and other places had the opportunity to hear the speech of Rammanohar Lohiya in Benaras in 1945. There was a large participation of Nepalese students. They came to know from his speech that they had to do something for their country.[47] When someone reminded Lohia that he had not said anything about Nepal, he said that it was the duty of the Nepalese to come forward and do something.[48] As R.H. Joshi points out, "After some time, Lohia called us to the house of Sri Prakash Gupta and discussed with us what we should do in Nepal and about the way to proceed ahead. Tanka Prasad Acharya, the leader of *Praja Parishad,* also took part in the discussion. It took place towards August and September, 1946.[49] B.P. Koirala arrived after fifteen days. The Nepalese students had participated in it. Nepali

National Congress was established on January 25/26, 1947. The students studying in Calcutta and Benaras came to participate in it and had the opportunity to share information.[50] Student unions were not widespread in those days. They were often localized. In the beginning, we also formed a 'Hill Student's Union' and expanded it to form Himachla Student's Association in 1948.[51] In Nepal, political leadership had been taken by student leaders like. Tanka Prasad Achary, Chuda Prasad, Ram Hari Sharma, Dasharath Chand, Ganga Lal etc. Seasoned leaders like B.P. Koirala, Dilli Raman Regmi, Matrika Prasad, Koirala and Man Mohan Adhikari were also student leaders in their early days.[52] The students and leaders were complementary to each other in the cultivation of political culture. The Nepalese students studying in Calcutta and Benaras organized themselves and helped build political movement.[53] One often feels lonely in a foreign country and starts to search for an identity. In a city like Calcutta, with the domination of the Bengalis, the Nepalese students thought of forming a large group for their security and identity. Besides, Hiranya Shumshere and Subarna Shumshere opened a 'Democratic Front' in Calcutta with a view to overthrowing the Ranas. Nepal's Consulate General's office was located in Calcutta at that time. The Nepalese students were dissatisfied with his behavior. The Consular General used to spy on the Nepalese students. This provided an ample ground for political organization there.[54]

At a time when the revolutionary wave was sweeping in and outside the country, Secretary of the Himanchal Student's Union, Daulat Bikram Rana, intruded into the premises of the Consulate General's office in Calcutta and shouted anti-Rana slogans. Royal Consulate General Daman Shumshere Rana called the Indian police and had Daulat Bikram Rana arrested from the premises of the consulate.[55] The "Yugani" has this to say on this incident: 'Secretary of the Himanchal *Chhatra Sangh* intruded into the consulate: General's office and shouted anti-Rana slogans. Down with the Ranas!, Inqiulab Zindabad !, he shouted.[56]

These and various other reasons gave the Nepalese students in Calcutta an ample opportunity to express their political activities.[57] Nepali Congress was established on January 25 and 26 in Calcutta. We students had also participated in the conference. We were deeply impressed by the unfolding events and formed 'Hill Students' Union' by gathering the students from Sikkim, Bhutan, Darjeeling, Asam, Bhakshu, Burma, Ceylon, Nagaland etc.[58] It, however, could not function well. As a result, we formed *Himanchal Chhatra Sangh* with a view to obtaining representation of the students of the whole Himalayan region.[59] *Himanchal Chhatra Sangh* was established in the beginning. Later, we Nepalese students brought it to life again.[60] At four o'clock last Saturday, that is, on August 17, 1929, a meeting of the students from Darjeeling, Nepal and Sikkim took place at the Scottish College building under the chairmanship of Shri Yukta Rupnarayan Singh. The objective of the meeting was social gathering and the formation of students' union. At the meeting, Shree Yukta, T. Wangdi B. A. proposed the formation of the union which was passed unanimously.

The following was the structure of the union: President, Shree Yukta T. Wangdi B.A.; Vice-President, Lalit Kumar Basnet' General Secretary, Rup Nayarayan Singh B.A.; Cashier, Dharma Bhakta Pradhan and Woman member, Ms. Fulmaya Pradhan.[61]

Himanchal Chhatra Sangh was restarted on the initiative of the Nepalese students. Its objectives have been stated in the "Himanchal Magazine" as follows:

(1) to bring about social, cultural and academic consciousness among the students;

(2) to publish newspapers, books and magazines;

(3) to promote amity among the members of the association and other students at large;

(4) to enhance the interest of the students in sports;

(5) to cultivate close friendship with students in general;

(6) to organize logic contest, symposiums, and study teams etc.[62]

In this way the *Chhatra Sangh* had played a great role in organizing and enlightening the students.

The Himanchal magazine has this to write about the Himanchal *Chhatra Sangh:* "The 31 year old students" union has braced itself up for renewed activities. It was established on 17 August, 1929 as a social gathering and an effort for the safeguard of students' right and interest. We students give its credit to Shree Rup Narayan Singh and Shree T. Wangdi. The union has been in existence because of their efforts. We may not be able to write about all the works it has done. But our matter of concern is what it may have to do in the future. The *Himanchal Chhatra Sangh* which has come into existence in Calcutta has not only contributed in the field of literature, it has also brought a new surge of unity and organization among the students and other Nepalese staying in Calcutta. As the Himalayas have given us life, so has done the *Himanchal Chhatra Sangh* to us in giving our rights to live. It will give the message: "As a human being you have the right to live"[63] The *Himanchal Chhatra Sangh* had published articles propagating its future programme stressing on students' unity and national development. The articles runs as follows:

> *The time flies. With the flight of time, there is a call for progress. Those nationalities or nations which did not listen to its call were left behind in the race for progress. It may be destroyed at the cruel hands of time. The Nepalese have been through this plight.*
>
> *Students are the conscious organs of a society. They have to rip open the festering wounds and heal the sores eating into the vitals of their race, society, nation and the country. The responsibility of removing the dirt and smudges of backward Nepalese society to create a true and beautiful country and to raise the Nepalese to the level of human beings. This issue of*

the Himanchal *is the symbol of the effort made by the* Himanchal Chhatra Sangh *to instill intellectual consciousness among the students. It is up to you to evaluate if we have been able to take a single step forward in our effort to cross the vast sea of duty. It will not be out of place to ask the blessings from our predecessors for the success in our efforts. With their inspiration, we should consider it worthwhile if we do not lag far behind in our journey even if we are not able to flow with time.*

As our country has fallen behind in progress, we have also fallen behind in all the fields. When we cast our eyes to other countries, we wonder why we were in animate with progress. We have many problems. Education is only one of them. It is related not only with Himanchal Chhatra Sangh *but with the hundred of thousands of people of the country.*

In view of the lack of education in our country, the major responsibility of education has fallen on our shoulders. When we start something with a concrete programmes, we will certainly attain success. We will be able to bring about cultural, social, and intellectual development both in and out of the country singing a sacred hymn of unity, which we need so much ......

Let us hope that the attention of the association will be drawn towards it and will be successful in leaving the footsteps of progress behind. It is our last hope that the theme of unity propagated by the Himanchal Chhatra Sangh *will spread far and wide both at home and abroad.*

Nepalese students study in various academic institutes of India. Nepalese studying in Calcutta, Darjeeling, Kashi, Allahabad, Asam, Durbhunga, etc. have made their own local unions. Though they have similar objective, they have different names, let alone a central organization. That is why we ask: "Why we should not be united."

We should identify our problems as opportunities. We should not think about where we differ. But we should find the points of unity. If we do so we shall find out that most of our problems are similar. We can evolve consensus in most of the issues if not in all of them. We should revive the sense of adjustment

> *and cooperation among us. Divergence cannot bring about unification. If we are not united in ideas, we cannot find solution to our multifaceted problems. If we can pay attention to these questions, the students will have different appearance. The present individualistic discordance will be replaced by collective cooperation awakening our spiritual consciousness.*
>
> *The invention of science has been making the world narrower each day. Should not we try to take out level of thought nearer to the progress made by the world? This is the question we have put before the analytical thinking of our friends."*64

The *Himanchal Chhatra Sangh* had expressed its view about national situation, problems and its goals through the "Himanchal Magazines." A frequent meeting and discourse with Indian and Nepalese leaders also took place. This association had made a significant contribution in the 1950 Revolution.[65]

The leaders of the association even tried to hold its conference in Kathmandu towards May-June, 1950. Some discussions were also held on this subject. Students studying in Banaras, Patna and Allahabad like Bunu Bijayalaxmi, Bishwabandhu, Jayawar Sing Pradhan, Rhidayaraj Sharma, Ganeshraj Singh etc. even sent their consent and greetings.[66] Ramhari Joshi reached Raxaul and sought permission from Kathmandu to hold the conference. However, Bijaya Shumshere telephoned next day and refused permission.[67] However, we did not lose heart. We decided to proceed towards holding the conference with greater preparation. We assigned Jayanarayan Giri to meet the students in India and bring them to Nepal. The responsibility to arrange things in Kathmandu was given to Ram Hari Joshi, Ishwarilal Shrestha and Arunchandra Pradhan. Ram Hari Joshi was the group leader. Ram Hari Joshi went to the palace himself, sought audience with King Tribhuwan through his adviser Govind Narayan Singh and informed him about the plan to hold students' conference in Kathmandu under the auspices of *Himancal Chhatra Sangh*. The King had a positive view about it and sponsored seven or eight trips of aircraft service for the transport of student representatives.[68] When the preparation was being made to hold the conference around September of October, 1951, the Chiniya Kaji episode took place. B.P. Koirala tendered his ıesignation, the cabinet of Mohan Shumshere was dissolved and the conference was also postponed.[69] Matrika Pasad Koirala became Prime Minister. An enlarged conference of the students took place in Kathmandu on Monday, December 24, 1951. Student representatives from Calcutta, Patna, Banaras, Allahabad, Delhi, Assam, Panjab etc. attended the conference.[70] A dispute arose on whom to invite to inaugurate the conference. Some were in favour of B.P. Koirala while others wanted it to be inaugurated by Shahibddin who was a member of the Federation and had sustained bullet injury on his leg during Chiniya Kaji episode and whom Mohan Shumshere had sent to[71] Patna giving Rs. 5000 for treatment. After long discussion, a decision was made to have it inaugurated by Laxmi Prasad Devkota.[72] This was the first such conference of the Nepalese students. Many students from home and abroad had participated in the conference. King Tribhuwan had sent good wishes to the conference.[73] The All Nepal Students' Conference scheduled to be held in December could not take place due to non-arrival of all the representatives. It was started at Tundikhel. Student representatives from Burma and various corners of India had come to participate in the conference. This was the first such conference ever held in Nepal.

4.5 Inauguration of Students' Conference by Poet Laxmi Prasad Devkota

The Nepalese students' conference started at *Thulo Tundikhel* at 3 O'clock. This conference was organized by the students of Nepal and *Himanchal Chhatra Sangh*. It was inaugurated by the poet, Laxmi Prasad Devkota.

Laxmi Prasad Devkota made a speech full of erudition. Following this, President of Nepal *Chhatra Sangh,* Surendra

Raj Sharma, requested Prof. Amrit Prasad Pradhan to take the chair and made reference to the role of students in the revolutions of the past. Representative of the *Himanchal Chatra Sangh* Jaya Narayan Giri shed light on the objective of the conference and said that the conference was held purely to promote mutual goodwill among the students. Minister for education Sharada Shumshere Rana in a statement said that the responsibility to disseminate education had evolved on the shoulders of students owing to the backward academic state of the country. The education minister hoped that the mutual cooperation and unity of the students would take the country forward along with the path of progress. Prime Minister, other cabinet ministers, students of almost all the schools of the valley and thousands of other people were present at the conference. In the beginning, the *Himanchal Chhatra Sangh* helped promote understanding and unity among the students by organizing various programmes. Initially, it had laid stress on the students' interest and national issues. Later, it began to acquire a political tilt. Even the political parties started to give attention to the students' union after the revolution of 1950. One of the important achievements of the *Chhatra Sangh* was to take initiative in forming All Nepal Indian Students' Federation by unifying all the students scattered around India.[74]

The *Himanchal Chhatra Sangh* had a social basis. It used to observe Saraswati Puja, Holi, and Bhailo once a year and did philanthropic works like publishing *Himanchal* magazine from the money thus collected. In the beginning, it looked after the welfare of the students and drew their attention to the plight of the country. Later, when political parties began to be opened, it began to have political influence.[75]

4.6 Interview Taken by *Himanchal Chhatra Sangh* with Prime Minister Bishweshwor Prasad Koirala

The interview took place at Kanak building at appointed time. There were many other people waiting for interview.

But we were given the first priority. As soon as we entered, the Prime Minister showed his curiosity to learn about the background of the *Himanchal Chhatra Sangh*. The chief secretary of the Sangh, Prithvi Raj Giri, gave a short description of its background and said that the association was not new. It was established 31 years ago and it was not sectarian. It had worked for the promotion of brotherhood in association with other social organizations (See Appendix V).

4.7 Student Organization from 1950-1960

4.7.1 Sanskrit *Chhatra Sangh* (Nepal)

India was the main area of democratic activities of Nepal before 1947. But sporadic incidents regarding democratic movements had taken place in Nepal from the early period of the Rana rule in Nepal. We feel pleasure in our heart to record some events in history which had put the Ranas in a tight rope. But the Ranas would not lose much in terms of power. It was the Nepalese who got rigorous punishment. That was why the Nepalese people had used the Indian soil for democratic movement before 1947. Banaras is one of the places inspiring the Nepalese people for democratic movement. The educated Nepalese youths were inspired to understand the situation of the country and get involved in politics. In this process, the students of Sanskrit Bidyapith pledged to launch a movement at a gathering in *Mangal Gauri Dharmashala* in 1947. The environment of Queen's College made it possible. Returning from Banaras after their exams, the students of the Sanskrit School submitted an ultimatum to the government demanding reform in the Sanskrit education by the end of July that year.[76] The government did not fulfill the demands and the students of the Sanskrit Hostel started a picketing. The Sanskrit Students Union had taken the leadership of the movement.[77] As for the Sanskrit students, they had started to get organized for quite a long time. It can be vindicated by various incidents taking place within the hostel.[78] The students hailing from Mechi to Mahakali stayed together in the hostel and had interaction among them. They were able to identify the problems of the country during the discussion. This helped build the movement.[79] The harsh attitude of the government also provoked the students to launch the movement. *Jayatu Sanskritam* movement gained momentum after Padma Shumshere termed Sanskrit as a dead language.[80]

The students of Sanskrit were organized for a long time. The Sanskrit Students' Association was established only during the movement of 1947. The students of Sanskrit are found to have a distinct feature. It is considered a symbol of common ideology. Some say that the students' movement was divided into different factions only after 1955/56.[81] Others, however, believe that it suffered from split only after 1959/60. One section of the students assisted King Mahendra after the incident of 1960. They also observed illumination that night.[82]

Towards 1953, the Sanskrit Students' Association was a students' organization having representation of different ideologies.[83] The Sanskrit Students' Association was established in 1947. It is probably the first students' organization in Nepal. This very organization is found to have endeavoured to create public opinion against the Ranas. The whole Sanskrit Hostel came forward in the movement of 1950. The entire students of the hostel had come out in the field of the movement.[84] The Sanskrit *Chhatra Sangh* was established in 1947. It was common forum for all the students having different ideologies. It started the propagation of political culture from the very heart of Kathmandu.[85] The students of the Sanskrit *Chhatrabash* were organized for a long time. The movement of 1990 makes it clear that they had a significant contribution in each political incident in the history of Nepal. Though the Sanskrit Students' Association was divided into ANNFSU and NSU, it has been a characteristic feature of the Sanskrit students to have a unified participation in all the academic, national and international events taking place in the country. Its credit should go to Sanskrit Students' Association.[86]

The students of *Sanskrit Bidyapith* had maintained an organized existence. They used to hold discussion and to arrive at certain conclusions according to the country's objective and situation. On this basis, a sketch of an organization was prepared at the initiative of Rajeshwor Devkota, Kashinath Gautam, Kamal Raj Regmi etc. The association was established in 1947. The movement for Jayatu Sanskritam started and the students got organized. Towards the end of 1948 and the start of 1949, the students became more actively involved in giving continuity to the intellectual activities. The constitution of the Sanskrit Students' Association was written in 1950. Sri Prasad Gautam had drafted the constitution. Mr. Gautam played a significant contribution in this association from 1947-1955. He ran a hand written magazine called *Chhatra Batu*. In a letter written by Ram Prasad Neupane, there is a picture of a flag on the cover and there are some poems in the pages.

Its first convention was held in 1952. It had 30 to 40 branches. It held its first conference in 1955. It elected Sri Prasad Gautam its president. It published a magazine called *Chhatra Sandesh* in 1955. It held its second conference in Dang. It elected Keshab Dipak as its president. The representatives of the Students' Association split in 1959 and they created another organization. They also set up a different office for the Association in 1960.

The Pitambar Dahal group opened an office hiring a room in Bagbazar for Rs. 25 per month. Bashudev Tripathi, Rewatiraman Khanal, Thakur Parajuli, Baburam Paudel etc. were its members. The progressive side hired a room in Bhotahity. The six persons who had splintered away were expelled from the hostel. The democrats undertook fasting in 1960. The incident of December 15 took place in the meantime. According to one source, the leftists observed illumination in the hostel that night. In 1961 two different conferences took place, one in Lal Durbar and the other in Bishwa Jyati. The parliamentary session was to take place in 1962. But the directive Act prevented it from taking place. Later, a national conference was held which elected Chetonath Acharya as its president. The leftist group is said to have link with King Mahendra. Altogether 31 issues of Jayatu Sanskritam monthly were published from 1960, 1963/64. The Sanskrit *Chhatra Sangh* was divided after Bashudev Tripathi left the organization in 1963."[87]

4.7.2 Greeting from King Mahendra Bir Bikram Shah

"Sanskrit language is the basis of the Nepalese culture. There is no doubt in it. The attempt to revive this language is to foster the Nepalese culture. We wish the magazine *Jayatu Sanskritam* scheduled to be published by Sanskrit *Chhatra Sangh* a success in leading the country along the democratic path keeping to the good traditions of our society."[88]

Here is an article published in the joint issue of Arunodaya entitled "A short Note on *Sanskrit Chhatrabash* and Democratic Activities." In fact, the organizational activities here started even before 1940. It identified itself as the first students' movement in Nepal's history by igniting national awakening movement in 1947 through 'Jayatu Sanskritam' movement having a definite political goal against the Ranas. In the process, it also became involved in anti-Rana activities by establishing 'Sanskri Students' Association' in the same year in order to bring about democratic awakening among the Nepalese youths. It helped the civil disobedience movement in 1956, opposed the retrogressive step of the king in 1960, and actively participate in the students' movements of 1979 and 1990. It also did everything possible to participate in the massive people's movement of 1990 launched to overthrow the autocratic and undemocratic Panchayat system. Many students underwent hardship in this process and the movement also became successful."[89] The students of *Tin Dhara Sanskrit Pathshala* pledged to make every effort to get their just demands fulfilled. This determination gave birth to Sanskrit *Chhatra Sangh* (Nepal).[90] Thus, the *Sanskrit Chhatrabash* gave the lesson of open and organized struggle to the Nepalese people for the first time in the history of the nation. At a time when it was crime to utter even a single word against the Ranas, it was indeed an epoch making event to launch an open and organized struggle against the policy of the government and for own's own rights.[91] As early as 2008 B.S., the students of Sanskrit in the capital were consolidating and expanding the Sanskrit *Chhatra Sanghi* openly and in an organized manner. Work also started outside the Kathmandu valley for the expansion of federal organization[92] The Sanskrit *Chhatra Sangh* has always supported the just demands raised by each and every student organization. The Sanskrit *Chhatra Sangh* has given the greatest contribution in coordinating students' organizations like National Students' Federation, Nepal Students' Union and other students' organizations. The local branches and workers of the Sanskrit *Chhatra Sangh* were also extending their cooperation to the just steps taken by the local student organizations.[93] Though the Sanskrit *Chhatra Sangh* had expressed its commitment to stay away from the partisan politics and to pursue a policy of equality and amity, it wavered to this and that side according to the tilt of the office bearers of the central executive committee. Despite this, it can be said to have a different character from those of the then Nepal Student's Union and National Students' Federation.[94]

4.7.3 International Relation

In this way the Sanskrit Students' Union expanded its relation to students' unions in foreign countries, consolidating the organization at home in accordance with its policy of detachment from partisan politics. The Sanskrit Students' Union was also successful in helping the foreign students to enhance their knowledge about Nepal and vice-versa through the mutual exchange of publications and letters.[95] The first student to go to Europe to attend the World Students' Congress held in Warsaw, Poland, was Achut Raj Regmi.[96]

4.7.4 Assistance in National Building

The Sanskrit *Chhatra Sangh* (Nepal) extended its hand in

making the people understand the importance of nation building and rekindle their interest to it.[97] One feels that the Sanskrit Chhatrabash had given continuity to the work started by Sanskrit *Chhatra Sangh*. Here goes the paragraph as occurs in the joint issue of Arunodaya:

The *Sanskrit Chhatrabash* is found to have made itself stand on the side of human rights, democracy and multi-party political system ever since 1947. There in lies the main achievement and significance of this organization. I would like to bring this context to end hoping that this institution will continue to render important contribution in the field of human rights, democracy and multi-party political system even in days, years and centuries to come.[98]

4.8 Nepal National Students' Federation

Nepal National Students' federation is a representative organization of all democratic and progressive students. This is the first students' organization which was established in 1950. From its very beginning, the NNSF has been playing a significant role in the field of struggle launched for students' welfare and people's democratic rights. Our students' organization has a glorious history of taking special initiative in the joint students' movement of Nepal. The red flag emblazoned with a book and a star has become an endearing flag for the Nepalese students.[99] Though there were a few places where only students rose in struggle, the students established their contact with different political parties and participated in the movement. Realizing the need for the students to go ahead with their own programme, All Nepal Students' Federation was set up with the assistance of the then Communist Party of Nepal in 1949. Since the party was underground and the movement was taking the form of armed struggle, the students too, became active accordingly. The students' movement raised itself from the status which it had before 1950 and moved ahead towards social change, democracy and nationalism in an organized manner. The students began to get agitated and organized in their own way in the new situation following the change of 1950.[100]

Nepal National Students' Federation (NNSF) is one of the organizations set up prior to 1950. The Federation participated in the anti-Rana people's revolution of 1950.[101] The organizational expansion of NNSF took place rapidly after the exiled leaders of the Communist Party returned to Nepal in the free atmosphere created by the successful revolution of February 18, 1950. It will be no exaggeration to say that this organization continued to work, though indirectly, as a sister organization of the Communist Party of Nepal. The propagation of the Russian revolution drew the NNSF to the Russian Axis.[102] Like other parties, this organization, too, could not free itself from the weakness of embracing the programmes of the party it supported. It considered its main objective to oppose the Nepali Congress by terming the 1950 Revolution a hoax and organizing protest against the murder of Chiniya Kaji in 1951.[103]

The NNSF had its first, second and third conferences in 1955, 1965 and 1971 respectively. It worked as a member of the Central Action Committee in 1978/79. It held its fourth national congress on September, 1979.[104] The fourth conference had designated the flag, objective, and the structure of the central committee which are as follows:

(a) Flag

A map of Nepal on the blue background and an open book with a heptagonal star at the left corner. The contour of the map in white and the colour of the book and star red.[105]

(b) Objective

(a) To inculcate the feeling of patriotism in the students of the country.

(b) To try for achieve, accessible, scientific and democratic education system for all the students of the country.

(c) To try for the promotion and development of national culture, national tradition, and national arts.[106]

The Nepal Students' Federation was established, in 1950 at *Sarawatisthan* in Svayambhu, Its founding secretary was Prachandaraj Singh Suwal. (The committee had no provision for a president) The NNSF had an active participation in the people's movement against the family autocracy of the Ranas. NNSF had organized a massive rally in 1951 at Bhugol Park, Kathmandu against Dehli Agreement, Intrusion of the Indian Military and against black lows. Student leader Chiniya Kaji had died a martyr when the police opened fire on the crowd at the order of B.P. Koirala. We have been observing this day each year as the Martyrs' Day. In addition to NNSF, the following students' organizations were also considered most powerful as early as 1953: The Students' Union, considered near to the Nepali Congress and the Sanskrit *Chhatra Sangh* having representation of all kinds of students.

The NSF had received full membership of International Students' Union (ISU) in 1953 owing to its active role in the country and outside.

About 200 student representatives had participated in the first national conference of the NNSF held in 1955. An 11 member central committee was elected under the chairmanship of Bashu Dev Dhungana.

ANNSF, Nepal Students' Union and Sanskrit Chhatra Sangh had organized a unity national conference at Kathmandu in 1956 with a view to creating a strong students' organization. The conference had named the unified students' union All Nepal National Students' Federation. The conference had elected a 13 member central committee under the chairmanship of Bashu Dev Dhungana.

In a short time following the unity congress the organization, which had played a great role in national and internal fields, became nearly paralyzed owing to reactionary penetration, internal squabble and the passivity of the leadership. A national convention was scheduled to be held in Butwal on January 10, 1960 with a view to revive and reactivate it. But it was postponed due to the military action taken on December 16, 1960 by King Mahendra.

Realizing a need for a strong and revolutionary students organization to provide a new direction to the students' movement in the context of the capitulation of the NNSF, an inter-campus students conference was held in Kathmandu from 1964 amidst a cruel suppression and terror by the Panchayat system.[107]

The Communist Party of Nepal was established on April 22, 1949. This party began to be active in the propagation of Marxism-Leninism and in the movement against the Ranas. It had its direct impact on the progressive Nepalese students. It provided inspiration to the Nepalese students to get organized in a better way. As a result, All Nepal Students Federation was clandestinely established in 1949. This organization was successful to meet the requirement for a central organization among the Nepalese students. It played an important role in the political movement of 1950 which had spearheaded action against the then autocratic rule of the Ranas.[108]

A protest demonstration was held with black flags when Indian Prime Minister Jawaharlal Nehru visited Nepal. A joint mass meeting of the Nepalese students was held in Bhugol Park in 1951 in order to expose the Delhi Agreement, intrusion of Indian troops into Nepalese soil and various immoral activities of the government. Chiniya Kaji attained martyrdom and others were injured. In commemoration of this day, the ANNFSU students have been observing ever since as the Martyrs' Day. In this way, this students' organization became renowned and won affiliation with international students' unions like WFDA and ISU.[109] Around 1956, some students studying in Kathmandu valley set up "Inter-College Students' Union" to conduct their activities. This students' union and ANNSF had a unity conference. As endorsed by the conference, both the unions were merged into "Nepal National Students' Federation" (NNSF).[110] In

1956, King Mahendra had inaugurated the conference of the Nepalese students at the present Nepal Eye Hospital in Tripureshwore.[111]

During this period, the NNSF organized protest demonstrations to oppose various unequal treaties made against Nepal's sovereignty, military mission of India in Nepal and military agreement of 1952, authorizing India to keep its check posts in the northern borders.[112] The NNSF had exposed the unequal treaties signed by the Nepalese government with India like agreement on vegetable ghee, Gandak agreement and trade agreement. It had also opposed other acts of immorality and murder that had taken place inside the country.[113] The military action of 1960 had an impact on all the associations and organizations of the country. The prevailing national and international situation affected their organized activities. The NNSF was also affected. In the meantime, NNSF, the organization of the Nepalese progressive students, went to the fold of the Russian revisionist. It created division within the progressive students.[114]

It is a wellknown fact that the Nepal Students' Federation established along with the Communist Party of Nepal had participated in the anti-Rana activities. The students had come to the street in 1951 in opposition to the Delhi Agreement signed to strangle the Nepalese people' revolution. The students are found to have special role in the movements organized against education law in 1952, Gandak Agreement of 1953, military agreement with India and the agreement authorizing India to set up check posts in northern borders. In addition to this, we also remember the movements organized by the students against Koshi agreement in 1956, import of vegetable ghee and other unequal treaties.[115] The party leadership was occupied by revisionists and royalists after the second national congress of the party. It had its affect within the NNSF.[116] A non-Marxist idea of separating students' movement from the peasants' movement was introduced.

Despite this, the NNSF led the movement against the import of vegetable ghee in cooperation with other revolutionary elements.[117] The leadership of the Communist Party capitulated before the King following King Mahendra's anti-democratic step in 1960. NNSF, too, supported the step terming it as basic democracy.[118] The militant Nepalese students held the first conference at Mujaffurpur in 1961 in line with the directive of the Durbanga plenum of the Communist Party of Nepal. The CPN had its conference in 1962. It passed the revisionist programme of National Democracy amidst shrill slogans of 'sovereign parliament'. In this way the renegade and revisionist elements usurped the party leadership rendering the NNSF directionless.[119] When revisionism prevails party leadership, it is natural for other professional and class organizations to have its impact. The royalists, liquidationists and revisionists, thus, had predominance in Nepal National Students' Federation.[120]

The students' movement expanded its areas of sphere and raised various issues such as the increment in the salary of campus lecturers, school teachers, instructors of Sanskrit schools, welfare of ordinary people, price rise and law and order. Federation was the motive force behind these activities. The Kathmandu valley had witnessed various strikes including the one launched in 1953 demanding reduction in the price of chilli. The residents of the city never hesitated to support the movement. The special issue of *Mulprabaha* concerning the Second Conference of Nepal Progressive Students' Union has reviewed the NNSF as follows:

> *The student mass opposed the Delhi Agreement in order to establish democratic system by completely overthrowing the Rana regime. Young student leader Chiniya Kaji died a martyr in this very movement. In this background the Nepal National Students' Federation was established for the first time in the history of the students' movement in 1951 with a view to safeguard the interest of the students and to restore democratic rights. The then communist party was in favour of the*

> *complete abolition of the feudal system and the establishment of a fully democratic system. Most of the students were also guided and inspired by this idea. Under the leadership of the NNSF, the students, therefore, played an active role in the peasants' movement against the Gorkha recruitment. The students fought as the vanguard force in the civil disobedience movement launched in 1957 against the conspiracy not to hold the election for the "constituent assembly". As the feudal elements infiltrating into the ranks of the students, usurped the leadership of the Federation and supported the obnoxious anti-democratic step of 1960, the student mass became leadershipless and directionless for some time.*[121]

The Federation was born in struggle, grew in struggle, will be tempered in struggle and will rip apart the black curtain of night and march forward unfurling its flag in the dawn. The revolutionary students of NNSF have launched an undaunted struggle against *Pancha* reactionaries. In this way the Federation has swept aside the rubbish, maintained its revolutionary tradition and safeguarded peoples' self-aspect. As the organization becomes weak if we struggle against the Panchayat system, we should use only those rights given by it to us, the constitution as democratic and that we should go on expanding democracy as nothing but the voice of the flunkies of Panchayat reactionaries. The Federation has fought and will fight against all kinds of reactionaries unflinchingly.[122]

Since the establishment of NNSF, it has been continuously fighting for democratization in education and other national and international issues. Though it underwent a period of stagnation following 1960, it has been able to claim a prominent place among the progressive students after its reorganization in 1969. It has maintained its militant image despite various attempts of the reactionaries to mislead it from its principles and revolutionary tradition. The incidents taking place in the intervening period have proved that the democratic feelings of the people cannot be strangled by any force howsoever strong. The conviction of the people to democracy has become stronger due to, among other things, the deep crisis brought about by the Panchayat system and the attempt of the *Pancha* reactionaries to escape from it. The Panchayat system is responsible for the present plight of the country and the only way out of the crisis is the restoration of democracy.[123]

As a member organization of International Students' Union (ISU) and World Democratic Youth Federation (WFDY) the NNSF expresses its solidarity with the global youth and students' movements taking place against imperialism colonialism, neocolonialism, racism, apartheid, fascism and Jewism and it stands for peace, independence and socialism. Similarly, the NNSF expresses its full support to the 12th youth and students festival being organized in Moscow under the slogan" Anti-imperialist Solidarity, Peace and Friendship.

The NNSF will continue to struggle on common issues of democratization in education, restoration of democracy in the country and the movement for peace against imperialism and for world peace.[124]

The NNSF has always been fighting for the students' movement and the people's democratic movement. It has set bright examples by playing an active roles in the joint struggle launched in 1978/79, in referendum in 1984. The prison terms spent by its leaders from its very foundation period are its proofs.[125]

The above activities and incidents prove that the NNSF was influenced by the conviction and ideology of the Communist Party of Nepal. With its militant steps in various national and international issues, it has given significant contribution in making the Nepalese democratic movement successful. In various stages of the movement, the Federation was compelled to take both simple and harsh steps about people's livelihood, law and order and development. The issues of the import of vegetable ghee, reduction of the price of chilli, civil disobedience movement of 1957 are some of the examples in which the Federation had played an active role.

4.9 Nepal Students' Union

Nepal Students' Union has added a very important chapter in the history of the organization of the Nepalese students. A founder and an active member of the Nepal Students' Union, Bashudev Rishal explains the background of its establishment and the nature of its activities in the following terms:

> *The Nepalese people were desperate to break free from the domination of the Ranas. But we were clear that the root cause of poverty, illiteracy and superstition of the country was the autocratic Rana regime. The failure of occasional revolts against the Ranas such as the* Praja Parishad *incident had a bad impact on us. In such situation, we students gathered at Kopundol and organized a club. It worked in the direction of assisting the people in their struggle against the Ranas. In the revolution of 1950, it organized Nepal Students' Union and enlisted the participation of the Nepalese students in the revolution. It was active in various issues until 1960. In political conviction the Nepal Students' Union shared the ideology of the Nepali Congress.*[126]

According to the records, the Nepal Students' Union was inaugurated by Late King Tribhuwan in 1950. It was chaired by Surendra Prasad Sharma. At a later stage, it is found to have been subservient to the government. It had created obstruction in the work of All Nepal Students' Federation. Some references are also found that it had opened an inter-college students' union in 1956 saying that it had objectives similar to ANSF's. It was chaired by Sundar Raj Joshi.[127]

In the meantime, the Nepal Students' Union was also established in 1950. Surendraraj Sharma, Asthamangal Bajracharya, Yamuna Lal Maskey were elected the chairman, secretary, joint-secretary respectively, Gajasundar Pradhan, Gorakchhya Bahadur Nhuchhe Pradhan, Puskarnath Sharma, Bashudev Rishal, Balaram Pyakurel, Chetnarayan Shrestha etc. were the executive members. Krishna Man

Shrestha, Jiwan Lal Satyal, his sisters and Devendra Shrestha etc. were the most active students during that period. They actively participated in the academic and other movements.[128] The Nepal Students' Union, Nepal Students' Federation and other Nepalese students studying in India had played a significant role in the armed and peaceful revolutionary movement of 1950.[129] Mr. Ganesh Ballav Pradhan who had once worked in the capacity of Secretary of Nepal Students' Union has made the following remark about Nepal Students Union:

> *Nepal Students' Union came into existence after the revolution of 1950. The leftist lobby of the union splintered away in 1956 and formed Students' Union. After some time this very union changed its name into Nepal National Students' Federation. A Kathmandu valley conference of Nepal Students' Union took place in 1959. It also opened its branch in the name of valley committee. It also held its national conference the same year. According to its constitution, it had a central committee and a secretariat of five members. The members of the secretariat were, Ganesh Ballav Pradhan, Sri Rang Pathak, Jaya Krishna Panthi, Shankar Ghimire and Sitaram Bhandari. There was no provision for a chairman. There was a general secretary in the secretariat. Ranga Lal Pathak was the general Secretary.*
>
> *Nepal Students' Union launched a movement in 1959 as part of Sanskrit* Chhatra Sangh. *It had academic demands. We stayed at Kalmochan Ghat for one and a half months. We observed a one day fast on the last day. We broke the fast after our demands were fulfilled. It expressed its solidarity in the civil disobedience movement of 1951 by undertaking picketing for one day. The students working under the Nepal Students' Union were diligent and skillful in their work. They traveled to villages canvassing for the Nepali Congress candidates in the general election of 1958. One of the leaders of the Nepal students' Union who was only 24 years was proved to have been 25 years with the help of his horoscope. He won the election and became deputy whip of the*

> *parliamentary party of the Nepali Congress. It vindicates the strength and ability of the students under Nepal Students' Union. We went to the districts to open the branches of the NSU following the victory of the Nepali Congress. Its central committee and valley committee were formed in 1959. The national and valley conferences of the union took place the same year. Its constitution was also drafted. The Nepal students' Union had organized and strengthened the student mass of the country by protecting class interest of the people, systematizing democracy, increasing the number of students nation-wide and taking appropriate steps regarding various national and international issues. Its office was located at New Road, just above the Joshi Shopping Centre. It was banned following the incident of 1960. The same night a group of policemen broke the office and confiscated all the documents and other items. The activities of Nepal Students' Union was thus brought to an end.*[130]

Nepal Students' Union has performed significant works in the areas of Nepalese students' organization and movement. The works of the Nepal Students' Union in increasing the number of students in schools and colleges, enhancing the cooperation among the students' organization, solving the education problems of the students' helping the students of the Sanskrit *Chhatra Sangh*, participating in civil disobedience movement of 1951 and extending a hand to the Nepali Congress in forming democratic government are unforgettable. The royal step of 1960 brought its dissolution also.[131]

Nepal Students' Union was established in 1950 and existed until 1960. During this period, it gave a significant contribution in academic and democratic field. It played an important role in accomplishing the general election of 1958 and the formation of a democratic government. It had its impact on us young students who were drawn to politics. It was banned following the royal step of 1960.[132]

There were four students' organizations in Nepal then. They all stressed on democratization of Nepal. At that time,

Bashu Rishal from Nepal Students' Union, Achutraj Regmi from Sanskrit *Chhatrabash*, Bijay Prasanna from Students' Union and Bashu Dev Dhungana from NNSF went to participate in the conference of the World Students' Union being held in Warsaw, Poland.[133] It is a proof that Nepal Students' Union had also participated in the international students' conference held in Europe.

4.9.1 Link with B.P. Koirala

Leader of the Nepali Congress B.P. Koirala who was organizing the Nepalese people in India with a view to spark revolution, met with the Nepalese students during one of his secret visits to Kathmandu. It was a matter of good fortune even for B.P. Koirala who was able to have link with young students.

The revolutionary pamphlets were carefully smuggled into Nepal from Banaras and Patna and were distributed to the people with the help of the students working under the Nepal Students Union. The students under the Nepal Students' Union even undertook great risks, which demanded courage.

B.P. Koirala instructed them to stick posters on the walls of Singhadurbar despite strict vigilance of the Ranas. At a meeting of the Students Union, a student said that he would stick those posters. The student was able to stick the anti-Rana posters on the gate of Singhadurbar camouflaging himself as a military man taking his turn on the night duty. Next day when the Ranas saw the posters they felt insecure, and that's exactly what B.P. had intended.

Eventually, the peoples' revolution of February 18, 1950 brought an end to the rule of the Ranas. After King Tribhuwan came back from India, some retrogressive elements carrying naked Khukris created disturbances against democracy. They even broke the king's photographs and shouted vulgar slogans. At that time also, it was the students who had to come forward shouting slogans against reactionaries.

4.9.2 Chiniya Kaji Shooting Incident

It is natural for a few years following the revolution to be sensitive to the nation and nationality. Situation had become fluid on some occasions owing to political rashness.

A protest rally was held at Bhugolpark in October, 1951 at a direct initiative of Nepal Students' Union and in cooperation with other students unions. People's leader B.P. Koirala had repeatedly appealed to the Nepal Students' Union and other students' organization to concentrate on professional interest and not to be puppets of political parties. The academic situation of the country was not only chaotic, it had also become an arena for dirty politics.

The rally held in October, 1951 went round the city demanding law and order and converged at Bhugolpark for a mass meeting. Students' leaders like Surendra Raj Sharma from Nepal Students' Union delivered speeches. But immediately after the winding up of the function, the police arrested Basu Risal and other four students and whisked them to Basantapur police station in a van.

The excited crowd of the students pelted the Hanumandhoka Police Station with stones, demanding for the release of the arrested students. After an exchange of stone throwing between the students and the police, a group of police appeared at the gate and appealed to the students to calm down. Students stopped throwing stones. After about fifteen minutes, however, some infiltrators threw stones to the armed police from behind the crowd. The shower of stones resumed again. So, the police also continued stoning, and fired three shots at the crowd.

Chiniya Kaji, Shahibuddin and Ram Man Shrestha who had come to see the spectacle were injured in the shooting. The police took the injured to the Bir hospital as soon as the crowd dispersed. B.P. Koirala who was Home Minister reached Bir Hospital as soon as he heard about the shooting. The condition of Chiniya Kaji had then become serious. He died after some time. Ram Man Shrestha returned home after minor treatment and Shahabuddin was taken to Patna to be treated at the government expenses. B.P. Koirala resigned on moral grounds.[134]

The 1950 revolution proves that any thing can be accomplished if an organized effort is made. The Nepal Students' Union is its proof. This union had organized a students' conference in the country in cooperation with Himanchal *Chhatra Sangh* and thus instilled them with a new courage. The incident of 1960 also destroyed this.[135] The ideology of Nepal Students' Union was similar to the ideology of Nepali Congress. Nepal Students' Union was able to achieve great success in the movement launched for improving the political and academic condition of the country, finding solution to political crisis, increasing students' number in colleges and schools, participating in international conferences, holding students conference in the capital under the auspices of Himanchal *Chhatra Sangh* and the village to village canvassing in the general election of 1958. Nepal Students' Union was banned on January 15th, 1960.[136]

4.10 Nepal Students' Union

A kind of confusion prevailed in Nepalese politics following the revolution of 1950. People's aspirations could not be met. Political instability grew inside the country. Political parties were busy consolidating themselves rather than solving these problems. Nepal Students' Union was established out of political instability and need of the time. The students had their own level of awakening.[137] According to Moshin, "We were motivated to engage in politics from leaders like Tanka Prasad Acharya who had been engaged in politics for a long time. The students' union was organized. We began to work more for politics than for students' welfare."[138] The students who were politically influenced detached themselves from *Chhatra Sangh* and formed Nepal

Students' Union.[139] A contradiction emerged within the *Chhatra Sangh* on whether students should be tools of political parties. In such a situation Himanchal *Chhatra Sangh,* monopolized the leadership and sidelined those who opposed them. We perceived the differences and separated from the union.[140] We then fielded our candidates in the union of Trichandra College. We had a better hold here. We won the election. Chandra Dhar Uprety's name figures prominently among those who provided help to us. Nepal Students' Union could be formed only because of the help of these friends.[141] In the meantime there was a clash between the police and the onlookers of a football match inside Singha Durbar. Some students were injured in the scuffle, including Chandra Dhar Uprety. Some were even imprisoned. The government provoked the students. They submitted demands for stable government, law and order, treatment of the injured and the release of the imprisoned.[142] The demands of the students were not met. They started agitation. An action committee was formed in which other unions also joined except the *Chhatra Sangh*. We prepared a schedule for the agitation. The strike spread. There was a second clash with the police. Chiniya Kaji died a martyr. Saibuddin received bullet injury on his leg. Some others were also injured.[143] Though the student movement could not develop further, it gave some experience to the students inside and outside of the country. They felt that it is easier to work if they stand united. As a result Nepal Student Union merged with Federation and Nepal national Students Union was formed. Even the students leaders of All India Students' Federation had come to participate in this function.[144]

Students' Union Nepal affiliated with Red Communist Party was also one of the most powerful students' organizations around 1953. With a view to forming a powerful students' union, ANSF students' union Nepal and Sanskrit *Chhatra Sangh* organized a historic unity conference in Kathmandu in 1953. The united students' organization was named Nepal National Students' Federation. It was chaired by Bashu Dev Dhungana. It also elected 13 member central committee. In this way the Students' Union was merged into NNSF.[145]

Students' unions were also called inter-college students' unions. Because of the possibility of clash between two students' unions, unity conference took place between the inter college students' union and All Nepal National Students' Federation. According to the decision of the conference, the joint students' union was named All Nepal National Students' Federation.[146]

4.11 All India Nepalese Students' Union

In fact, the students studying in India conducted various activities which culminated into democratic movement inside Nepal. Banaras was the main center of activities.[147] Kashi has an outstanding place in the historical progress of Nepal and the Nepalese. The start of the last revolution took place here. In view of the growing resentment among the Nepalese students it will not be an over statement to say that it was the birthplace of another revolution also. Many Nepalese students went to Kashi owing to the lack of educational institutions in Nepal.[148] Prior to 1950, the Nepalese students who were studying at various places in India were paying attention both to study and political activities. The only goal of the Nepalese students then was to bring about democracy in Nepal. Following the revolution of 1950, however, the students began to work on the basis of political conviction. Students belonging to one organization began to be non-cooperative with the students belonging to another organization. The same environment prevailed even in India.[149] In India the Nepalese students had formed the only student union called Nepalese Students' Union. It was confined to B.H.U. It had a modest membership. There was lack of mutual cooperation.[150] While studying in India we were impressed by the collective unity and programmes of other students. Realizing the need for unity, understanding and nationalism among the Nepalese students. Banaras *Chhatra Sangh* had played a pioneering role in this task.[151] Voice was raised in this regard in the student's conference held in Allahabad in 1951/52. A short description on this follows:

An impressive conference of the representatives of the Nepalese students took place in Allahabad last year against the anti-education policy of the Nepalese government. The representatives of almost all the Nepalese students participated and unanimously opposed the anti-education policy of the Nepalese government. Moreover, the students also formed an action committee to struggle against the unjust policy of the government and for the protection of their rights and interests. This conference had also sent a delegation of students to the Prime Minister and the Education Minister in order to oppose the government's policy and submit their demands. The delegation was led by Mr. Ram Bahadur Rawal.

When the government did not heed to the demands of the students of Nepal to raise their voice in support of the demands, all the students' organizations rose up in our support. A joint action committee was formed combining the Nepalese students studying in India and those studying in Nepal. The unity, perseverance and powerful processions and rallies cowed the Nepalese government ultimately forcing it to yield before the pressure of the students.

It follows from this that we should support the demands of the Nepalese students in making a united front against any kind of anti-national activities of the government. The second thing is that an all India level Nepalese Students' organization is needed in order to conduct struggles and agitations, propagate our culture and civilization and to bring about a unity among us who are studying at different places of India.[152]

The *Chhatra Sangh* was established at B.H.U. in July 1964. It had a provision in which the Nepali lecturer of the university would be the president and the vice president would be made out of the students studying there. This *Chhatra Sangh* was confined to B.H.U., having nothing to do with other students. But the Nepalese students had realized that if an organization could encompass all the students studying in India, the unity and courage of the students would be enhanced and most of the students' problems would be solved.[153] The executive committee of the Banaras *Chhatra Sangh* had given priority to this in 1952-53.[154] The structure of the executive committee is as follows:

Totra Raj Pandey, President; Mr. Jiwan Lal Satyal, Vice-President; Mr. Diwakar Bikram Rana, Secretary; Mr. Gunjman Sherchan, Deputy-Secretary; Mr. Chuda Bahadur Hamal, Cashier; Mr. Durga Bahadur Burma, Secretary for Literature and Publicity. Mr. Gauri Shankar Sainju, secretary for Social Service.[155]

On this occasion, the students outside of the B.H.U. had also discharged a historical duty by making their representation. They are as follows:

Mr. Yajgyna Prasad Acharya, Arts College; Mr. Mahesh Kumar, Arts College; Mr. Bishnu Prasad Risal, Science College; Mr. Mahendra Prasad Nuraula, Aurved; Mr. Indu Prasad Sharma, Sanskrit *Mahabidyalaya*; Sri Kumari Kokila, Women's College; Ms. Tula Shah, Women's College; Mr. Bishnu Prasad Parimal, Kamachha; Mr. Mrigendra Prasad Nepal, Kamachha; Mr. Bhawani Prasad Sharma, Harischandra; Mr. Bishwanath Banstola; D.A.V.; Mr. Madhab Prasad Sharma, Sanatan Dharma College; Mr. Ganga Prasad Sharma, Queen's College; Mr. Bishwanath Upadhya, Law College; Mr. Laxman Prasad, Commerce; Mr. Chirinjive Prasad Risal, Music College; Mr. Purajya Prasad Acharya.[156]

In the executive assembly Diwakar Bikram Rana said that all the students studying in India should have the right to get organized in Nepal *Chhatra Sangh*, not only those who are studying in B.H.U. All the students supported him.[157] He proposed to expand it into All Nepal Banaras Students' Union. It was unanimously approved. Programmes were carried out and the election commission was formed. It declared the election date. Maha Prasad Risal was made election officer. He finally informed that the date of the election was changed and it would not take place on the fixed day. Those who were in favour of postponing election were, Maha Prasad Risal, Surendra Bahadur Basnet, Chirinjivi Risal, Rabindranath Sharma.[158] The programme was sound. But the election date was changed owing to internal discrepancies. But one faction of the students proceeded with their work.[159]

This faction intended to form another students' union instead of expanding the one already fixed. It put a brake on the development of Banaras *Chhatra Sangh*.[160] As decided previously, a conference of the students studying in Banaras was held and "All Nepal Banaras *Chhatra Sangh*" was formed. The executive committee was formed form the general body. Diwakar Narsing Rana was elected its president. In his view, this organization had no affiliation with any of the parties and it was related only with the students' interests.[161] After the formation of All Nepal Banaras *Chhatra Sangh*, Diwakar Narsingh Rana submitted a report which reads as follows:

The Nepali *Chhatra Sangh* is entering into the eighth year. During the past eight years, the *Chhatra Sangh* has gained remarkable strength. It is moving along the path of progress. The students' union which was not able to go beyond the boundary of the university, has added a page in its history by becoming Banaras-wide. Moreover, the Nepal *Chhatra Sangh* has established a record by launching a struggle for the interest of the students. There is no doubt that the *Chhatra Sangh* performed organizational work among the students in a true sense of the term. The *Chhatra Sangh* laid its hands on various works though the degree of success varied. In a nutshell, the successes it has scored outweigh the failures.[162]

We proceeded with our programmes. We also made correspondence with the students studying in different parts of India with a view to establishing All India Nepalese Students Union. As a result, student representatives such as Diwakar Narsingh Rana from Banaras, Jagat Mohan Adhikari from Luknow, Mahesh Kumar Upadhyaya from Gorakhpur, Gyanender Bahadur Karki from Himanchal *Chhatra Sangh*, Calcutta, Narayan Keshari Shaha from *Chhatra Sangh*, Calcutta, Ram Narayan Shrestha, Surya Bahadur Thapa, Pius Raj Pandey, Ran Bahadur Rawal etc. from Allahabad, gathered together and formed a coordinating committee.[163] We organized a conference in Banaras on behalf of the coordinating committee. Many students, representatives from Bombay, Nagpur, Patna, Durvanga, U.P., Delhi etc. came to Banaras to participate in the conference. The students raised necessary funds for the conference from among themselves. The conference took place for three days. It was inaugurated by Maya Devi Chhetri, M.P. from Darjeeling. "All India Nepali *Chhatra Sangh*" was formed. An election was also organized.[164] The conference elected, Gyanendra Bahadur Karki, J.N. Giri, Yajna Prasad Acharya, Jagat Mohan Adhikari, Diwakar Bikram Rana, Harihar Raj Joshi, and Khadgajit Baral president, voice-president, cashier, secretary, publicity secretary, secretary for literature, and secretary of sports respectively.[165] The objective of this organization was to unify the progressive ideology, to promote Nepali culture and other social activities, and to strengthen democracy and nationalism in Nepal. B.P. Koirala was the chief guest in the first anniversary of the union. He delivered an impressive speech in Nepali and called upon the students to be organized. On the occasion a Hindi drama entitled "Mother" was also staged.

Benaras was the main area of political activities of B.P. Koirala, Dilli Raman Regmi, Puspa Lal Shrestha and Man Mohan Adhikari. The students studying in India were greatly impressed. In addition to this, Nepal *Chhatra Sangh* had already been established in B.H.U. But it was limited to Banaras only. The number of students living in Benaras for study was about 1200. The students, carried the dream of institutionalizing democracy and bringing about an all-round development in Nepal. With this objective, All India Nepalese Students' Union was established in 1955. Diwakar Bikram Rana, Yajnya Prasad Acharya, Chuda Bahadur Hamal had played an active part in it.[166] It held its election in 1956. The progressive panel became successful and enthused the organization with political concept.[167]

The All India Nepalese Students' Union had a goal of solving educational problems, promote studies, develop character, project itself as an ambassador of the people to strengthen democracy in Nepal and to lay stress in solving national and international problems. Whatever it did was for the welfare and interest of Nepal and the Nepalese. Its second conference took place in Bombay in 1958-59. It was inaugurated by B.P. Koirala.[168] An active member of the then All India Nepalese Students' Union, Yajgyna Prasad Acharya, has this to say:

> *Banaras, Patna, Allahabad, Calcutta etc. were the main places in which the Nepalese students studied. But there was no unity among the students. Two opinions emerged even in the Banaras* Chhatra Sangh. *There were some students who said that only the students of Banaras should be included in it. They were, Surendra Bahadur Basnet, Jiwan Lal Satyal, Rabindranath Sharma, Chirinjivi Rijal, etc. Those in favour of including the students outside Banaras were Diwakar Narsingh Rana, Yajnya Prasad Acharya, etc. Those students who had differing view on Gorkha recruitment formed another union. All Banaras* Chhatra Sangh *was formed in 1954. Students' representatives from eleven places such as J.N. Giri, Khadgajit Baral, Gyanendra Bahadur Karki, Ram Bahadur Rawal, Maha Prasad Risal unanimously decided to form All India Nepalese Students' Union in 1955. As King Mahendra was in India visit then, the conference was scheduled to be inaugurated by the King himself. But it could not materialize because of lack of time. The King, however, provided ten thousand rupees as an assistance. M.P. from Darjeeling Maya Devi Chhetri inaugurated the conference. Election was held*

following the conference. Gyanendra Bahadur Karki was elected president. The conference put forward three demands: (i) There should be a national university in Nepal. (ii) The Nepalese government should give financial support for cultural gathering of the Nepalesc students in India. (iii) A decision should be made on Gorkha recruitment. B.P. Koirala was the chief guest of the first anniversary of All India Nepalese Students' Union. Students who were studying in Bombay such as Bharat Mohan Adhikari, Kamal Koirala, Mohammad Mohsin, Banwarilal Mittal, Urmila Garg etc. Organized the second conference in Bobay. It was inaugurated by the first elected Prime Minister B.P. Koirala. The students in foreign countries always play a positive role in the promotion of democracy and nationalism.[169]

The Nepalese students in India were not meeting frequently since 1995. It was therefore, decided to hold the formal conference of All India Nepalese Students' Union. Its second conference was organized in Bombay in 1960. It was inaugurated by B.P. Koirala.[170]

Here are the major highlights of the conference inaugurated by B.P. Koirala:

4.12 All India Nepalese Students, Conference

Prime Minister B.P. Koirala left Kathmandu for Bombay in October, 1960. On the same day, Mr. Koirala inaugurated the second conference of the All India Nepalese Students' Union.

The letter of felicitation sent to the congress by King Mahendra was also read out.

In his inauguration speech, Prime Minister B.P. Koirala said:

We should now accomplish the general election and the responsibility of it has come to us. In my view there are basically two types of responsibilities on us. (i) Abolition of feudalism and (ii) Creation of an industrial society.

We are taking steps towards safeguarding the rights of the farmers over their lands. This is a great revolutionary step which will break apart all the relationships that have evolved under the existing land ownership. The steps being taken by the present government such as abolition of Birta, *taxation of excess land, giving of receipt to the farmers are bringing about great upheavals in the country. Not only each village, this step will affect each family. Great organized efforts are taking place against this progressive march.* Birta *holders, land lords and* Zamindars *are conspiring against history. Kings and princes also symbolize feudalism and feudal exploitation. History has no regard for them.*

The present responsibility towards which I just drew your attention and the challenges of the future are bound to bring India and Nepal closer. The basic problems of India are similar to Nepal's. The two countries have similar outlook to the problems and so are the ways of their solution. Out international views also conform with each other. You, therefore, are requested to make a serious study of how India solves its social, economic problems in addition to your pursuance of knowledge. The politics of India, its parliamentary system, its laws and acts are all subjects of our studies. You should pay attention to these things also during your stay in India. I hope that this study and experiences you have gained here will be useful for the country.[171]

4.3 The Student Organization From 1960-1990

The reactionary rulers with military action toppled the then multiparty parliamentary system in 1960, and imposed ban on all the political parties, and the class organizations and enforced the partyless Panchayet system. Then other democratic forces came out to the field of struggle to seize back their lost rights and interests.[172] The autocratic rulers used every oppressive means like killing, arresting and torturing to suppress the voices of the students. Despite such savage attacks, the students' struggle continued on.[173] Following the military action of 1960 and imposition of ban on political parties along with other class organizations, political leaders were arrested, some went underground and others were forced to go to self-exile. Such a situation invited anarchy in the country. In that terrific condition, the students continued their struggle against the Panchayat system.[174] Although it looked simple from the outside, the student movements would be motivated inwardly by political changes. The slogans and demands would be simple such as for the systematization of examinations, well-management of course materials books and libraries, transport, facilities, building of bridges and roads and protest against rise in fees etc. But all such demands would be politically inspired and centered to political interests.[175]

The Panchayati government itself created situation for the students to wage struggle against it.[176] In those days, the students did play a helping role for political parties. The Panchayat government taking the students as class-organization adopted the policy to conduct them under government direction and brought out statute for student organizations declaring "National Directives Law 1961". Most of the students became dissatisfied with such a system, because it would not serve their political objective.[177] So the students demanding rights to organize nation wide free student unions launched movement against the government with the demands very simple looking on the surface but directed to the political goal.[178] At that time, the students, however could not stage street demonstration and organize in large mass. However, they continued to struggle for their rights, interests and well-being. They did not lose courage under any difficult situation. They continued their struggle demanding for nation wide free student union and for the restoration of democracy.[179] For conducting the movement they had formed different units under different names, such as Patan Student Union, National Student Federation, Nepal Student Community, Nepal National Student Council etc. Such units had played a great role in founding National Level Student Organizations.[180]

4.14 The Role of Student Unions (Committees)

After the 1960 military operation, most of the leaders of the outlawed political parties remained either locked up in prisons or exiled in India. In such a situation, the compulsion of leadership fell into the hands of the students. The 1967 'National Directives Law' provoked the students. Hence, the concept of a free student union began to spread for district and zonal level unions also through aforementioned student unions and organizations. The students came to Kathmandu to study from Janakpur district and they worked for the promotion of political culture background organizing Gauree Shankar Student Committees. This student committee was the first in the history of the student committees. It was a matter of pride.[181] Gauree Shanker Student Committee is taken as the first and the oldest in the history of the student organizations. It was founded in 1961.[182] Since the students could not get their demands fulfilled for the foundation of a United Single Student Organization by calling a nation wide conference, they thought it necessary to be organized even on the regional, or district or provincial basis.[183] Following the Gauree Shanker Student Committees' Gandaki Student Committee, western No 1 student committee, far western regional student committee, Sagarmatha Student Committee, Arghakhanchi-Gulmi Social Committee were founded.[184]

Through these committees student kept on struggling with the Panchayat government for political and their class interest putting different demands. These student organizations did not only express their political dissatisfactions but also remained active in different creative works such as memorial programmes of national heroes and builders, literary programmes, seminars, speech-seminars, talk-seminars, talk-programmer, games etc. with the publication of high leveled journals and magazines. Such programmes could be successful in developing sentimental intimacy and deep friendship among the students.[185] These student committees helped in building a very strong, consolidated and organized student force.

4.15 Democratic Socialist Youth League (DSYL)

The young students had made a great contribution to the continuation of democratic movement in Nepal by forming student organizations outside the country after the 1960 incident. In the same context, a group of youths supporting democratic socialism held a discussion in Biratnagar for the preparation of a separate organization and organized Democratic socialist youth league. Participants were deputed from the Kathmandu valley and Benaras, India.[186] In the course of establishing organizations, the Nepalese students living in Benaras and other places also founded "Democratic youth group" in about 1962. This group had sent its representatives to Kathmandu to help the student movement in the D.I.G. Naryan Singh incident in 1966. This organization always gave helping hands to every student movement sending its representatives with different materials like pamphlets, leaflets, posters, etc. in Nepal.[187] Democratic Socialist League was such a first student organization in which the democratic revolutionary students living in and out of the country were involved. In fact this organization was the origin of creating revolutionary minds in the students.[188] It also worked to expand its organizations in different parts like Butawal, Bhairawa, Pokhara, Gorkha etc.[189]

In the gathering held in Biratnagar, the participants formed an executive committee of "Democratic Socialist Youth". It also adopted different resolutions related to national and internal issues. Among them, two resolutions were not only very contextual but also bold in the difficult political situation that was prevalent in the country in those days. They were as follows:

(i) Forcing the government to release ex-Prime Minister and senior leader of the Nepali Congress B.P. Koirala to launch democratic Movement in Nepal under his direct guidance.

(ii) To work for the establishment of democratic socialist system by ending the dictatorial monarchy.

It was a challenging matter to adopt such resolutions by the democratic socialist youth league in the Panchayati concept of those days.[190]

After the sacking of the parliamentary system in 1960, the outlawed political parties remained busy for the restoration of the parliament. All the Nepalese students were working unitedly until 1963. But after the nationwide conference held in Biratnagar, they began to be mobilized according to their respective political parties. In the same way the supporters of the Nepali Congress organized their own student organization called, Democratic Socialist Youth League.[191] The objective of the organization was to keep consultation with Nepali Congress, understand people's problems and put demands to fulfill them, call strike, press the government to release political leaders, to end the Panchyat system and bring about socialist democratic system as planned and founded a new organization Nepal Student Union in 1970, which continuously contributed to the nation up to the democratic movement of 1990 making it a success.[192]

The students who were working in a free as well democratic environment were greatly affected by the 1960 military action. The Panchayati partyless system was enforced. Then the students began to work as representatives of different parties. The then Panchayat government tried all means to suppress, arrest, torture the students and split or disintegrate the students unity. It also provoked them by making new rules and regulations against the students' interests.[193] The Panchayati government attempted to keep control over the students by including student organization in the category of class organization under the National Directives Law, 1961. But it made the students to center their mind to start a movement. Then the student launched movements demanding for Free Students Unions and restoration of democracy and kept fighting for more than three decades.[194] As the students can raise voice in different forms to serve political interests, their organizations are the main base to conduct movements for their demands. So different committees in the country and aboard were founded in different names.[195] Inspired by such effective steps of the students All Nepal National Free Student Union and Nepal Student Union came in to existence.

These student organizations could play the role of opposition parties in the Panchayat era.[196] Panchayat government also had known the importance and strength of student organizations, so it tried lot to keep such organizations under its guidance and control. But leaving aside some exceptions, it could not succeed to do so.[197] Later on, the Panchayati government with an intention of strengthening the Panchayati system established its own student organization naming Nationalist Independent Student Council.[198] Its blatant activities provoked the opposition student organization to adopt more rigid policy seeking new issues against the government. The activities of the Nationalist Independent Student Council created such an environment in the student sector that the opposition students were compelled to wage a decisive struggle which led to the achievement of Free Union declaration of referendum and finally the restoration of democracy in 1990. These are the results of the students' struggles begun after the 1960 incident. It was also the students' struggle to make the political leaders openly involved in the popular movement of 1990 and lead the movement which succeeded to end the autocratic Panchayat system and to restore democracy in 1990.

4.16 The then Three Main Student Organization

The student movements for the achievement of "Free Student Union were conducted through different ways. As a result, three student unions come to exit. Goverdhan Rana has described the student movement in his book in the following way:

> *During the period when almost the democratic students were in prison in the course of 1965 A.D. students movement, the leftist students remaining outside the jail one-sidedly announced that the first 'All Nepalese Student Conference' was held in a house near Shovabhagabati, Kathmandu, and had formed on adhoc committee under convenorship of a 9th class student of Shantinikunja High School Atmaram Kharel, called Sujan Kharel. The formation of separate organization of the leftist students jeopardized the united movement of the democratic and leftist students resulting a feud between the two groups. The leftist students held a next gathering in Poush, 1966, and on May 20, 1968, they held a 2nd conference of 'All Nepalese Students' at Kirtipur. This conference made a decision to name the organization as 'All Nepal National Free Student Union' and an executive committee was formed with the same name.*[199]

On the same subject a book titled as *Nepalese Student Movement and A.N.N.F.S.U.* has described as follows:

> *The adhoc committee formed by the 'valley inter-college student conference of 1964 A.D. decided to call All Nepal Free Student Conference in 1965. According to the resolution passed by the 'Laknow Gathering' the progressive students successfully held an underground conference with a view to establish a national level student organization at a peasant's home on the side of the Bishnumati stream. This conference organized an eleven member central committee under the convenorship of Sujan Kharel. When some of the leaders of the Nepali Congress released statements of surrender to the Panchayat system in about 1967, the students affiliated to their politics began to disintegrate and distrust the student organization. They heinously served the interest of the government by disrupting every student movement using different means. The second national conference was held under the convenorship of Tribhuvan University Student Union at Kirtipur on May 20, 1968. In this way 'All Nepal National Free Student Union.*[200]

The above mentioned statements clarify that the

Nepalese students were divided into two, the leftist and democratic political blocs. The third bloc was that of the autocratic Panchayat government. In the same way, there appeared three organizations of the Nepalese students briefly mentioned below:

4.16.1 All Nepal National Free Students' Union (ANNFSU)

A convention of progressive students including the distinguished political leaders in Lukhnow, India was held by the end of 1964. The convention passed a very important resolution to establish a students' union making totally free from the then Soviet revisionist trend and decided to reorganize Nepal National Student Federation.[201] The preparatory committee organized by the valley inter-college student conference in 1964, convened a conference in May, 1965 and formed an eleven member central executive committee under the convenorship of Sujan Kharel. This very conference was supposed to be the first conference of the "All Nepal National Free Student Union.[202]

ANNFSU is an organization of patriotic, democratic and progressive students and, in essence, it is a revolutionary democratic organization. It has been clearly presenting its democratic principle, intention and objective. This organization has been known as an organization to have unity between principle and practice through its activities.[203] According to the mouth piece of the ANNFSU, it was brought in the existence as a common and independent organization of all the progressive democratic and patriotic students of our country. More to say, it came to exist as a representative organization of all the justice loving Nepalese students against the autocratic Panchayat system. It has been upholding the ideal and character of a democratic organization since its founding.[204] This organization shall play a leading role in making all the young student force take steps towards new democratic movement.[205] The Nepalese student movement has been upholding the glorious revolutionary tradition since the founding of ANNFSU. Many of its members have cheerfully sacrificed their life against both the national and international exploiters and aggressors. This student organization has played a prime role in the Nepalese youth movement against the anti-people, anti-national and anti-democratic activities of the rulers and for the interest of the majority people, national sovereignty, freedom and nationalism along with movement for the interest of the students. This fact has been proved by the history of the Nepalese student movement.[206]

ANNFSU was founded in 1965. This organization has been said to be a common organization of all the patriotic, democratic and progressive Nepalese students in its manifesto.[207] In a clear-cut sense, it is working as sister organization of the Communist Party of Nepal. It could not remain out of disputes since its foundation. The division, groupism and split in the communist party greatly influenced the student community also. The division and dispute in the political party reflected in the student organization. And different trends began to appear in the ANNFSU itself. As a result, the process of split and division into different groups in different names began to exist.[208] Due to the disputes in the left movement, deviation of leadership, lifelessness and suppression of Panchayat government, the organization became passive after its 4th conference. At the same time, taking the advantage of the weakness of the organization, the Panchayat government imposed ban on the student organizations in 1973.[209] Leaders of the communist party with disputes and difference became divided into several groups. The party's sister organization ANNFSU also naturally divided into different groups like other sister organization. So it is clear that the student unions were to run under the guidance of the parties. The unions have not independent existence, when the parties break and leaders become separate the union also break or new unions exist. This trend of unions is not good to the students.[210] The student communities are very strong in a nation which has inter-relationship with politics, and political parties have inter-relationship with students. In the modern democratic culture both of them work as complementary part of each other. As it becomes easier and quicker to present nation's necessity and wants before the people through students, it seems necessary to establish student organizations according to the ideology, politics and policy of any political party. Since the leaders of the communist party of Nepal were split, and they formed different new party organizations of their own ideologies, it is not a bad aspect to appear their sister organizations according to and on the basis of the party organizations.[211] In the same way ANNFSU also was divided into different groups and they opened their separate offices.[212] After 1960, the leadership of the leftist student movement in Nepal was held by ANNFSU, but when the communist party was divided into different groups the leftist student union also was divided accordingly into several groups.[213]

The political glimpse of Nepal (*Nepalko Rajnitik Darpan*) of Grisma Bhadur Devkota mentions about the division of ANNFSU in this way:

> *The third conference of ANNFSU was held at Okubahal in Lalitpur on June 3, 1969. This conference made a decision not to make ANNFSU a stooge of any political party but rather develop it as a common independent democratic organization of all the progressive, democratic and patriotic students and run it on the basis of a certain programe of its own. A dispute also arose an issue on whether to recognize it to be the second or third conference of ANNFSU. So a five member commission comprising Mohan Chandra Adhikari, Shiddilal Singh, Khadga Bahadur Gharti, Nirmal Aryal etc. was formed to settle the dispute. This commission gave a conclusion to take it to be the third conference. As a result, ANNFSU could not stand on unity. Several groups appeared in it. The fourth conference was also held in Lalitpur in 1972.*

One of the groups of ANNFSU held its 5th conference in Ayoddhya, India in 1976. The representatives from 31 districts had taken part in the conference. And the same group held its 6th conference at Thaiba, Lalitpur in 1979.

In the same way another group held its 5th conference in the name of united 5th conference at Chabahil, Kathmandu on March 22, 1979.

Out of the above two factions, the third group held its conference in Kathmandu on April 20, 1979. This group changed its name to "Nepal Progressive Student Union."[214]

In this way the single ANNFSU founded in 1965 was split into three groups, about which a brief description which has been made is as follows:

4.16.2 All Nepal National Free Student Union (6th) (A.N.N.F.S.U.-6th)

ANNFSU (6th) is a common and independent organization of all the left, progressive, patriotic and democratic students to fight against all kinds of exploitations, oppressions, and injustice of the retrogressive or reactionary forces and for the achievement of people's democracy and national independence.[215]

Its objectives was to make all the left, patriotic and democratic students organized, disciplined and powerful to take steps for the protection of nationalism, sovereignty, territorial integrity and for the democratic rights of the people.[216]

Its flag was a five-conned white star on the upper part (near the stand) and an opened pen pointing to the star on the reel background.[217]

Its leadership political organization is 'masal' led by Mohan Vikram. This organization takes the monarchy to be the main enemy, it blames all the other groups taking part in the elections to be revisionists and claims only itself to be a revolutionary one. This group has supported the policy of boycotting the Panchayati elections and referendum, and in the student circle, it has been disseminating "Mao Tse Tuung thought".[218]

In this organization also differences appeared and consequently, it was split into different groups:

(i) ANNFSU (a group under presidentship of Bhanu Sharma)

(ii) ANNFSU (a group under convenorship of Prabhunaryan Basnet)

(iii) ANNFSU (6th) came into existence. These factions had adopted a policy to be united and had also formed a coordination committee to this direction in 1989.[219]

4.16.3 All Nepal National Free Student Union (Unity-5th)

Its political leadership party organization is CPN (ML), the present CPN (UML). It was natural for this organization to be influenced by the unstable as well as immature political thinking of its party organization (ML). Boycotting referendum in 1980 and Panchayat elections etc. were its serious political mistakes.[220]

Its objective was to remain working for the achievement of the right, interests, and dignity of all the student community and for the protection and promotion of them.[221]

Its flag was a five conned white star on the upper left angle and a white open pen painting to it on the red background.[222]

4.16.4 Nepal Progressive Student Union (NPSU)

Its mother organization is CPN (Marxist). This organization, except releasing statements, has not taken any concrete step.[223]

Its objective was to take active part in any people's struggle for democratic rights,

To be ready to pay any cost for the protection of nationalism, sovereignty and territorial integrity of the country,

To make effort for democratic education system, promotion of mental, physical and moral qualities of all the students and remain struggling for the interest, rights and dignity of all the student community and to keep a friendly relationship with the people of all the parts of the world for peace progress, and independence.[224]

Its flag was an opened panel on an white opened book painting to a star on a red background having two times wide and three times long on the ratio.[225]

The cause of renaming the ANNFSU as "Nepal Progressive Student Union" as the *Madales* organized in the name of so called ANNFSU (Unity 5th) and ANNFSU (6th) conference spoilt and calumniated the secured name of 'ANNFSU', we have proposed to give it a new name as "Nepal Progressive Student Union". This is not any new organization but only a new name of the Nepal National Student Federation and (NNSF) and ANNFSU which have come maintaining their revolutionary tradition since long.[226]

The other Progressive Student Unions were apart from the above mentioned:

4.16.5 Nepal Revolutionary Student Union (NRSU)

Despite being many honest friends involved in 'ANNFSU' the other masked and wrong elements spoiled the history of dignified as well as glorious name of ANNFSU and degraded it to a worthless crowd (Deusim). An inter organizational struggle was carried out against such activities. Since all the struggles could not work for any improvement, and there remained no alternative, "Nepal Revolutionary Student Union" came into existence in 1969 in the underground condition under the direction of the communist party of Nepal.[227] This student organization of the left and progressive students tried to make alive and uphold the revolutionary tradition against the feudalist capitalist ideas. This organization has stood on the side of workers, peasants and different exploited classes of people joining hands with them in every democratic and progressive movement being effortful for the unity of students and for national independence and territorial integrity and left opportunism since its founding.[228] It is mother organization of Nepal workers and peasants party. Its flag holds star, pen and the map of Nepal.[229]

This organization NRSU remaining under ANNFSU involved in the 1975-76 and 1978-79 student movements and took part in the first union elections. Later on, there was a dispute over the question of the conference of ANNFSU and the students of NRSU tried their best to solve the dispute to keep ANNFSU united, but it was divided into two, despite the efforts of NRSU. So NRSU also was compelled to launch its own programmes and open activities.[230]

It also tried to involve and play active role in the struggle for the interest of students, and in the struggle against autocratic, partyless Fascist Panchayat system and against superpower hegemonies, imperialism and expansionism.[231]

4.16.6 Nepal National Student Federation (NNSF)

Nepal National Student Federation (NNSF) is progressive student organization founded in 1950. It has contributed to every event including the revolution of 1950. The military action against parliamentary system in 1960 badly affected NNSF also. Despite the foundation of ANNFSU in 1964, NNSF did its works as usual without any effect in its activities. It has been successfully playing its role among the left and progressive students.[232]

When Manandhar and Verma were divided into two factions, one of the splits of CPN, NNSF also was divided in two factions in 1981. Both of the factions were equally involved in the 1990 democratic movement. When Manandhar, Verma and T.L. Amatya became united, they named their parties as CPN (United), in 1992, NNFS also became united as one.[233]

Its flag was opened book and a five conned star on the left corner into a map of Nepal lying of green background with white outline of the map while the book and it star were of red outline.[234]

Its objectives:

(i) To arouse patriotic sentiment among all the Nepalese students.

(ii) To work for a cheap, easy-accessible, scientific, progressive and democratic education for all the students or the Nepalese people.

(iii) To work for the protection promotion and prosperity of national culture, tradition and arts etc.[235]

4.16.7 Nationalist Independent Student Council (NISC)

After the military action against the parliamentary system on December 15, 1960, the partyless Panchayat system with the intention to keep control over the class organizations under the "National Directives Law" also founded. "Nepal Student Organization" in 1962.

Hemanta Bahadur B.C. was the first government nominated president of this Panchayat system supporting student organization.[236]

Since all the students were unitedly struggling against the National Directives Law, the Government founded Nepal Student Organization (NSO) became not only damnable but also notorious in the student community.[237] The Nepalese students demanded for free union and began to struggle for it. The Panchayat government tried to suppress and disrupt it. In the same context an angry rally of students which was staged against the D.I.G. Narayan Sing event attacked the NSO's central office at Bagbazar in 1966. As a result and achievement of the Narayan Singh event and the attack on NSO's office by the opposition students, the Panchayat government was compelled to announce the dissolution of the national directives law and Nepal Student Organization (NSO).[238] The government had understood the importance of the student force and organization. So it wanted to keep control and use this force for the partyless Panchayat system by suppressing and disrupting the opposition student organization, but could not be successful to do so. Then, later on, the government founded its own student organization named Nationalist Free Student Council to use it in favour of the partyless Panchayat system and against the opposition students. After the military action of 1960, the partyless Panchayat system system was enforced. All the political parties were banned. A complicated situation prevailed. In that difficult environment, only the students became the main force to raise voice for human rights and democracy.[239] The students went on strikes demanding for student organizations based on already enjoyed democratic culture and for the settlement of all the problems of the educational sector. The students began to hold gatherings, discussions and even conferences on different occasions. All the students would not be treated or seen equally. There were different blocs, some left or progressives and some democratic students. The campus classes would often be hampered by force by the students.[240]

During the period of 1963-1965, the Nepalese student politics got uncertainty and faltering environment. The students' minds were centered to politics rather than teaching and learning. There was a fearful and terrific situation for those students who would like to be present in the classes and continue their learning.[241] In that ongoing situation the left and progressive students convened a conference of students delegates. But the other students opposed it questioning how and where from the delegates could come without holding any elections, and the spoke for the freedom of students from any political party.[242] The students became divided after the left and progressive students one-sidedly held the conference in 1967. Then the democratic students began to work separately. In such a situation the other neutral students who wanted to continue their study also were compelled to have their own organization.[243] Especially in Trichandra Campus, there appeared three groups. The number of neutral students was not less than the progressive and democratic students. So the neutral students also called a gathering and discussed for founding a new free organization of the neutral students. When King Mahendra was on a visit to Kanchanpur. I also got an opportunity to meet him there.[244] He also had a good-will for the progress of the education sector and said, he would help for its promotion. Then the neutral students held a gathering at Trichandra Campus. As decided by the gathering the Nationalist Independent Student Council (NISC) was founded in 1967. This student organization came to exist due to the feud between the progressive and democratic students.[245] In this way the Nationalist Independent Student Council was registered in the government and came in to existence in 1967. There was no hand or involvement of domestic or foreign power in founding this organization and it was the students who did so. As it was registered in the government, they might have blamed it be the supporter of Panchayat system. The non-student-activities of the students were responsible for founding this new student organization, Nationalist Independent Student Council.[246] After consulting the students from Mechi to Mahakali, an adhoc-committee was formed in 1970. The founder members of this adhoc committee were Padam Thakurathi, Khilendra Pratap K.C., Shivahari Paudel, Gambhir Pradhan, Narayanraj Gurughrana, Jitbahadur Arjyal, Parmeshor Shakya, Ramkrisna Panta and Hari Bahadur Chaudhary.[247] The conference used to be held once in two years. The first conference was held in the Rastriya Nachghar, Jamal, in Kathmandu in 1971. In this conference, delegates of different campuses from forty-five districts had taken part. The present RPP Chairman, Rajeswor Devkota had inaugurated the three-day conference. Its plenary session was held in Mahendra Yubalya, Lalitpur on the 2nd day, and on the 3rd day the conference was ended electing Rabindra Chakrabarti as Chairman of its advisory committee and Padam Thakurathi as central committee chairman of the organization.[248] The second conference was held in Birgunj. Kamal Thapa was elected chairman of the organization and the central advisory committee was changed into directives-committee by amending its statute. The 3rd conference was held in Janakpur and Dilanath Giri was elected its chairman, the 4th conference held in Biratnagar elected Niranjan Thapa its chairman.[249]

In fact, the student organization used to work as political organization in the Panchayat era. Similarly, the Nationalist Independent Student Council also had given emphasis on the promotion on educational sector along with the priority to the protection of nation and nationalism.[250] The 'NISC' had helped to start new education system in 1971 realizing that the old Macaulay education system could not help develop the country.[251] Since it was implemented without any preparation, both the teachers and students were not clear about the new education system and the opposition students got points to oppose it. Indeed, the new education has been unsuccessful due to political reasons.[252]

When India took over Sikkim 'NISC' had demonstrated protest rallies. Slogans like "India may take over Nepal, all the Nepalese should unite for the protection of our country' were chanted. 'NISU' also was involved in the 45 day long student strike demanding students' rights, interests and different facilities in the Tribhuvan University in 1975. It also put the demands that Nepal should get the facility to use Radhikapur road. NISC with its invitees from Thailand, also had conducted an afforestation programme at Sitapaila and Kakani. It had emphasized on the need of National Development service program for the university students who could learn about the villages.[253] NISU had its units in the sixty-two districts. Its central office was at Ratna Park.

Objectives

To protect nationalism along with rights and interests of students and create a free environment for teaching and learning activities in the university, to end the warring situation among students and continue the teaching learning condition.[254]

Constitution

I swear by the fire, the water, the air and the soil of my country that I shall dedicate myself for the interests and rights of all the students of our nation. I shall never let the dignity of my nation and nationalism to be blurred and shall always remain effortful to create a prosperious educational environment.[255]

'NISC' had not used any flag of its own. Really, NISC did not contribute to any democratic movement. It worked according to the then situation and the political system. It did not play any role to bring about democracy in Nepal.[256] The "NISC" had no principle or ideology like that of other student organizations. It used to work under the guidance of the establishment.

Later on, vices and perversions appeared in this organizations, specially after 1973 'NISC' was divided in to several groups behind different Panchayatist leaders such as Mohmud Mohsin, Tulri Giri, Damodar Shumshere etc. and began to show their strength against one another bringing the whole NISC into disrepute.[257]

It began to work under the leadership of C.D.O., zonal commissioner, ministry, *Panchas* etc. It was organized without any central policy, ideal or principle and rules of its own. It became like a tool of the Panchayatist leaders due to whom it became uncontrolled and unrestrained. It became unpopular among other student organizations and people.[258] After 'Back to Village' central committee was formed, NISU was brought under the class organization to guide it, but it was very late 'NISC' was giving priority to people's well being, nationalism and educational issues. According to Mohamad Mohisin in this organization the clean political personalities like Padma Thakurathi, Kamal Thapa etc. were also involved. But due to some uncouth and unbridled characters, the other reasonable as well as intelligent students also had to be faint-hearted. The leaders of the then Panchayat system did not try to understand the importance of the strength of student community. Instead they favoured to dissolve it to save the Panchayat system. The demand of 1979 student movement was the dissolution of 'NISC' and it was dissolved by the recommendation of the royal commission.[259] The Panchayat government handled it from the beginning, they divided it behind different Panchatist leaders, and moreover it was defamed by NSU and ANNFSU finally to be dismissed by the government in 1979 in the excuse of not renewing its registration on time. It was a registered bonafide organization. It was mentioned in its constitution that it should have to be renewed before the last of June every year. The main demand of the 1979 movement was its dismissal and the government dismissed it in the recommendation of the Royal Commission, which found an excuse of not being, renewed its registration.[260]

4.16.8 Some Comments about the Nationalist Independent Student Council (NISC)

The situation was such that the Panchayatist government would not stay without any student organization of its own. The Panchayatists also wished to have its student organization to show that it was a popular as well as democratic political system. So, to fulfil this objective, an organization called Nationalist Independent Student Council (NISC) was established in 1968 under the chairmanship of Padam Thakurathi by collecting different students who had previously worked in the student organizations and it ran under the frame-work of Panchayat system. All the activities of this organization would be secretly conducted through zonal commissioners and C.D.O. The indirect objective was to invade anti-Panchayat activities and organizations. It was not unnatural of NISC to be its character of Panchayat system as it was patronized by the Panchayat government. This organization 'NISC' gradually became infamous because of its irresponsible, immoral and terrorists activities. The higher level authorities of the Panchayat government and those who would claim to be nationalists and royalists used to protect all such activities of NISC putting them above the law by keeping the people and the king in darkness. This organization with the help of hard lined Panchayaists and administration became more active to involve the students, the people and especially the democratic forces. As a result, it became so infamous and notorious that any bad work that would be done by anyone in the country began to be called 'Mandale work' as an objective for hatred. All the political parties and press-media criticized and opposed the 'NISC' for such activities. But the terrorist nature of it remained unchanged. Those who used to protect such activities of NISC making it much scandalous became more prosperous.

The period from 1975 to 1979 can be taken as a period of Mandale terror. The education sector was much terrorized by the vandalism of NISC. Finally this organization was ended by the order of Royal commission on May 21, 1979, during the 1978/79 historic student movement. This organization was established by the Panchayat system, and ended by the Panchayat system itself.[261]

A conference of the new and old Mandles was held at Simaltar in Bhairahawa on November 21, 1980 to reanimate the 'NISC' already dissolved on May 21, 1979.[262]

The Nationalist Independent Student Council (NISC) is a royalist and Panchaytist organization. This kind of organization imbued with national thought and free from any foreign thoughts and influence is indispensable in the country in such a geo-political situation like our Nepal. To change the name of Nationalist Independent Student Council is to commit suicide.

After it was used to suppress the student and peasant movements by the administration, the same organization of the ruffians was given national recognition in 1971. Then this organization of vandals and ruffians began to spread terrorism working like police without uniform and C.I.D.s in the campuses to disrupt the students and to implement the wrong education plan by force. After organizing this group, all the units and national organizations of the student unions were gradually banned. Then after 1971-72, the idiot ruffians of this organization spread a terror by committing different crimes like killing, looting, raping etc. all over the nation. They continued their wanton aggression on every sector of educational and social life till 1979. Niranjan Thapa, Kamal Thapa, Padam Thakurathi, Deepak Bohara and company were the ring-leaders of this notorious organization. This organization was the main target and the course of the 1978-79 student movement. Due to the student protest against this organization, the Panchayat government itself imposed ban on it on the recommendation of the royal commission. Then the word *Mandale* had been an adjective and a synonym to denote government sponsored student wing.

4.16.9 Comments on the then Student Leaders about 'Nationalist Independent Student Council' (NISC)

(i) As the students of NSU and ANNFSU began to move for democracy, the Panchayat government established NISC to mobilize it against the students. In this organization both the vandals or ruffians and good elements were working. This organization was established for counter defense, there were so many members who used to show their physical strength. Such activities would compel the opposition politics to adopt a strong policy against them.[263]

(ii) NISC was established with the objective to consolidate and strengthen Panchayat system.[264]

(iii) Student community is an intellectual community. The students uphold this or that ideology and principle. In the same way, NISC was also established. This organization supported Panchayat politics and remained appeased to other political parties. The opposition students got an opportunity to react against the NISCs acts and uncouth activities due to which the other student organizations could intensify democratic movement. The negative character and activities of NISC compelled the other student organizations to launch strong as well as speedy movement for democracy.[265]

(iv) We always took the 'NISC' as a student organization supporting Panchayat system. We only opposed their nature and wrong activities.[266]

(v) In the name of student organization, NISC has remained as a contemptible organization in the history of Nepalese students. It worked as a stooge of the autocratic Panchayat system and weakened the national strength. Whatever this organization did in the name of nationalism was all against democracy.[267]

(vi) The one sided uncouth activities of the NISC forced the students to be united and launch democratic movement and aroused fearlessness and courage to fight against injustice.[268]

(vii) 'NISC' was the organization of those students who supported the autocratic Panchayat system. To work in favour of Panchayat system was its lawful and reasonable duty. But its open activities against other student organizations were anti-democratic ones.[269]

(viii) NISC also includes in the history of Nepalese student organizations. It used to suppress democracy and democratic activists in the name of nationalism. But nationalism and democracy are supplementary to each other. Taking only one of them is against the interests of the nation.[270]

4.17 Nepal Student Union (NSU)

After the incident of 1960, the Nepalese students unitedly remained struggling against the autocratic Panchayat system. For instance, its aims were to go against the National directives law, to demand for free student union, to force for the dismissal of D.I.G. Narayan Singh from his post, to give candidates the chance for the elections of Tribhuvan University Union from different student groups etc. The sole objective of all these activities was to end the then Panchayat system and restore democracy.

Theoretically, an ambition to strengthen, unite and consolidate their own organization arose among the students after 1967. The progressive group holding a one sided conference in 1967 founded "All Nepal National Free Student Union". And, later on, disputes arose in this organization and it also divided into several groups according to the political leaders. The Panchayat system took the opportunity to grab the advantage of the division and established its student organization named "Nationalist Independent Student Council."[271] Since the democratic students did not take part in the students conference held in 1967, we, the other progressive students were obliged to take a decision to found 'ANNFSU' by which the students were completely divided in two political ideologies, the left and democratic blocs.[272] In such a challenging as well as competitive situation, the democratic student groups also realized the need of a national level student organization of their own and established 'Nepal Student Union' in April, 1970. When 'ANNFSU' splitted into different groups; 'NSU' grabbed the advantage.[273] The political parties began to keep control over the students when the student union became strong in the Tribhuvan University. Then voices of political parties and leaders began to be raised through the students. After Kamal Chitrakar was elected in the T.U. Union, the democratic group began to work according to its own policy. In such a situation it was contextual to have separate student organizations and focus their works on the restoration of democracy.[274] This makes it clear that NSU was inevitable to be organized, and it came to exist in April, 1970.

The United Student Movement perpetuated from 1960 was first disrupted by the progressive students when they separated themselves from the entire student community working in the 'All Student Union' by founding 'All Nepal National, Free Student Union in 1968.Then it was natural for the democratic students to realize the necessity of a separate national organization of their own. And the victory of the democratic panel in the T.U. Student Union election in 1969 was also an encouragement to create an environment in favour of democratic students. The students elected in the T.U. Union and the student leaders of the democratic group held a meeting in January, 1969. The meeting realized the need of a national level student organization of the democratic students. So, for the national level conference preparatory committee, Debendralal Nepali, Arjun Narshing K.C., Chirnajeebi Wagle, Rishikesh Gautam and Miss Durga Acharya were to be sent from T.U. Union."[275]

According to the pre-announced programme, the leader of Nepali Congress, Krishna Prasad Bhattarai inaugurating the historic conference of the students on April 19, 1970 A.D. said:

> *At first, we had organized Nepali National Congress with a limited number of our friends. But in this student conference such a large number of participants even in this extra-ordinary situation of today shows that you will be very successful to reach the goal. On 7th Baishakh the second session was held at Pashupati, Rammandir and a decision was made to name the student organization as 'Nepal Student Union (NSU). The police interfered on the spot and some participants were arrested from there. The constitution of NSU also was proposed and was passed. Those who were successful to escape from being arrested continued the conference and elected an executive committee of 'NSU' under the chairmanship of Bipin Koirala.*[276]

Marshal Julum Shakya, an the active founder of the union has said about the foundation of 'NSU' in the following way:

> *Devendralal Nepali, a candidate from the democratic group, was elected in the T.U. Union election in 1969. At the same time B.P. Koirala was released on April 8, 1969. Subrarnar Shumshere gave a wording to collect fund for the interests of students. So, looking the then prevalent environment the democratic student bloc formed a preparatory committee to this purpose. Bipin Koirala, Marshal Julum Shakya,*

> *Damannath Dhungana, Rishikesh Gautam, Develdralal Nepali, Shiva Bahadur Khadka, Ram Chandra Paudel, Jawahar Joshi, Basanta Gurung and Arjun Narasing K.C. were elected to the preparatory committee. This committee, after holding necessary discussions, consulted with the democratic students all over the kingdom. After having detailed discussions formed zonal wide primary-committees by mutual consensus and held national conference in Kathmandu, NSU was organized at Bhuikhel, Swoyambhu on April 19, 1970. Krishna Prasad Bhattarai inaugurated the conference. The next session was held at Jalvinayak Chobhar on the same day. The third session was held at Rammandir, Pashupati on April, 20. The constitution of NSU was passed by the same session. As police surrounded the session, some participants were arrested, some escaped, and some remained underground. On 22nd April, NSU held an election for the central executive committee in the central department of economics, in T.U., Kirtipur at 8 O'clock in the evening. Marsal Julum Shakya and Bipin Koirala were the candidates. Bipin Koirala won the election. Bipin Koirala became the first president of NSU. So, NSU officially came into existence from the same day. Two delegates and three observers from each district were present at the election programme.*
>
> *The objective of NSU was to unite all the democratic students of the kingdom in the organization and consolidate to strengthen it against Panchayat system. The primary objective was to strengthen the campaign to bring about democracy in Nepal. According to the same objective set in 1990 A.D., NSU continued to struggle for democracy and finally became successful to bring all the students and political parties under the commandership of Ganeshman Singh in 1990. and with the united efforts of all the students and political parties Nepal could enter the new era of democratic system.*[277]

The first president elect and founder of NSU Bipin Koirala says about NSU in this way:

> *Krishna Prasad Bhattarai who had been freed from jail on April 8, 1969, inaugurated the NSU conference at Bhuikhel, Swoyanbhu on April 19, 1970 A.D. The second and third*

> *sessions of the conference were held at Chobhar and Rammandir respectively. The election of the central executive committee was held in the hall of central department of economics, T.U. at Kirtipur on 9th Baishak. Marshal Julum Shakya and Bipin Koirala were candidates for the presidentship. Bipin Koirala won the post. The Panchayat government did not give recognition to NSU in the excuse of being an illegal organization. The court's bench under the Judge Durganath signed us, punished and continued arresting us. The lawyers Ganeshraj Sharma and Kushum Shrestha, advocated in our favour and, the Supreme Court decided the case making NSU a legal organization on 9th July 1970. There began the process of forming NSU units all over the country. Fifty-two district units were immediately formed.*[278]

NSU was founded in 1970 to have right for nationalism, socialism, democracy and for the interests of students. NSU played a vital role in the movements of 1971, 1972, 1975, 1978–79, 1987 and 1990 A.D. In short, NSU is the only one student organization which continued its struggle up to 1960 for democracy and got success to consolidate democracy movement of 1990.[279]

To step in the Nepalese political field in those difficult days during the Panchayat autocracy was itself a revolutionary identity of NSU.[280]

A brief description of harsh-laws against NSU, the decision of the Supreme Court and release of students:

> *The Supreme Court gave a decision in favour of the students on the habeascorpus-writ filed in the division benches by students against the chairman of tribunal Durgadas, Police DSP of Kathmandu, Home and Panchayat Ministry, District Court of Kathmandu and jail office. The Supreme Court ordered for the release of 48 students who were already convicted and imprisoned, and clarified that such student organization did not need to take any admittance from the government.*[281]

A welcome ceremony was held on 7th September, by NSU

for the respect of the released students who were arrested in connection with the conference for the foundation of NSU and the senior lawyers who had contributed to NSU by advocating from the side of students at the Supreme Court.[282] The chairman of the welcome ceremony and NSU President Bipin Koirala speaking at the ceremony said 'The students have been struggling for the rights and interests of the students for the last 8 or 10 years. The government arrested the active NSU students before NSU had taken its official shape as well as size. The government dramatically filed charges against the students and suspended fundamental rights and interests not only of the students but also of the whole Nepalese people.[283]

At the same ceremony, senior lawyers Krishna Prasad Bhandary and Ganeshraj Sharma speaking on behalf of the lawyers said, at the time whenever the people's legal and fundamental rights are exploited, we will try our best from the side of the people to have their rights best enjoyed. In the end the NSU information and publicity secretary Ramchandra Paudel thanked all the invitees for their presence at the welcome ceremony.[284]

NSU has remained as a sister unit of Nepali Congress. The flag with red background at the center of which lies a sign of flaming torch and a pen into a white circle belongs to NSU.[285]

4.18 Nepa' Student Union (NSU) (a)

NSU was founded in Kathmandu on 19 April, 1970. It was inaugurated by Krishna Prasad Bhattrai.

Its flag- A flaming-torch and a pen into a white circle at the center on red background.

Its ideals- Student unity, nationalism, democracy and socialism are its ideals.

Its objectives- To solve student-problems by students

themselves as far as possible. To establish relationship with international unions and organizations representing its own objectives, views, concepts and beliefs etc.

The second conference of NSU was held in Naryanagar, Chitawan, on 14 September, 1971. It was inaugurated by Bakhansingh Gurung.

The third conference was held in Gnagasagar (*Dharmashala*), in Janakpur on March 12, 1979. It was inaugurated by B.P. Koirala. There were three candidates for the post of NSU president. Benu Prasai, Dil Bahadur Gharti and Bimalendra Nidhi. But Bimalendra Nidhi was made president. So no free contest was held for the presidentship.

This conference admitted NSU to be a sister unit of the Nepali Congress led by B.P. Koirala and expressed commitment to uphold the ideals and principles of the Nepali Congress.[286]

4.19 Nepal Student Union (NSU) (b)

The third conference of NSU 1970 was held in Kathmandu on 10 March, 1979. This conference was inaugurated by Bakhansing Gurung. Its objective was to promote the rights and interests of students along with democracy and nationalism and its flag was a flaming-torch and pen into a white circle at the center on re-background. This conference held on 10-11th March elected a 21 member central committee under the presidentship of Kul Bahadur Karki.

Bakhansingh Gurung while inaugurating the conference stated that NSU without being a tool or stooge of any outlawed political party or political person can only discharge its present national responsibilities by being the main assisting force and symbol in the national democratic movement as a whole.

NSU president Kul Bahadur Karki's statement at a press conference is as follows:

> *The duty of the student union is to protect and promote democracy, nationalism and sovereignty giving priority to the interests of students but not to work against the wish and sentiment of students being stooge of any individual. But NSU became a room of certain political individuals due to its relationship with the political party. So we all the democratic students claim that this union is the real NSU and the one which was established in 1970. We tried to maintain the dignity of the union and the democratic students.*[287]
>
> *This fact clarifies that NSU was divided by the political leaders to fulfil their vested interests. So an element of division became active in Nepali Congress. That has been expressed through various media and events on different occasions.*

Some comments made by newspapers about NSU are as follows:

> *After some leaders of Nepali Congress had given statement with unconditional surrender to the Panchayat system in about 1967 the NSU students related to their politics began to destroy and disintegrate in student organization (NSU). They always worked for the benefit of the government by contemptibly disrupting every student movement in different excuses. The congress students split off from ANNFSU, and founded NSU on 19th April, 1970; the same NSU is continuing still today.*[288]

Specially due to the struggle against the Indian expansionism and American imperialism by the leftist students, the Nepali Congress supporting students, according to their character did not become ready to involve in such struggles and began to seek a new way of their own. This faction also organized about 51 district and zonal level units after 1968, and founded their new organization, NSU, on 19th April, 1970, it was inaugurated by Krishna Prasad Bhattarai. The conference declared nationalism, democracy and socialism as its main objectives.[289]

The student movements of 1964, 1966 and 1969 against the suppression of the government are most important and are worthy to be written in golden letters in the history of Nepalese student movement. The foundation of NSU in 1970 is the result of the same movements. Through this organization, we can struggle for the achievement of democracy and its protection by uniting all the students of the country.[290]

> *We, the Nepalese students have founded 'Nepal Student Union' after a long struggle. It will certainly play a vital role to bring about changes in the country.*[291]

Nepal student union is an organization of the students and youths who have dedicated, and sacrificed their lives for the establishment of human rights and democracy. Its history represents the history of revolution and martyrdom of the Nepalese students for nationalism and democracy.

NSU had to remain struggling for nationalism and democracy under the suppression and torture for a long time since its beginning. Thousands of students were kept in jails and dozens became martyrs. The cruelty, the bullets and batons could not supress the student movements, but rather showed the way of unity and determination against the dictatorship. The weighty role played by NSU in bringing about democracy in Nepal on the call of Nepali congress being its sister organization has made its own indelible history.[292]

4.20 Some Other Student Organizations

Apart from the above mentioned student organizations, some other new student organizations also came to exist after the student movement of 1978-79. The objectives of these organizations are not found different from the formerly organized ones. All the student organizations were established and they worked under the influence of ANNFSU. There was also Panchayat supporting organization.

4.20.1 Nepal *Rastriya Chhatra Sang* (Nepal National Student Organization)

After the announcement of referendum in 1980 the Pančhayati leaders by collecting several students from different campuses held a gathering in Kathmandu and decided to organize students in support of partyless Panchayat system. They founded 'Nepal National Student Organization' as an adhoc committee under the chairmanship of Bhuwan Pathak. This organization contributed a lot to the Panchayat system during the referendum period.[293] Its objectives were:

(i) The sources of inspiration of "Nepal National Student Organization (NNSO), are the motherland of Nepal, the center of faith, the crown. All the educational institutions of Nepal are the working fields and all the Nepalese students shall be the successors of the achievements of this organization.

(ii) To build a free and fair student force dedicated to the nation, crown nationality and partyless Panchayat system.

(iii) To make all the students know the importance of discipline and study.

(iv) To make the students aware of the vested interest of selfish elements who try to diverse them from study and education.

(v) To keep the students away from the anti-national sentiment and groupism.

(vi) To mobilize the organized student force in building the nation.

(vii) To prevent the educational environment from being blurred and to maintain hearty relationship between the students and the teachers.[294]

4.20.2 Nepal *Rastriya Viddharthi Parishad* (Nepal National Student Council)

A gathering of students from different districts studying in different campuses in Kathmandu decided to found a separate organization naming, Nepal National Student Council (NNSC)" in August, 1979.

This gathering formed a three member adhoc committee under the chairmanship of Binod Thapa with Prithivi Raj and Bhuwan Pathak as its members.

4.20.3 Nepal *Rastriya Viddyarthi Sangathan* (Nepal National Student Organization)

The objective of this organization was capitalism and the stooge supporters of democratic socialism are the enemies of humanism and indicative of exploitation as well servitude. Therefore, we are infavour of purely Marxist economy and highly democratic life idealism. This organization was related with 'Multi Party Democratic Forum', a small party.

This student organization was established on 7th February, 1980. It formed a seventeen member central committee under the chairmanship of Narendra Raj Prasai. A gathering held under the chairmanship of Narendra Raj Prasai formed Sarswati Campus primary executive committee under the chairmanship of Ganga Vikram Lama on 23rd March, 1980.[295]

4.20.4 Nepal Lefties Student Union

This student organization came to exist in Kathmandu on 29th October, 1979. Its objective was to make a unity of all the Progressive Student Organizations. Until this was achieved, it was to work in harmony with all the progressive student unions holding discussions at the same time.[296]

4.20.5 Sunsari Free Student Union

It was organized in Kathmandu in November, 1979. Its objective was to voice against the inhuman suppression by the government in Sunsari district and to support the people's resistance. A ten member committee was formed under the chairmanship of Nilmani Pokharel.[297]

The 1978/79 student movement brought a new trend in Nepalese political movement. It became successful to convince the people that there was also political alternative of the partyless Panchayat system. The Nepalese student movement also became a successful force for the announcement of referendum holding the Panchayat system in confinement. The students also achieved the right to form free student union and the Panchayat supporting student organization called "National Independent Student Council (NISC)" was forced to be dissolved.

In the referendum of 1980, Panchayat was declared to be the winner, but the students did not accept it and continued their movement until 1990 which was successful to restore democratic system by dismissing the partyless Panchayat. Although this movement was led by political leaders, the main role was played by the students.

2.4. All India Nepalese Student Union

The conference of "All Nepalese India Student Union" was held in the compound of the Jawaharlal University in Delhi on 20th January, 1980 and had elected an executive committee comprising (1) Ananda Gurung (Jayapur), President, (2) Deva Shrma Paudel (Chandigar, Northern Region) Vice President, (3) Rabindra Nath Bhandary (Delhi, West and South region), (4) Madan Kumar (Banaras, Eastern Part, Banaras), General Secretary, (5) Arun Sayami (Jawalpur), Treasurer, (6) Ganesh Ghimire (Kurukchetra) Literary Secretary, (7) Hisila Yemi (Delhi), (8) Puruswottam Pokhrel (Delhi) Cultural Secretary, (9) Devadatta Kharel (Kanpur) Public Contact Secretary, (10) Kedar Bahadur Karki (Ludhiyana) and ex-president of the union Baburam Bhattarai advisors.

It was said: AINSU, is a common organization of all the democratic and patriotic Nepal students studying in India and it is out of influence of any political party or any individual.[298]

4.20.7 All India Nepalese Student Association (Conference)

All India Nepalese Student Association (Conference) was held a convention in Patna, India on 22nd, 23rd, February, 1980. It was inaugurated by Bhadrakali Mishra. Inaugurating the convention, Mr. Mishra said: "A constitutional assembly elected on the basis of adult franchise only can solve the political problem prevalent in the country."

The other participants in the conference, president of International Student Organization of Banaras Hindu University Rahul, the ex-minister of Bihar Buddhadev Singh, Marxist Communist Party representative Kiswary Prasanna Singh, Sudhir Kanta of Youth People's Party, Akhtar Husen of Lohiya thoughts, Cangadhar Jha of Saptari, Pradip Giri of Siraha, Ramchandra Mishra of Mahottary and Kedar Sandilya also had expressed their views at the convention.

The convention elected the members of an executive committee comprising of (1) Deva Chandra, Resident, (2) Krishna Ache, (3) Tikaram Wagle, (4) Jitendra Mhasheth, Vice-Presidents, (5) Dr. Rabindra Kumar Singh, General Secretary, (6) Mahendra Nayak, (7) Dhurba Nath Tripathi, (8) Radha Prasad Thakur, (9) Prakash Mitra Secretary, (10) Chandreswor Prasad, Treasurer, (11) Dilip Kumar Jha, (12) Baburam Pathak, (13) Govinda Ghimire, (14) Homnath Dahal, (15) Nirmal Kumar Sharma, (16) Sachitananda Mishra, (17) Ramnaresh Mahato, (18) Radhakanta Mishra, (19) Kamales Kumar Mishra.[299]

The Nepalese students continued movements for democracy in Nepal by forming different organizations inside and outside the country from 1940 to 1990 A.D. During this long period different wrong elements also could use the students in anti-democratic campaign for their vested interests which became a serious crisis for the nation and at the same time the character of the political system and the government also was unmasked before the people.

Then, finally the democratic movement became successful to bring democracy in Nepal by farming a single forum of different student organizations on the call of different political leaders and under the commandership of Ganesh Man Singh in 1990. After 1990 different new student organizations have also been formed according to the division of old political parties.

References:

1 From an interview with Yadunath Khanal on 1998/7/2, Kathmandu.
2 From an interview with Dilliraman Regmi on 1997/7/20, Kathmandu.
3 From an interview with Bishnu Bahadur Manandhar on 1997/7/28, Kathmandu.
4 From an interview with Man Mohan Adhikary on 1997/4/9, Kathmandu.
5 From an interview with Kamal Raj Regmi on 1997/5/10, Kathmandu.
6 Soorya Lal Amatya, Jagadish Agrawal & Krishna P. Pradhan, *A Study of Student- Problem in Tribhuvan University*, (Kirtipur: TU Rector's Office, Research Division, 1980), p. 3.
7 *Ibid.*
8 *Ibid.*
9 *Ibid.*
10 *Ibid.*, p. 4.
11 *Ibid.*
12 *Ibid.*, p. 5.
13 From an interview with Shambhu Ram Shrestha on 1998/9/2, Kathmandu.
14 Amatya, Agrawal & Pradhan, f.n. No. 6, p. 6.
15 From an interview with Bharat Raj Joshi on 1998/9/5, Lalitpur.
16 Amatya, Agrawal & Pradhan, f.n. No. 6, p. 5.
17 *Ibid.*
18 *Ibid.*
19 *Ibid*, p. 10.
20 *Ibid.*
21 *Ibid.*
22 From an interview with Diwakar Bikram Rana on 1998/9/7, Kathmandu.

23 From an interview with Bharat Raj Joshi on 1998/9/5, Lalitpur.
24 From an interview with Ram Hari Sharma on 1996/2/10, Kathmandu.
25 From an interview with Krishna Prasad Bhattarai on 1998/4/9, Kathmandu.
26 From an interview with Bishwa Bandhu Thapa on 1998/4/9, Kathmandu.
27 From an interview with B.C. Malla on 1996/9/3, Kathmandu.
28 From an interview with Bishwa Bandhu Thapa on 1998/4/9, Kathmandu.
29 Bhim Bahadur Pande, *Tes Bakhat ko Nepal, Pahilo Bahg* (The Then Nepal), Vol. 1, (Lalitpur: Research Center for Nepal and Asia Studies, 2039 (1982), p. 205.
30 *Ibid.*, p. 120.
31 Bhuwan Lal Pradhan, *Nepal ko Jana Kranti 2007 B.S.* (People's Revolution of Nepal 1950 A.D.), (Kathmandu: Rumu Prakashan, 2047 (1990), p. 209.
32 Balchandra Sharma, *Nepal ko Aitihasik Rup Rekha* (An Outline of the History of Nepal), (Banara: Madav Prasad Sharma, 1969), p. 407.
33 Pradhan, f.n. No. 31, pp. 105-06.
34 *Ibid.*, pp. 209, 290, 292 & 299.
35 *Ibid.*, p. 241.
36 From an interview with Krishna Prasad Bhattarai on 1998/4/9, Kathmandu.
37 From an interview with B.C. Malla on 1996/4/14, Kathmandu.
38 *Ibid.*
39 From an interview with Bishwa Bandhu Thapa on 1998/4/9, Kathmandu.
40 *Ibid.*
41 From an interview with Krishna Prasad Bhattarai on 1998/4/7, Kathmandu.
42 From an interview with Man Mohan Adhikari on 1997/4/9, Kathmandu.
43 From an interview with Parshu Narayan Chaudhari on 1998/5/1, Kathmandu.
44 From an interview with Govinda Prasad Lohani on 1998/5/10, Kathmandu.
45 From an interview with Keshar Jung Rayamajhi on 1997/4/15, Kathmandu.
46 From an interview with Ram Hari Joshi on 1996/4/14, Kathmandu.
47 *Ibid.*
48 *Ibid.*
49 *Ibid.*

50 *Ibid.*
51 From an interview with Keshar Jung Rayamajhi on 1997/415, Kathmandu.
52 From an interview with Hikmat Singh Bhandari, on 1997/415, Kathmandu.
53 *Ibid.*
54 *Ibid.*
55 Pradhan, f.n. No. 31, p. 345.
56 "Kashi Bishwa Bidyalaya Nepali *Chhatra Sangh*," *Quarterly Yugbani*, Vol. 24, (Wednesday, 1948 A.D.), p. 12.
57 From an interview with Hikmat Singh Bhandari on 1997/5/3, Kathmandu.
58 *Ibid.*
59 *Ibid.*
60 From an interview with Keshar Jung Rayamajhi on 1997/4/15, Kathmandu.
61 *Annual Magazines from 1964-1965*, (Calcutta: Himanchal Chhatra Sangh, 1950), p. 5.
62 Constitution of Himanchal Chatra Sangh, Annual Himanchal, 1950, p. 1.
63 *Annual Magazines from 1964-1965*, f.n. No. 61, pp. 35-36.
64 *Ibid.*, p. 48-49.
65 From an interview with Ram Hari Joshi on 1996/4/14, Kathmandu.
66 *Ibid.*
67 *Ibid.*
68 *Ibid.*
69 *Ibid.*
70 From an interview with Ram Hari Sharma on 1996/2/10, Kathmandu.
71 From an interview with Devilal Shrestha on 1997/2/10, Kathmandu.
72 From an interview with Ram Hari Joshi on 1996/4/13, Kathmandu.
73 From an interview with B.C. Malla on 1996/4/15, Kathmandu.
74 From an interview with Diwakar Bikram Rana on 1998/9/7, Kathmandu.
75 From an interview with Hikmat Singh Bhandari on 1997/5/3, Kathmandu.
76 From an interview with Kamal Raj Regmi on 1997/5/10, Kathmandu.
77 From an interview with Sri Bhadra Sharma on 1996/1/25, Kathmandu.
78 *Ibid.*

79 From an interview with Kamal Raj Regmi on 1997/5/10, Kathmandu.
80 From an interview with Padma Shankar Adhikari on 1997/5/15, Kathmandu.
81 From an interview with Nawa Raj Kattel on 1997/3/15, Kathmandu.
82 From an interview with Pitambar Dahal on 1997/3/11, Kathmandu.
83 *Bidhyarthi Shamachar*, Vol. 17, (Kathmandu: Central Publication and Publicity Department, ANNFSU, 1993), p. 27.
84 *Arunodaya, Nepali Literature 1963-1990*, Vol. 26, (Kathmandu: Tindhara Sanskrita Chatrabas, Joint issue 1-2, 1991), p. 74-75.
85 From an interview with Bashu Dev Tripathi on 1997/12/3, Kathmandu.
86 From an interview with Rajeshwor Devkota on 1997/7/5, Kathmandu.
87 From an interview with Nawaraj Kattel on 1997/7/5, Kathmandu.
88 *Jayatu Sanskritam* (monthly magazine), Vol. 1, No. 1, (Kathmandu: Sanskrit Chhatra Sangh, Nepal Prakashan, 1960), p. 1.
89 Nabraj Kattel, "Jayatu Sanskritam Andolan," (Movement of Jayatu Sanskritam), *Arunodaya*, (Kathmandu: Chatrakarya Samiti, Sanskri Chhatrabas), pp. 137-38.
90 Gobhardhan Rana, *Prajatantrik Andolan ma Nepal Bidhyarthi Sangha* (The Nepal Students' Federation in the Democratic Movement), (Kathmandu: Nepal Students' Federation Western Zones Co-ordination Committee, 1994), p. 36.
91 *Ibid.*
92 *Ibid.*
93 *Ibid.*, p. 41.
94 *Ibid.*
95 *Ibid.*
96 From an interview with Bashu Dev Dhungana on 1997/3/10, Kathmandu.
97 Rana, f.n. No. 90, p. 41.
98 *Arunodaya*, Vol. 6, f.n. No. 84, p. 86.
99 NNSF: An introduction, Central Committee Nepal National Students' Federation, 1996, p. 1.
100 Jhalak Prasad Subedi, *Nepali Vidyarthi Andolon ko Addha Satabdhi 1997-2047 V.S.* (Half a Century of the Movement of the Nepalese Students, 1940-1990 A.D.), (Pokhara: Subedi Prakashan, 1992), pp. 9-12.
101 Rana, f.n. No. 90, p. 46.
102 *Ibid.*
103 *Ibid.*

104 *Ibid.*, p. 47.
105 *Ibid.*
106 *Ibid.*, p. 46.
107 *Bidhyarthi Shamachar,* f.n. No. 83, p. 27.
108 A Brief History on the Nepalese Student's Movement and all Nepal National Free Students' Union (Sixth), (Kathmandu: Thirteenth Central Committee, 1997), p. 5.
109 *Ibid.*
110 *Ibid.*, p. 9.
111 *Ibid.*
112 *Ibid.*
113 *Ibid.*, p. 10.
114 *Ibid.*, p. 11.
115 *Larko Bulletin,* No. 2 Mouth Piece of Bhaktapur District Committee on Nepal Revolutionary Students' Association, 1997, pp. 1-2.
116 *Bidyarthi Bulleting* (ideological, half-yearly), Vol. 25, No. 1, NRSU, Central Office Bhaktapur, 1997, p. 2.
117 *Ibid.*
118 *Ibid.*
119 *Ibid.*
120 *Ibid.*
121 *Mul Prabaha,* Special Issue on the Second Conference of the Nepal Progressive Students' Union, 1997, p. 35.
122 Bulletin of Nepal National Students' Federation, No. 1, Oct., 1982, Ombahal, p. 4.
123 *Ibid.*, Bulletin No. 17, 1975, p. 5.
124 *Ibid.*, Bulleting No. 19, 1984, p. 8.
125 *Ibid.*, p. 6.
126 From an interview with Basu Rishal on 1998/5/10, Kathmandu.
127 Subedi, f.n. No. 100, p. 12.
128 Pradhan, f.n. No. 31, No. 2, p. 62.
129 From an interview with Bhuwan Lal Pradhan on 1997/3/7, Kathmandu.
130 From an interview with Ganesh Ballav Pradhan on 1997/2/20, Kathmandu.
131 From an interview with Srirang Pathak on 1997/2/22, Kathmandu.
132 From an interview with Marshal Julum Shakya on 1997/3/17, Kathmandu.
133 From an interview with Bashu Dev Dhungana on 1997/3/10, Kathmandu.
134 Rana, f.n. No. 90, pp. 30, 31, 33 & 34.

135 From an interview with Jaya Krishna Panthi on 1996/9/4, Kathmandu.
136 From an interview with Shanta Ram Bhandari on 1997/12/2, Kathmandu.
137 From an interview with Mohamad Mohsin on 1998/3/7, Kathmandu.
138 *Ibid.*
139 From an interview with Ganesh Ballab Pradhan on 1997/2/20, Kathmandu.
140 From an interview with Dr. Mohamad Mohsin on 1998/4/17, Kathmandu.
141 *Ibid.*
142 From an interview with Ganesh Ballav Pradhan on 1997/2/20, Kathmandu.
143 From an interview with Dr. Mohamad Mohsin on 1998/4/17, Kathmandu.
144 From an interview with Bashu Dev Dhungana on 1997/3/10, Kathmandu.
145 *Bidyarthi Samachar,* f.n. No. 83, p. 27.
146 Nepalese Students' Union and A.N.N.F.S.U. (Sixth) Short History, (Kathmandu: A.N.N.F.S.U. Thirteen Central Committee, 1998).
147 From an interview with Diwakar Bikram Rana on 1998/9/7, Kathmandu.
148 Chatra, Banaras: Nepali Chatra Sangh, Hindu Bishwabidhyalaya, Kashi, 1954, p. 125.
149 From an interview with Diwakar Bikram Rana on 1998/9/7, Kathmandu.
150 Chhatra, f.n. No. 148, p. 128.
151 From an interview with Diwakar Bikram Rana on 1998/9/7, Kathmandu.
152 Chhatra, f.n. No. 148, p. 133.
153 From an interview with Diwakar Bikram Rana, on 1998/9/7, Kathmandu.
154 *Ibid.*
155 Chhatra, f.n. No. 148, p. 122.
156 *Ibid.*
157 From an interview with Diwakar Bikram Rana, on 1998/9/7, Kathmandu.
158 *Ibid.*
159 From an interview with Chirinjive Rijal, on 1997/10/14, Kathmandu.
160 *Ibid.*
161 From an interview with Diwakar Bikram Rana, on 1998/9/7, Kathmandu.

162 Chatra, f.n. No. 148, pp. 114-15.
163 From an interview with Diwakar Bikram Rana, on 1998/9/7, Kathmandu.
164 *Ibid.*
165 From an interview with Yajnya Prasad Acharya, on 1997/11/6, Kathmandu.
166 From an interview with Mahesh Kumar Upadhyaya on 1998/9/15, Lalitpur.
167 *Ibid.*
168 *Ibid.*
169 From an interview with Yajnya Prasad Acharya on 1997/11/6, Lalitpur.
170 From an interview Mohammand Mohsin on 1998/3/7, Kathmandu.
171 Grishma Bahadur Devkota, *Nepal ko Rajnitik Darpan, Pahilo Bhag* (Political Mirror Nepal) Third Edition, (Kathmandu: Dhurba Bahadur Devkota, 1979), pp. 546-47.
172 *Student Voice* (Vidhyarthi Awaj, 8) ANNFSU, Central Committee, Central Committee's Official Magazine, (Year 7, 1985), p. A (ka).
173 *Ibid.*
174 From an interview Bipin Koirala on 1997/11/14, Kathmandu.
175 From an interview Dambar Bir Thapa on 1998/9/13, Kathmandu.
176 *Ibid.*
177 From an interview Maheswornan Shrestha on 1998/9/15, Kathmandu.
178 From an interview Kamal Chitrakar on 1997/6/3, Kathmandu.
179 From an interview Janardan Acharya on 1997/6/14, Kathmandu.
180 From an interview Nirmal Aryal on 1997/6/17, Kathmandu.
181 From an interview Bipin Koirala on 1997/11/14, Kathmandu.
182 Rana, f.n. No. 90, p. 93.
183 *Ibid*, p. 92.
184 From an interview Bipin Koirala on 1997/11/14, Kathmandu.
185 Rana, f.n. No. 90, p. 93.
186 *Ibid.*
187 *Ibid.*
188 *Ibid.*
189 From an interview Ramchandra Poudel on 1998/7/3, Kathmandu.
190 Rana, f.n. No. 90, p. 130.
191 From an interview Bipin Koirala on 1997/11/14, Kathmandu.
192 From an interview Miss Shailaja Acharya's on 1997/11/20, Kathmandu.
193 From an interview Kamal Chitrakar on 1997/6/3, Kathmandu.
194 From an interview Viswokanta Mainali on 1998/3/7, Kathmandu.

195 From an interview Daman Nath Dhungana on 1997/6/20, Kathmandu.

196 From an interview Janardan Acharya on 1997/6/14, Kathmandu.

197 From an interview Hiranyalal Shrestha on 1997/6/22, Kathmandu.

198 From an interview Kamal Krishna Joshi on 1997/6/20, Kathmandu.

199 Rana, f.n. No. 90, p. 106.

200 Nepalese Student Movement and ANFSU, f.n. No. 146, pp. 13-14.

201 *Ibid.*

202 Nepalese Student Union, f.n. No. 146, p. 13.

203 *Student Voice*, f.n. No. 172, p. 19.

204 *Ibid*, p. 56.

205 *Vidhyarthi Jagaran*, ANNFSU, Dolakha d.c., Mouth Piece, 1984, p. 44.

206 *Student Voice*, f.n. No. 172, p. 69.

207 *Ibid.*, p. 56.

208 *Ibid.*, p. (B) (kha).

209 *Bidyarthi Samachar*, f.n. No. 83, p. 28.

210 From an interview with Sambhuram Shrestha on 1998/9/2, Kathmandu.

211 From an interview with Mokunda Bahadur Shrestha on 1998/9/4, Kathmandu.

212 From an interview with Nirmal Kumar Aryal on 1997/6/17, Kathmandu.

213 From an interview with Mukunda Bahadur Shrestha on 1998/9/4, Kathmandu.

214 Grishma Bahadur Devkota, *Nepal ko Rajnaitik Darpan: Janmat Sangrah ra Tyspachi* (Political Mirror of Nepal: The Referendum and After), (Kahtmandu: Umesh Bahadur Devkota, 1983), pp. 75-76.

215 Nepalese Student Union, f.n. No. 146, p. 50.

216 Devkota, f.n. No. 214, p. 76.

217 *Ibid.*

218 Report of 4th National Conference, Bhaktapur District Committee on Nepal Revolutionary Students' Association, 1991, pp. 11-12.

219 Subedi, f.n. No. 100, p. 68.

220 Report of 4th National Conference, f.n. No. 218.

221 Devkota, f.n. No. 171, p. 79.

222 *Ibid.*

223 Nepal Revolutionary Student Union, f.n. No. 218, p. 14.

224 Devkota, f.n. No. 171, pp. 79-80.

225 *Ibid.*

226 *Ibid*, pp. 80-81.
227 *Larko Bulletin* No. 2 Mouth Piece of Bhaktapur District Committee on Nepal Revolutionary Students' Association, 1998, p. 2.
228 Report of 4th National Conference, f.n. No. 218, pp. 11-12.
229 *Larko*, f.n. No. 227, p. 1.
230 Report of 4th National Conference, f.n. No. 218, p. 12.
231 Devkota, f.n. No. 171, p. 82.
232 From an interview with Prunaman Shrestha on 1998/7/27, Kathmandu.
233 From an interview with Sunil Manandhar on 1998/7/27, Kathmandu.
234 Devkota, f.n. No. 171, p. 71.
235 *Ibid.*, pp. 71-72.
236 Rana, f.n. No. 90, p. 122.
237 *Ibid.*
238 *Ibid.*
239 From an interview with Padam Thakurathi on 1997/10/15/, Kathmandu.
240 *Ibid.*
241 From an interview with Rabindra Chakrabarti on 1997/10/25, Kathmandu.
242 From an interview with Padam Thkurathi on 1997/10/15, Kathmandu.
243 From an interview with Rabindra Chakrabarti on 1997/10/25, Kathmandu.
244 From an interview with Padam Thkurathi on 1997/10/15, Kathmandu.
245 *Ibid.*
246 From an interview with Rabindra Chakrabarti on 1997/10/15, Kathmandu.
247 From an interview with Mohamud Mohsin on 1998/3/7, Kathmandu.
248 *Ibid.*
249 From an interview with Niranjan Thapa on 1998/3/15, Kathmandu.
250 From an interview with Kamal Thapa on 1998/3/20, Kathmandu.
251 From an interview with Rabindra Chakrabarti on 1997/10/15, Kathmandu.
252 From an interview with Trailokyanath Upreti on 1997/8/8, Kathmandu.
253 From an interview with Niranjan Thapa on 1998/3/15, Kathmandu.

254 From an interview with Padam Thakurathi on 1997/10/15, Kathmandu.
255 From an interview with Rabindra Chakrabarti on 1997/10/25, Kathmandu.
256 From an interview with Padam thakurathi on 1997/10/15, Kathmandu.
257 *Ibid.*
258 From an interview with Dr. Mohamand Mohisin on 1998/3/7, Kathmandu.
259 *Ibid.*
260 From an interview with Padam Thakurathi on 1997/10/15, Kathmandu.
261 Rana, f.n. No. 90, pp. 13-24.
262 *Ibid.*
263 Subedi, f.n. No. 100, pp. 33-34.
264 From an interview with Basudev Tripathi on 1997/8/15, Kathmandu.
265 From an interview with Hikmat Singh Bhandary on 1997/5/3, Kathmandu.
266 From an interview with Tanka Karki on 1997/5/19, Kathmandu.
267 From an interview with Bala Bahadur K.C. on 1997/7/25, Kathmandu.
268 From an interview with Viswokanta Mainali on 1998/1/19, Kathmandu.
269 From an interview with Mahesworman Shrestha on 1998/9/15, Kathmandu.
270 From an interview with Birendra Bhakta Shrestha on 1997/6/2, Kathmandu.
271 *Ibid.*
272 From an interview with Janardan Acharya on 1997/6/14, Kathmandu.
273 From an interview with Sambhu Ram Shrestha on 1998/9/2, Kathmandu.
274 From an interview with Nirmal Kumar Aryal on 1997/6/17, Kathmandu.
275 Rana, f.n. No. 90, p. 135.
276 *Ibid*, pp. 140-41.
277 From an interview with Marshal Julum Shakya on 1997/3/17, Kathmandu.
278 From an interview with Bipin Koirala on 1997/11/14, Kathmandu.
279 From an interview with Bal Bahadur K.C. on 1997/7/25, Kathmandu.
280 Rana, f.n. 90, p. 174.
281 *Ibid.*

282 *Ibid.*, p. 175.
283 *Ibid.*
284 *Ibid.*
285 *Ibid,*, p. 139.
286 Devkota, f.n. No. 171, pp. 73-74.
287 *Ibid.*
288 Nepalese Student Movement, f.n. No. 146, p. 14.
289 Subedi, f.n. No. 100, p. 36.
290 *Deurali Bulleting*, (Kirtipur : Nepal Students Union, Kirtipur Multiple Campus, 1964), p. 93.
291 *Sakranit Bulletin*, Issue-2, (Kathmandu : Nepal Students Union, 1970), p. 63.
292 Rana, f.n. No. 90, p. A(ka).
293 Devkota, f.n. No. 171, p. 82.
294 *Ibid.*, p. 81.
295 *Ibid.*, p. 82.
296 *Ibid.*
297 *Ibid.*
298 *Ibid.*, p. 84.
299 *Ibid.*, pp. 84-85.

CHAPTER FIVE

The Student Unrest

(1950-1990)

5.1 Introduction

Nepal has not been an exception so far students movement is concerned. In most of the developing countries students prepared a background for political movements by opposing colonialism and imperialism, whereas Nepal prepared background of student politics by opposing autocratic Rana regime. It would also not be an exaggeration to say that Nepal's student movement was due to the influence of Indian politics. Indeed, the Indian movement against British Imperialism or the Indian Independence movement had helped much in the Nepalese movement against the Rana regime in Nepal.[1]

It seems that the students movement was not directly launched against the political system of the country. The students simply expressed their dissatisfactions with the weakness of educational sector and, later on, political demands were added to their demands under the influence of political parties. Mainly the students movements would start for the educational reasons. The educational reasons were based on;[2] (i) International educational environment with which the students express their dissatisfaction, such as teachers weaknesses, lack of good-library management, lack of course books and reference materials, scholarship system and freeship, facility of transportation, formation of students units and their conduction etc.

The hike of fees has been found to be main reason for the students to express their grievances. Voices against the hike of fees are specially raised by the students coming from remote parts, like villages of Terai and hilly regions. Most of them come from very remote parts and are aquatinted with every difficulty and problem their guardians face.The unrest and anarchic environment in the educational sector is also related to the establishment of student organization.[3] All such problems lead the students towards movement in which political demands also are added. The movement of 1979 was successful to bring the Panchayat system to critical mode. By this movement all the people such as peasants, businessmen, workers, service-holders and simple people were also influenced.[4] Similarly, the people were involved in the movement against the so-called new education system introduced in 1971. The movement at that time was suppressed, but the student started their movement again in 1975. They went on strike. The Panchayat government interfered with the movements by using different violent and immoral means. Even then the students continued their movements with utmost unity. The result was that the king announced referendum to select political system. This is taken as the most important event in a country like Nepal.[5] In epitome, the causes of Nepalese student movements are seen related to educational, cultural, economic, social and political reasons. Student movements also have been found related with the same reasons. The student movements in Asian countries including Nepal are found mostly related with politics. The students' organizations came to exist for the cause of politics and the opposition political parties are found giving supports to the students in various ways.[6] It is natural and contextual for the educational institutions to be politicized in such a country which has a very short history of higher education.[7] The Nepalese student movements are divided mainly in three chapters.

(i) The period before 1950 (during the Rana regime)

(ii) From 1950 to 1971 (From the post democratic revolution to the advent of National Education System Plan, NESP)

(iii) After the National Education System Plan to (1990).

5.1.1 The Student Movement Prior to 1951 (The Rana Period)

The autocratic Rana government had made tradition as a main basis to rule the country. They had restricted any modern development in the country, so that the people's eyes would not open and they remain in darkness. So little development took place in the sector of education. There was a kind of "Reign of terror" in the country.[8] The government always wanted to keep the people in darkness. The Rana government had the fear that in case people became educated, waves of awareness would undulate among the people and they would be politically and socially consciousness to depose the Ranarule. Prime Minister Chandra Shamsher had also regretted for the establishment of Trichandra College, realizing that it would make the people conscious of their legal and political rights.

The condition of Nepal in the sector of education literacy was very poor before 1950. So, the Nepalese students played a vital role to topple the Rana regime forever.

The Nepalese who were studying in the educational institutions in India and were involved in the free India movements also worked to arouse consciousness and educational awareness among the people. After 1930 the Nepalese youths promised to disseminate education and its importance in Nepal in two ways, one from India and the other from inside the country, with a view to end the Rana regime, making the people conscious through education.[9] Especially the Nepalese youths began to go in to exile after the rise of Rana regime. A large number of them would go to Banaras for study. During the Rana period most of them would live in India, especially in Banaras as political refuse to escape punishment from government. Their role became vital to make the 1950 revolution a success.

The Nepalese studying in Banaras expanded their organizations in different parts of India like Calcutta, Delhi, Patna, Bombay, Lackhnow, Allahabad, etc. to effectively drive their anti Rana campaign in Nepal. Among them, the Benaras 'Student Union' and the, Himanchal student union of Calcutta. were the main organizations.[10] Changes in Nepalese political system were unavoidably necessary and it was eminent but this was possible only with the help of the political leaders. B.P. Koirala wrote an article entitled "Among the people and peoples' rule" and published it in 1946 to arouse political consciousness among the people. The article largely influenced the educated Nepalese youths.[11] In that ongoing context some students studying in Benaras held a conference on October 31st. 1946 and founded "All India Nepali National Congress", and then a gathering was held in Bhavanipur, Calcutta. Students from different parts of India such as Benaras and Darjelling, had taken part in the conference. In the same year the Nepalese students studying in the Benaras Hindu University founded "Banaras Hindu University Nepalese Student Union". This organization began to support the Nepali Congress.[12] This organization also took part in Jogbani conference on 9-10 April, 1946. Then Biratnagar workers' movement was started on the call of congress party. Many students took part in the movement abandoning even their examinations.

The workers and students came in contact with Nepalese political leaders in Benaras and were greatly influenced by their politics. They also could learn much from the 'Independence movement of India'. Such events helped the Nepalese youths learn and know the reality about the autocratic Rana government of Nepal. The Indian political environment influenced the Nepalese students very much. As the result, they understood that it was necessary to cross through several phases in question of nationalism and freedom like the Indian Independence Movement. They also knew that education and educational institutions could play a vital role to this purpose. Some students who had returned to Nepal after their education in India began to demand to make the Nepalese education modernized and widespread for all. They started a movement. However most of the students were forced to go into exile. They joined the Nepali Congress in India. Later on they became successful to play an important role in question of nationalism and democracy in Nepal.[13] The fact that consciousness should be increased among the Nepalese people through education was realized by them after knowing about the educational condition and environment of India. The Indian educational institutions established by the Indian people were being conducted more progressively and systematically than those established by the British government. So, the Nepalese youths also established Mahavir School in Nepal in 1935 with the affiliation of Indian National Education Institution (*Bharatiya Rastriya Viddyapith*). The children were sent to schools with the intention to make them politically conscious. When people began to be conscious of the situation in the country and the number of students grew, the Rana authority charged the school as a means of exciting people against the system. They closed the school on the 20th of October, 1936 and arrested 28 teachers and kept them into jail.[14] In the same year some enthusiastic young students founded 'Nepal Praja Parishad' and began to work against the Rana Government. The government restarted to severely suppress the activities of the 'Parishad' in 1940, but its effect became positive to the Nepalese democratic movement in the long run. The Nepalese people's movements before 1951 are found focused against Rana regime. The students inside Nepal and those who came from India completing their study with experiences from the Indian Independence movements got organized against the Rana government. In the same period the communist party of Nepal also came into existence under the leadership of Pushpalal. Then the Nepalese students took part in the anti-Rana movements guided by the joint leadership of the communist party and the Nepali Congress. An armed revolution was started since the day King Tribhuvan took shelter in India. The student community was directly involved in the armed struggle against the Rana government and finally the autocratic Rana regime came to and end forever in 1950.

5.1.2 From the Revolution of 1950 to the Advent of National Education System Plan (NESP)

The century-long Rana regime ended in 1950 and a democratic system, was established after the revolution. Different classes and professional organizations were founded. The students also organized their own unions. In the same period the communist party founded its sister organizations of students, peasants and intellectuals. According to the call of the communist party, Nepal National Student Federation was organized.[15] Similarly, Nepali Congress also organized its supporter student organization called "Nepal Student Union". The number of schools and colleges began to grow in the country. In the initial period of democracy, the students could neither break the traditional ways nor use the new ways and modern thoughts in their works. In such a difficult transitional period, whatever roles they played were worthy and contextual to the age.[16]

After the revolution of 1950, different professional and class organizations would stage protest, rallies, mass meetings and different programme of their own, but the activities and role of students' organizations had a different and special character from the other. On 6th November 1952, the police fired on the student rally in Kathmandu and a student was shot dead. This event fuelled the student activities against the government. The then Minister B.P. Koirala was regarded responsible for the death of the student. So he resigned from his post.[17] B.P. Koirala failed to solve the problem holding talks with the student organizations. The student movements took a political mode as a result of which the government of Prime Minister Mohan Shamsher was dissolved, and another government was formed under the premiership of Matrika Prasad Koirala. It indicates the student dissatisfaction and movement affect the new political set up in the country.[18] In those days there was not any university in Nepal. The colleges, had been affiliated with Patna University. So the students' activities were focused on politics rather than educational ones. The students earnestly demanded for the establishment of a university in Nepal also. So a university statute was declared in 1959 with the founding of the Tribhuvan University, and the Tribhuvan University law was passed. The university law at first gave recognition to the student organization.[19] The rules of the student organizations were prepared within the context of the law. In 1960, the first elected government and the parliament were dissolved with the imposition of bans on the student organizations including all the political parties and class organizations.[20] Then the partyless Panchayat system was introduced. After this undemocratic action, the student movements began to be more organized and strong. The Panchayat government had kept a watchful eye on any rallies, mass meetings or organizations. But the students without any fear remained working for the objective of the restoration of the democracy. Although they could not openly come out to the streets with strong organizational way, they went on struggling for their rights and interests. They did not lose courage even in the difficult situation. So, they launched movements for free student organization.[21]

In fact, the 1960 political event had created situation of terror and a fearful environment all over the country. The student could not help without opposing and resisting it. The Panchayat government began to suppress the students' dissatisfaction with the declaration or the "National directives law 1961" to guide the students' organizations under the same law. In this law, a concept of student union for the support of the Panchayat system was encompassed. But the students were more dissatisfied and provoked since the law would not help the students to achieve their political objective. So they began a campaign against the law. They strongly demanded for the opening of a nation wide free student union and started a movement against the Panchayat system. This became the primary demand of every student movement. But the government did not easily accept this, as it was against the principle and intention of the partyless Panchayat system.[22] The students did not lose spirit and they went on demanding the rights of National Free Student Organization. Indeed, the period from 1960 to 1979 was very difficult for the students to launch movement. During this period, they had to carry out the political programmes of the under-ground political parties and their leaders along with the student activities and programmes. Whatever bitter events took place in the student politics during this terrific period has occupied an important chapter in the history.[23]

The students were determined to hold Tribhuvan University Union elections, which were held in 1961. This election became successful to form students' platform and unity against the partyless Panchayat system.[24] The students used to put demands, stage protest programmes and express dissatisfactions through the union.[25] Although the demands of the students would be outwardly related with educational sector, their aims were political and their demands would automatically take political shape. In this context, the Panchayat government declared the National directives law with the intention of keeping the students under government control, which became the main point of disagreement for the student community. The students tried hard to have National Free Student Union to counter the government's intention as soon as possible.[26] MaheswORMAN Shrestha, Janardan Acharya, Kamal Chitrakar, Birendra Bhakta Shrestha, Dambar Bir Thapa, Bhakta Govinda Shrestha etc. were very active in this regard.

There are a number of evidences to prove that these student-youths had suffered a lot in different movements for the establishment of free student organization.[27] Their contribution to this purpose shall remain bright in the history of the Nepalese student movement forever. From minor to the major events often became the cause of student unrest. The student, at first, would express dissatisfaction and later on it would create an environment of student movement.[28]

The first greatest student movement after 1960 military action and introduction of partyless Panchayat system was the student strike of 7th May, 1963 which caused the expulsion of Bhakta Govinda Shrestha from Trichandra college for not paying fees. The students who were in his favour called a strike demanding his re-admission. Other colleges also took part in the strike in support of his readmission. The students had mainly three demands in which rights to organize free student union was included.[29] The situation became more complicated and Bhakta Govinda Shrestha started hunger strike. This was the first event, which began to knock the Panchayat government and the system. The king was compelled to give direction to the government to form a commission for investigation and give a right decision of the case.[30] The strike was called off, but the main demand for free student organization remained with the question mark.[31] The students again began a movement on 17th March, 1963, submitting demands for free student organization before the then Prime Minister Kirtinidhi Bista. They also made a plan to call valley-wide student gathering and hold discussions on different issues. On 7th May, 1964 the first Nepalese students convention was held. They observed 'Students' Day' with slogans and demanding for 'Free Students Organizations', releasing the students form detention and closing the Gorkha recruit center etc. The convention was ended on 11th May.[32] During the period of the convention a large number of students were arrested. Again the students began a strike demanding the release of all the students. The government was forced to release all the students. The students movement of that time had been fully motivated by politics due to which the Panchayat government was compelled to release the students from detention.[33]

The students of colleges and schools of the Kathmandu valley called a strike in 1965 demanding improvement of education system, organization of Free Students Union, systematisation of fees, scholarship and freeship, transportation facilities, etc.[34] The student strike took a serious mode. Most of the schools and colleges remained closed. The students adopted an extremist policy. The police arrested them from colleges and schools and most of them were imprisoned. Later, their demands were fulfilled, the strike was called off and the students were released. They were granted identity cards at certain percentage less charge and the rights to form free student organizations also.[35]

In 1968 again the students movement became more terrific. This movement has occupied an important and new place in the history of Nepalese students movement. A valley inter college conference was held in 1965. But the arrest of a large number of students had certainly brought a difficulty in the student politics.[36] In 1966, an election of students union was held in which Pro- Moscow Communist Students got victory. This created a situation of conflict.[37] The panel led by Bal Mukunda Kharel became victorious in the T.U. union election.

This created a situation of conflict between the government sponsored group and the group supported by others. At last, the government had no other way left to deal with the 'undesirable elements' than dissolving the organization.[38] In September 1969, DIG Narayan Singh, event took place. A cultural programme was being held in National Cultural Hall of Rani Pokhari by the Department of Commerce of Trichandra College. DIG Narayan Singh entering in the make-up and dressing room, behaved in a rude manner. There arose a dispute between the students and the police officer. The students demanded action against him. At that time the government suppressed the students' demand,[39] but the students were provoked and they started strike. A large number of students were arrested adding fuel to the fire. Finally the government was compelled to dismiss the DIG from his post and the students were released. Then the students movement was ended.[40] From this action the students knew the real strength and situation of the government. This event increased the courage of the students.[41] However, the

Panchayat government intended to suppress the opposition of students by organizing Nationalist Free Students Council (NFSC) in favour of the Panchayat system.[42] The students became more united and the student movements became stronger and more revolutionary indeed. As a result, many students went on strikes which gave an impetus to the democratic movement.[43] In 1968, the S.L.C. question papers were found wrong due to which the S.L.C. examination was postponed for certain period. In that situation the college students also demanded for holding examination of only one subject a day. The students tried to convince the concerned authorities about their demands for three days, but the authorities turned deaf ears to them. So the students in a bit of anger vandalized the office of the Controller of Examinations.[44] Later, the authorities accepted the demands for holding examination of one subject a day.[45]

The students started a movement against the incursion by India into Susta territory of Nepal in 1969.[46] The police baton-charged the students proceeding towards Singha Darbar and a number of them sustained injuries.[47]

On 5th and 7th December, 1968 mass rallies were organized in Lalitpur and Bhaktapur. The participants rallied in the street with fire-torches at night in Lalitpur.[48] Then on 14th February, 1969, the students' main wing staged a movement demanding reformation in the education system.[49]

On 10th July, 1969 the police arrested Ramchandra Paudel and the government directly interfered with the student community creating an anarchic environment in the educational institutions. A five-member delegation met the Minister of Education and demanded the release of Ramchandra Paudel, but the government paid no notice to the demand. Then a fifteen day movement was launched. On 8th July, the T.U. union president and treasurer issued a statement demanding to post Nepalese security guards on all the border areas of Nepal and to close down the Indian check posts in the Nepalese territory.[50] The political movement was started by the students on 11th and 12th July. Many students including the union president and treasure were arrested. Then the student movement took a serious mode on 13th July. A large number of students from schools and colleges took part in the movement. Although the left and progressive students had started the movement, the democratic students also fully supported it.[51] The police baton charged the students on 13th July. The T.C. College students were provoked and they started the movement again. Then the college was closed for some days. On the 23rd of July, two students started hunger strike; they were Tekendra Bahadur Karki and Pitambar Dahal. On the same night the arrested students were released, the strike was called off. The aim of the movement was to force the government to dismiss DIG Narayan Singh form his post.[52] The left and progressive students became very successful to launch every movement in an effective and strong way with fruitful results.[53]

The movements were so effective to threaten the government that the authorities had to remain alert for saving the Panchayat system. After such events, the importance of students organization appeared to be very necessary among the students. The progressive students became successful to organize their group.[54] There was little influence of a political party on the students. The political workers and leaders were scattered in exile, in prisons or under-ground. In such a situation the students were the main force to play opposition-political role. The political leaders would keep secret contact with the students and give necessary suggestions to the student leaders. Seeing the popularity and influence of the progressive students organization among the students, the other students having different ideologies also realized the necessity of their own organization. Specially, the democratic students took initiative to establish their own organization as it was suitable to have multi-organizations according to and based on the democratic ideals and principle.[55]

During this period, the progressive students initiated

agitation on many occasions and largely influenced the student community. With the T.U. students' union almost in their grip; they led movements to broaden their activities and to attract other students into their fold. The most important success which they achieved was that they made their presence felt. Meanwhile, the democratic students also initiated their organizational build up to counter the growing strength of the leftists. On 20th April 1970, they held an all Nepal students conference in Kathmandu. On the third and last day of the conference, Mr. K.P. Bhattarai addressed the Nepal Students Union. After this, a large number of students totaling about 100, were arrested, and they were imprisoned for over three months. Then, a writ petition was filed in the Supreme Court for their release. Later, they were released on 9th July, 1970. In 1971, The Nepal Students Union held a conference. It was basically aimed at strengthening the democratic forces in the country, especially among the students. However, the first organized attack on NESP was broadcast and the plan was severely criticized as irrelevant and inconsistent. After this incident, on many occasions, the students showed their opposition to the NESP.[56]

In the same context, the democratic students proceeded their process of founding their own organization. They held a conference in Kathmandu on 20th April, 1970 K.P. Bhattarai addressed the conference on the third and last day.[57] It was interferred by the police and some participants were arrested. About 100 students were imprisoned and they were released after three months. The students were released on 9th July, 1970, by the order of the Supreme Court. The court also decided that the students organization should not be banned. However, the government continued to arrest them in different excuses.[58] The Nepal students union held a conference in 1970. The conference was centered on politics rather than on the student problems.[59] The conference condemned and slammed the NESP saying that it was out of context of Nepal's reality. The students went on opposing the NESP for a long time.

At this point, an extract from the book, *A study on the nature of student problem in Tribhuvan University* describing the student agitation of 1972 and their demands seems worth mentioning:

Early in August 1972, a group of students attempted to organize a mass strike in opposition to the NESP. Their demands included suspension of the NESP, preservation of the rights of the students; better transportation facilities etc. Students also started picketing in T.U. College. On August 10th, the police arrested two students within the campus remises as claimed by the students. The arrests provoked the students and strengthened their cohesiveness, whereby later their movement shifted from concern with the educational matters to the political questions.

This situation resulted in the spread of strike in other colleges of the valley. Though initially the problem started with the grievances concerned with education system, political motives refueled the campaign later on. The strike was equally participated by the democrats as well as by the progressives. The students' list of demands included the following:

(i) The university code or conduct should be modified. Students should have a voice in proposing changes in the New Education System.

(ii) There should be a vigorous programme to provide employment for university graduates. There should be no hindrances in obtaining higher education.

(iii) The best four out of six internal assessment examinations should be counted for granting a degree. More emphasis should be placed on fieldwork activity in the university courses.

(iv) A new bridge on the way to Kirtipur should be built within three months and four buses to the Kirtipur campus should be added.

(v) There should be more books in the library.

(vi) All charges against the students should be dropped.

(vii) Various laws to control political activity should be abolished or modified.

(viii) The government should provide compensation for peasant victims of police firings.

(ix) There should be a free press.

(x) The Gorkha recruiting centers should abolished.[60]

The movement effectively spread all over the kingdom and forced the Panchayat government think seriously. The students' movement of the month of August has glorified the whole history of the student movement.

The strike became an example to prove any student movement can achieve success if the people of all walks of life also participated in the movement.[61] In this student strike, the revolutionary slogans surpassed the limit of the previous movements. Serious scuffles between the students and the police took place. Many students were arrested. Big rallies were demonstrated in the streets of Kathmandu city by which a new radicalism began among the student mass.[62]

But the administration did not intend to consider the demands of the students. This becomes clear by the statements released by the T.C. The Tribhuvan University also issued statements at times appealing to the guardians to send their wards suggesting them to study in a peaceful manner. In some campuses, destructive activities took place and the 21 day long movement caused a lot of property loss, T.U. administration was compelled to announce the closure of T.U. This event is regarded very important in the history of the T.U.[63]

The university issued statements time and again appealing to the students to stop the agitation and resume the classes. Even the guardians were appealed to send their wards to classes. Violence took place in some of the campuses, and property and equipment were damaged. After about 21 days of agitation, the university had no other way than closing the campus. Such a step was the first of its kind in the history of the university.[64]

The student movement did not cool down from the closure of campuses. T.U. called the students for holding talks to reach an agreement. As a result, a group of students agreed for talks. At the same time a large numbers of students were arrested. The student movement continued more violently. 45 days after the strike, compromising talks were held between the T.U. administration and the students and the detained students were released.[65] An agreement was signed promising to provide maximum facilities for the students. Thus t even though the student movement came to an end, it gained continuity because the administration, after fulfilling only the educational demands, kept the political demands under consideration. The administration agreed to consider the political demands. Then the classes were resumed and the teaching-learning process began after a long discussion.[66] Apart from this famous movement, many other sporadic movements would be staged almost daily. Different student groups affiliated with different political parties would stage separate movements to influence the students.[67]

The tone of student agitation during this period remained mostly political. The students were divided into various groups showing their affiliation with the erstwhile political parties. The elections of Tribhuvan University Unions were fought on the basis of anti-system tone and affiliations with political parties. The unions became the platforms for expressing ant-system views. The student meetings, conferences and their pamphlets were marked by anti-system articulation. In this regard, Baral states that "student organization during the period under review (1961-1972) was characterized such as facilities for transport, bridges cinema, concession etc.; but they acquired political color as and when the authority concerned ignored them. Thus, though students' opposition looked like a room-oriented opposition, it often tended to be anti-regime in character.[68]

NSU, ANNFSU and NSF formed a united action committee to initiate a joint movement in the month of July, 1972. They put forward Eight-point demands which included the release of political detainees, abolition of state-offence act, control of organizations act, National Directives law, security act etc. The movement became violent and spread all over the kingdom. The T.U. administration declared the closure of campuses for an infinite time and 17 students were expelled from T.U. A scuffle between the students and police took place in Pokhara, curfew was imposed in Biratnagar, and in Janakpur the police opened fire on the students' mass and two students, Kameswor and Kusheswor were shot to death at Jadukoha.

The students' movement of 1975, which was started with eleven-point demands putting the fundamental rights to be organized at the top of the first, has its own importance in the history of student movement.[69] The student movement since the imposition of partyless Panchayat system in 1960 in the opinion of Birendrabhakta Shrestha is as follows:

> *The student movement and its role after 1960 have occupied an import place in the history of Nepalese student movement. The students gradually weakened the Panchayat system. Very important substances would be expressed through trifle matters. The students would raise meaningful paints in simple ways and launch movements. Notwithstanding any success or failure, whatever the students did against the Panchayat system were the biggest threats to the government. The students' sacrifice, dedication, heroism and greatness has remained as a glory. They have also been an unending source of inspiration for the student community forever. The student movement was centered on the achievement of democracy after 1960. They started first movements demanding for free student union. The leading students in those days were Dambarbir Thapa, Janardan Acharya, Kamal Chitrakar, Maheshworman Shrestha, Mohan Prasad Pokharel, etc. As a result, T.U. union was organized. Later on, different student unions came into existence making threats against the government. The Panchayat government tried to control the student-politics in its grip by implementing New Education System Plan in 1971.*

But the NESP ironically provoked the students towards more strong and united movement against the government.70

5.1.3 The Student Movement from NESP Onwards

The student movement was divided into three phases from the political point of view. The student movements after the New Education System Plan (NESP) are found stronger and widespread.[71] The post- NESP student agitations appeared to be a kind of civil-war among the students. The 1972, 1975 and 1979 movements are the instances, leading towards the 1990 historic movement which finally became successful to bring about democracy in the country.[72] In such a situation they wanted to create a free teaching-learning environment but the Panchayat government would force to make them support the system in any away. The government began to keep the students within this plan as prisoners, but the students system and began to express dissatisfactions through strikes.[73] The nationwide student movements of 1972, 1975 and 1979 had compelled the Panchayat government to seriously think to reach a critical mode.[74] So, the first and second amendment had to be made and the movement of 1990 finally brought democracy by rooting out the 30 year old autocratic Panchayat System.[75]

The new education system plan instead of leading the nation on the path of development by consolidating and promoting the educational situation created an atmosphere of dissatisfaction and violence. Since 1971, when the NESP was enforced, there used to be student agitations for this or that cause almost daily. Among them, 1971, 1975 and 1979 movements are supposed to be the most important. These movements served as a strong background for the decisive democratic movement of 1990 to lead the nation towards the democratic era. The credit of the democratic movement of 1990 goes to the student community.[76] In fact, the NESP created an environment to force the students towards a mighty movement against the government.

5.1.4 National Education System Plan : An Introduction (NESP)

The government of a country formulates education policy as one of the major bases to make itself strong and be able for ruling the country in a systematic way. This is taken as the most important step in the educational history of Nepal regardless of its bad or good aspects, the NESP has given emphasis on high-level technical and vocation educational in the country. But what was wrong with the NESP was that it was prepared without holding wide discussions and implemented against the real context of Nepal.[77] The NESP was prepared by foreigners and was implemented by force of the rich countries to make them satisfied as a new experiment in our country.[78] In facts the New Education System Plan was implemented after a long study and wide discussions, but it became a failure politically.[79] The New Education System Plan was prepared and implemented realizing the needs of modern technical education in our nation. But it was ended by political games.[80] In those days the students would pay more attention to politics than to their education and study. The NESP was also directed to make the students center their mind on educational activities rather than politics, but it was opposed by the students themselves and eventually doomed to be a failure.[81]

From the above mentioned statements, it becomes clear that the New Education System Plan was implemented by the Panchayat government in a random way. As there was political instability in those days and the students were in opposition of the system, the government used the education sector to divert their attention. The so-called New Education System Plan (NESP) proved to be a curse for an underdeveloped country like Nepal. A lot of economic resources of the nation were squandered, and thousands of Nepalese students were hurled into a meaningless education system, depriving them of all-round development of their career on the other.[82] There was a situation of economic distraction as it seemed to be a barricade against Nepal's modern development. So, the students demanded for the removal of the New Education System Plan.

It would be contextual to briefly mention the NESP in the following way:

The main objective of the NESP was to produce citizens loyal to the system, country and crown.[83]

> *The basic objective of the NESP is to produce citizens who, with full faith in the country and crown, will conduct themselves in accordance with the Panchayat system and to meet the manpower requirements of the development through the spread of scientific and technical education.*[84]

So, it is clear that the objective of the NESP was to strengthen the Panchayat system. The education system and its policy should have to be conducted with a wider as well as national point of view and national perspective; but it was designed only to serve the political system, instead. Hence, it was natural to go against education system. Similarly, the NESP was not found to meet the national plan and requirement. It was out of national objective and had given priority to the elements beyond the educational sector.[85] NESP was designed by the high echelons without considering and knowing the situation of the remote villages and the people living throughout the country. As a result, many programmes were doomed to failure due to the lack of skilled manpower.[86] It seriously affected the progress of national development. The NESP seemed to have given encouragement to older tradition, culture and superstitions in the Nepalese society. The NESP clearly appeared to be unable to promote social, political and economic conditions to meet the necessity of the country. It became also clear that such irrelevant and weak education system would not benefit the Nepalese people and the country. The NESP had mentioned the main problems of the old education system in the following way:

(1) The education policies and objectives were not well defined and laid down clearly.

(2) The education system was based on the unproductive values of the society.

(3) The education system was wholly unrelated to the aims and objectives of the national plan. It was not work oriented.

(4) The education system did not stress on the need for consolidating education institutions. Hence quantitative increase of education institutions of various levels had been made at the cost of quality.

(5) The impact of the commutative weaknesses and shortcomings are reflected in the existing educational wastage which is fraught with grave socio-economic consequences.

(6) In the ultimate analysis, most of the problems outlined above seem to be the outcome of weakness inherent in the educational administration.[87]

Moreover, the country had restructured its political economy by adopting the Panchayat system, which is aimed at achieving national integration and egalitarian ideals. The change in the political system required new instructions manned by well trained and development oriented people which the then education system simply could not provide. The political system required the mass participation to achieve its broad objectives of economic equality which was possible only by properly educating the people and developing necessary skill and knowledge among them.

Therefore, with a view to achieving national integration and development of human resources consistent with the needs of the country, the overall change in the education system became urgent. The education system had to be aimed at developing a political community well committed to the crown and national loyalty, and proving a helping tool in the modernization of the economy through people's participation for the greater benefits of the common masses.[88]

The national education system was developed as stated.

"The plan is primarily aimed at counteracting elitist bias of the inherited system of education by linking it more effectively to productive enterprises and egalitarian principles. It, in brief, is committed to tackle irrelevant and disorganized varieties of education that still exist in the country. The plan calls for unifying education into one productive system. The concept regards education as an investment in human resources for the development of the country."[89]

The NESP has been designed and developed as a socio-economic and political necessity and is aimed at providing education to the common people with a view to imparting necessary knowledge and skills, so that it can prove productive and contribute to the overall national goal of creating an egalitarian and modern society.[90]

(1) To further, consolidate and strengthen faith and loyalty to the crown and country by harmonizing different economic and social interests, by integrating multi-lingual traditions into one all embracing nation, by further encouraging economic and social mobility and by transferring the geo-political entity of Nepal into a positive emotional integration.[91]

(2) To comprehend the old and new teaching methods currently in force in the country within national education system, and bring about uniformity in the intellectual traditions so that national solidarity may be developed and strengthened.[92]

(3) To supply trained manpower for national development and to generate a deeper faith in the national heritage and the Panchayat System.[93]

5.3 The Role of Student after National Education System Plan (NESP)

NESP; Policy Programmes and Strategies are mentioned as follows:

5.2.1 Policy

(1) The main object of higher education will be to produce trained manpower.

(2) Higher education will be correlated to job opportunities in the future.

(3) Vocational education will receive special emphasis with a view to meeting the needs of technical manpower for successful implementation of the national plan.

(4) Qualitative improvement of education will be synchronized with its quantitative growth. New educational facilities will be progressively made available to the remote areas.[94]

5.2.2 Programme

(1) Arrangements will be made to reduce the number of those taking up arts and humanities and increase the numbers who study technical subjects.

(2) The university will organize a separate admission test to determine eligibility for higher education.

(3) The number of students joining higher education institutions will gradually be reduced from the present 27 to 19 percent only.

(4) Of the students admitted in higher education 60% will be enrolled in vocational and technical institutes, leaving only 40% for the enrollment in general education.

(5) Stress will be laid on production and distribution of necessary educational materials in order to raise the standard of education.

(6) In the educational institutions, proper provisions will be made for the programming of extra-curricular activities, cultivating an intellectual atmosphere and promotion of active student participation in the nation building activities.[95]

5.2.3 Curriculum

(1) The higher education level curriculum will be designed to meet manpower requirements.

(2) Fieldwork of one year's duration will be compulsory before joining the next higher level after completing one level of higher education.

(3) The curriculum will be developed from an inter-disciplinary point of view.

(4) Along with the adoption of the principles of making education vocation-oriented, attention will be also given to the need for a standard curriculum in general subjects.

(5) The curriculum will include at least one paper in which the student will be required to submit an original writing on the basis of given facts and figures.[96]

5.2.4 Evaluation

(1) Examination will be further decentralized. Teaching institutions and teacher will be required to participate in and be responsible for the assessment of students.

(2) The present practice of conducting biennial examination will be scrapped in favor of the semester system.

(3) Accomplishments of the students will be evaluated partly by internal assessments and partly by external examinations at the end of every semester. In the early stage, internal assessments will be assigned a weight of 20%, which gradually will be increased to a maximum of 50%.[97] The 1971 National New Education System Plan had formulated clear rules and regulations for giving a new shape to the T.U. administrative system and for running the campuses in a smooth way along with determining the status of the T.U. teachers and tackling the student activities in a proper way.

5.2.5 Administrative Restructuring

Tribhuvan University was made an autonomous body functioning under the policies, rules and guidelines laid down by the National Education Committee. The National Education Committee was made responsible for implementing the National Education Plan.[98]

NESP generated structural changes in the delivery system of the university. As a result, quite a few changes were introduced in the organizational structure of the university from the campus level to the central level.

The university now has a pyramidal organizational structure with three tiers; the central office, the Deans' Office and campuses. This change also required restructuring in the decision-making and implementation processes and in the distribution of powers and duties.[99]

At the initial period, the central office was chiefly responsible for the formulation of the general policies of the university. As the university academic programmes were divided into a number of institutes, the Deans as the heads of the institutes were given adequate administrative powers. But the change brought after mid-term evaluation in 1975-76 resulted in the centralization of power of Deans with regard to personnel and finance.

At the lower organizational structure, all the colleges were put under one roof to operate under the university's academic and administrative organization. This was a major step towards creating uniformity in standards of the study programmes in various colleges and coordinating them effectively. Under the new organization much emphasis has been laid on maintaining and upgrading the educational standard in the country.[100]

In addition to these three levels of the administrative hierarchy, there are a number of academic and administrative staff offices and units for coordinating, guiding and evaluating various academic, research and administrative programmes of the Tribhuvan University.[101]

Some of the important organs and bodies are as follows:

(a) Curriculum Development Center

The chief of the center shall be the Rector, the main task of the center shall be to design and produce text books and materials.

(b) Student Welfare Section

This office works under the guidance of the Rector. Its main objective is to make the students mentally and physically capable. Its works are as follows:

- To guide and supervise the establishment of students union in different campuses and their activities.
- To look after the dormitories and cafeterias.
- To conduct sports and other extra-curricular activities.
- To recommend awards and stipends to the needy and meritorious students. And
- To help students solve their various problems.[102]

(c) Examination Section

The main duty of the Registrar is to conduct and supervise the T.U. examinations. In the semester system, the campuses conduct examination; however, this office takes responsibility to keep examinations records and arrange distribution of mark sheets and certificates.

(d) Faculty Board

There will be a faculty board under the chairmanship of the Dean in every faculty. The tasks of the board are to implement all the rules and regulations such as course-books, admission, and examination in a responsible way including promotion of other concepts of academic development.

(e) Subject Committees Instruction Committee

There will be separate departments of every subject under the faculty. Their main task is to help teach the designed course-books. A chairman from among the campus-teachers will be appointed. He will hold discussions on teaching courses with the related teachers and inform them about the academic year and teaching subjects.

(f) Teachers' Place Under NESP

In any university organization, the main role lies with

the teachers, because most of the students' unrest begin from the activities in the campuses and spread out from there.

The place of teachers in the university organization is a vital one because of two reasons firstly, a teacher is ultimately responsible for implementing the study programme, and secondly, he is the only person who maintains direct link and close association with the students. In the university's organizational structure the class-room is at the very bottom of the structure. But it is only here that the student/teacher interaction occurred most intensively.[103] A teacher's typical position can be gauged from the fact that though his work is limited to the class-room, and though he has no fixed position in the organizational hierarchy, his presence is felt at every level.[104]

The education plan, the policies and the programmes are all aimed at one direction to give the best possible education to the students. And this, of course, lies on teachers.[105] Their morale, knowledge and competency are the deciding factors for the success or the failure of the education system. Their place in the university and their commitment to the education system are the actual deciding factors.[106] The students perceive and judge the education system from what goes on in the class-room. Actually, it is the class-room which is the basic source of all sorts of grievances, dissatisfaction, indiscipline and unrest. Thus what role the teachers play is of great significance to know about the student unrests.[107]

The planners of NESP seem to have given appropriate attention to the importance of teachers in the education system. The plan states: "It is essential that talented people be attracted to the teaching profession and be induced to stay on in order to reform and improve the quality of education. In the plan period, therefore, high priority will be assigned to a programme aimed at ensuring the security of service, promotion, prospects and equitable pay scales." This indeed was the first time when the teachers' job security and other amenities were so clearly spelled out. This was an important step forward in making teaching job appealing.[108]

Apart from this, two other major developments occurred with the advent of the NESP, which not only recognized the status of the teachers but also entrusted them with powers parallel to those of the administrators.[109] Firstly, with the advent of the NESP, powers and authority relationships were remolded under the Tribhuvan University. The structural change introducing the three-tier system, Central Office, Dean's Office and Campus Level Administration was, significant. The significance of this change was heightened by the appointment of teachers to all the administrative and academic posts right from the Vice-Chancellor to the Instruction Committee members at the campus level. This was clearly guided by the concept that knowledge should prevail and knower should be at the top.[110] This concept opened room for the teachers to participate in all academic programmes for the formulation of the educational programmes. Closely associated with this is the provision for equipping the teachers with powers to evaluate student performance.

One of the major changes in the education system of the country was made in the examination system, whereby the old annual examination system was replaced by the semester system. The teachers were fully authorized to frame questions and to scrutinize the answer copies. This system was developed on the ground that being the expert in the subject and having close association with the students, teacher would be the best judge of the students' performance.[111]

Thus under the NESP appropriate measures were taken to upgrade the status of teaches and boost up their morale.[112]

5.3.6 The Place of Student under NESP

The new education plan had aimed to make the students concentrate their mind to the study of the courses, to make them develop their self-reliance and create a disciplined environment. The role and place of the students underwent significant changes under the NESP. The plan provided ample opportunities for students to learn for self-development, and also demanded discipline and serious commitment to study.[113] The basic policy-features and programme characteristics that determined the place of student under the NESP are explained below.

Professional Student

The communities engaged in educational institutions are called professional students. The NESP had an aim that the student communities should make their profession a dignified one and develop it. The NESP, specially emphasing on technical education made the students center their mind only to their educational activities.[114]

The NESP discourages professionalism through its various provisions. One of the most important characteristics of higher education is the emphasis on technical education. It says that, "arrangements would be made to reduce the number of those taking up arts and humanities and increase the numbers of those who taking technical subjects". It further says that, "the number of students[115] joining higher education institutions will gradually be reduced from the present 27 to 19 percent only".[116]

The quota system in the admission of students was also introduced. Closely interrelated with this is the necessity of passing through the entrance examination to higher education.[117] The plan makes it clear that the S.L.C. Examination is merely a test of whether the candidate has acquired the competence of secondary education. The universities will, therefore, conduct a separate entrance test to determine whether or not the candidates are fit for higher educations.[118] Another major feature is the make-up system of examination. Those students who fail in a subject or subjects in the semester examination can proceed further to the next semester at the same level. To get through that level or to be qualified to appear at the entrance examination for the higher level, students are required to sit in the make-up examination in the failed subjects during the remaining semesters of the level or after the fourth semester. The students are not required to attend the regular classes on those failed subjects.[119] The introduction of National Development Service (NDS) was another main feature of NESP whereby it was provisioned that field work of one year's duration will be compulsory before joining the new higher level after completing one level of higher education.[120] This was applied, however, only to those regular students who were studying at degree levels.

The introduction of internal assessment was a new provision which decided on the qualification to appear in the semester examination, and yearly examination was also introduced with a view to discouraging, 'Professionalism'.[121]

Student Welfare Section

A Student Welfare Section (SWS) with units at each campus was established at the central office under the Rector. The prime objective of this section is to take care of the entire programme meant to promote the physical and mental well-being of the students. It plans, organizes, conducts, supervises and coordinates the student welfare activities carried out at different campuses of the Tribhuvan University.[122]

In addition to such welfare activities, it was also expected to play the role of 'Grievance Communicating Unit' in the absence of the provision for students' union. It was to work as a 'Communicating Link' between the students and the university authority. At the campus level, one of the teachers is appointed as the chief of the unit who supervises the student welfare activities in close coordination with the students and the campus chief.[123]

Expansion of Educational Facilities

The NESP, not only changed the organizational structure of the Tribhuvan University but also opened new avenues of education by opening new Institutes, Campuses and Programmes providing greater opportunities for students to study the subjects of their interests.[124] Its policy specifies: qualitative improvement of education will be progressively made available to the remote areas.[125] If on one side it tried to restrict the number of students in higher education, at the same time, it also provided opportunities for the qualified students to study the subjects of their choice.[126] Under the NESP, Agriculture and Animal husbandry, Forestry, Engineering, Medicine and Applied Science were taught. This saved the students from hardships caused by the necessity to go outside the country for higher education in these subjects.[127]

Commitment to Study

The NESP was formulated in such a manner that it demanded spontaneous commitment to study. In the old education pattern, the students had to appear in annual examination, which was not promoting regular study.[128] Students generally used to study hard only on the eve of examination, and thus the very purpose of education was not fulfilled. But the NESP introduced the semester system under which students have to appear in examinations every six months and regular internal assessments are conducted all the year round. This required a regular study schedule on the part of students.[129]

The new teaching methods also added further responsibilities on the students; homework and preparation for assignments required regular study. Specially at the degree level of education, the introduction of compulsory thesis writing posed a new challenge requiring in-depth study of creation aspect of the students' subject of choice.[130] The plan stipulated that curriculum should include at least one paper in which the student will be required to write its own literary creation or put down his own creative thoughts on the basis of given facts and figures.[131] To facilitate the study, library facilities were also enhanced giving students a wider access to study materials and sharpening their desire to know more about the different subjects.

Job-Oriented Education

The objective of NESP: Higher education will be organized to meet the manpower requirements of the country based on nation wide estimate. Its aim will be to maintain a high standard of teaching and study.[132] The NESP aimed at correlating higher education to the available or to be available job opportunities in the country. The National Planning Commission provides the manpower estimates to the university on the basis of which the number of students for admission to different programmes are fixed. The plan states that arrangements will be made for correctly estimating the various manpower needs of the country. Accordingly, the Ministry of Education will fix the number of students who should be admitted to the various Institutes of higher education.[133] The NESP aims at counter-acting elitist bias of the old education system, by linking it effectively to productive enterprises. Though it cannot guarantee jobs to qualified degree holders, still, the linking of the education system to national manpower requirement provided enough assurance to students regarding future prospects.[134]

Code of Conduct

The maintenance of discipline among the students both inside and outside the campus premises is a *sine qua non* for the smooth operation of the teaching and learning process. The lack of discipline not only affects the whole set of academic programmes but also breeds a sense of insecurity, indifference and promotes absence of commitment. With a view to curtail the acts of in discipline, therefore, a code of conduct was devised.[135] The code of conduct is meant for creating a sense of discipline, keeping a high degree of morality and so make the students abide by the rules and regulations of the university.[136]

Extra-Curricular Activities

In addition to the emphasis on technical education in particular and on productive manpower in general, the NESP has made ample provisions for the development of the students' intellectual faculty by engaging them in other activities apart from class room study.[137] The plan makes it clear that in the educational institution, proper provisions will be made for programming of extra-curricular activities, cultivating of an intellectual atmosphere and the promotion of active participation in nation building.[138]

The provision of the Central Students Welfare Council was made for the formulation of plans and policies regarding student welfare, and their implementation. The Central Student Welfare Section is the Secretariat of this council.[139]

Student's Organizations

Initially the plan provided for the establishment of students' council at the campus level. Later, the System was abrogated and was replaced by the *Sadan* system.[140] According to the system, a number of *Sadans* were to be opened at each campus with the students of the campuses becoming the members of these *Sadans*. This system has ample room to engage the students in welfare and other constructive activities in an organized manner.[141]

Student Counselling

The importance of student counselling does not need any exaggeration. In view of its utmost importance, it was provisioned that every student would be assigned an academic advisor, keeping in view his/her subject of study.[142] The primary purpose behind this assignment of academic advisor was to provide advice and required guidance to the students regarding their academic requirements and problems from time to time.[143] This was not only meant to make available the services of the teachers to the students to help solve their academic problems put it was also conceived as a means to establishing a close support between the students and to teachers.[144]

Apart from this, student counselling was made one of the primary functions of the Deans at the institute level. The institutes were made responsible for imparting information, which would help the students in selecting their subjects of study keeping in view the future prospects. Besides, the students were also to be helped in getting jobs after completing their studies.[145]

Other Facilities

In addition to the above-mentioned provisions, the plan included other provisions to provide many other facilities to students with a view to help them in their academic pursuits. One of the important facilities was the institution of scholarships and free-ships to the talented and poor students.[146] This was meant to motivate the students to study seriously and to help the poor but talented student by making it possible for them to get free higher education. Care was also taken to make plans for expanding physical facilities as well as providing education materials in adequate quantity. The need for libraries and hostel facilities was adequately recognized and various programmes were formulated for the improvement and the expansion of physical facilities in campuses.

5.4 Causes of Student Unrest after the Implementation of New Education System Plan (NESP)

After the event of December 15, 1960 A.D., Nepalese students started movements making Educational Independence a main issue. The chief demand was for Free Students Union. The government did not pay any attention to the demand, rather it suppressed and disrupted the students. In this context the National Education System Plan was implemented. Then the students were more angered and they started movements directly opposing the Panchayat system itself. A brief description has been given about the causes of the student unrest after the implementation of NESP.[147]

5.4.1 Working of Supporting Institutional Arrangements

(a) The Students Unrest is a Result of Unsatisfactory Organization of Structure

The new education plan was implemented with a view to give new developed education by abandoning the unscientific old education in 1971. NESP had aimed to start new works according to the national needs and desire. The education policy was intended to provide new opportunities in keeping with the changed political context. But the education planners seemed not to pay any attention to the social structure of our country. "What sorts of reorientations were brought into the interlinked institutions with the revolutionary change in the education system of the country? What links were developed for the coordination of different institutions with the University for 'unifying education into one productive system? Very little attempt was made in these directions and, as a result; the university had to face many problems.[148] Prior to the preparation of the National Education Plan, the National Education Commission should have given attention to the national concept and people's wish, but it was neglected. Among the objectives of the NESP, production of skilled manpower was also the one.[149] The estimation of manpower requirements, had been clearly laid down. The Ministry of Education of His Majesty's Government will from time to time estimate the manpower needs of the country in consultation with the National Planning Commission (NPC).[150] However, NPC, because of its weakness, could never succeed in presenting the actual manpower needs. Its estimates proved nothing more than guess-work. Furthermore, the lack of process in the country's development activities also invalidated the estimation of manpower needs. As a result, a large number of graduates and post-graduated were produced by the university which only added to the already long queue of the unemployed.[151]

The estimates of manpower needs in Nepal for five years (1971-76) were based on the premise enunciated by the UNESCO in 1976 for the South East Asian Countries. They are:

(1) National Income will go up by 20% in the next five years (1971-76)

(2) The attrition in the existing stock of manpower will be at an annual rate of 5%.

(3) The need for high level manpower will be twice the growth rate of national income i.e. the ratio of increase in high level manpower to the increase in national income will be 2:1.

(4) Middle level manpower requirements will be 52% more than the high level manpower; i.e. the ratio of middle level manpower to high level manpower will be 1.5: 1.

(5) The basic level manpower requirements will be twice that of the middle level manpower; i.e. the ratio of basic level manpower to middle level manpower will be 2:1.[152]

The limitations of this mode are as follows:

(a) It does not provide occupation-wise estimates and

(b) This approach may lead to an over-supply of educated manpower if development activities are not executed at such a speed and in such a scale as to ensure the achievement of the projected growth of national income, while educational institutions turn out the estimated manpower by strictly following the model.[153]

Now to check the validity of these assumptions, we shall see to what extent the assumptions have turned out to be true.

(1) We can first of all evaluate the growth rate of the national income. The planning commission has not published the data relating to the national income. But

the reading of its annual economic survey reports presents a gloomy picture of the national economy. Moreover, the speech delivered by the Secretary of Finance in the Aid Nepal consortium puts the matter very clearly.[154]

(2) In the presence of inherent limitations of the model, it has been said that, ... model has served as guide to planners in giving emphasis on the preparation of basic and middle level manpower...[155]. Thus the model is only a guide, and estimates based on this model cannot be relied upon. It does not help in checking the manpower wastage.[156]

(3) In the absence of any other institution other than the NPC, all the institutes have to rely totally on it for manpower estimate. But the estimates of NPC, are nothing more than guess work.[157] It has been said, The Ministry of Education was supposed to supply the university with these estimates, in consultation with the National Planning Commission. What figures there exist are merely rough and ready ones, and they seem to rely more on the rule of thumb than on any systematic investigation or real field needs against the hypothetical ones.[158] The committee set up to evaluate the progress of the National Education System Plan, has also come to the same conclusion. It reports that, the Ministry of Education and NPC have not done the estimation of manpower as per the objective of the plan.[159]

(4) Since the model does not help in occupational estimates, the NPC's occupational estimates are more guess-work, which may be underlined by the fact that NPC does not give any input-output table.[160]

(5) NPC was supposed to revise its estimates along with the progress of development activities. This depends upon a well laid mechanism working for both NPC and the university. But there is no such system for collecting progress reports from all the campuses, which could be communicated to NPC.[161] The NPC on its part is unable to evaluate the progress of development activities to produce revised estimate. So, without any

> study of the market, the university continued to produce what it was told to produce only to add to the already large inventory of educated unemployed or educated under-employed in the country.[162] All this tells on the very concept of relating the university's production with the manpower requirements of the country. As such one cannot expect a high degree of correlation between manpower production and job opportunities.

In Nepal, HMG is the largest employing agency. Apart form a negligible percentage of foreign educated manpower, the university is the only source of supplying manpower to HMG. Because of this, the criteria and qualifications necessary for the different levels of personnel have also been developed keeping in view the degree awarded by the university. Though under NESP specific education and training was provided by the university in different fields, the public Service Commission continued inviting applications for section officer level posts from candidates who had a B.A. (Diploma) or similar graduate degree which could include a *Sastri* in *Sanskrit* and a bachelor in science. The graduate level point remained as it was in the past; though the degree level education was supposed to produce higher level manpower. As a result, post-graduates and graduates had to compete for the same post.[163] This was enough to cause frustration to both groups. In most cases higher degree holders succeeded in getting a majority of such posts, leaving only a few for highly competent bachelors. This forced the graduates to take jobs at lower levels. This is a direct wastage of national resource.

In the university organizational structure; the Deans holds the key position in providing academic leadership to their respective institutes. A Dean is the Chief of the Institute and all the academic and administrative functions pertaining to the institute are carried out by them. Apart from many important functions entrusted to the Deans, two functions worth a special mention. They are as follows:

(a) Guidance and counselling services are to be provided to the students regarding the employment opportunities in relation to the study of certain subjects.

(b) To help students in getting employment and to keep a record of the various kinds of work they are engaged in.

These two functions call for establishment of close links between the institutes and the community. The Deans as the heads of the institutes should establish such links. In this way the institutes can know the needs of the society, and the society is provided with appropriate manpower.[164] The Deans were also expected to provide such services to the students under which they would know about the subjects offering more employment opportunities. In addition, they were expected to keep the records of their allumin and run some sort of employment exchange service to facilitate the proper and timely employment of their graduates. This is very important in view of the absence of such services at the national level.[165]

(1) A study of the NESP gives an impression that it gives a tacit promise of job guarantee. But because of the weak delivery system, the educated persons were forced to turn to the streets, inculcating a sense of apathy and frustration among the students.[166]

(b) The Students Unrest as a Result of Inadequate Academic Arrangements

In the semester system, a commitment was made to provide sufficient educational materials both for the teachers and students. The NESP had the policy to have good library management laboratory, good management of classrooms etc. But in practice, it was just opposite. So many weaknesses and lapses were found. The campuses could not run smoothly due to the lack of necessary skilled manpower by which the students seemed to be frustrated. Similarly the compulsory rule of thesis for master's level students brought a great problem as all the students do not have aptitude for research. The NESP should have given options to the students who would be unable in writing thesis. But the NESP held the policy to compel the students to write thesis without providing adequate training and pre-exercise. The students felt suppressed from all around. The NESP became a bar against the development of students' intelligence and knowledge. If it was implemented after wide study and survey not so much problem would have appeared.[167]

About 50 percent of the total teachers have opined that the thesis writing is not good for all the students and it should be made optional giving the opportunity to only intelligent and capable students. They have also pinpointed some of the constraints in supervising the students for thesis writing. Lack of adequate laboratory facility in the science faculty and a large number of students in Economics and Commerce are the major constraints. The students, in general, are poor in writing and most of the teachers have complained that it is difficult to supervise such students. In Economics Instruction Committee, it has been reported that a teacher supervised as many as 30 students in 1978. In a situation when a teacher has to supervise 20 or more students for thesis writing, we cannot expect a good quality of writing. Indeed, it becomes a great burden to the concerned tracers. About 40 percent of the teachers expressed their difficulty in supervising the students.[168]

(c) Student Unrest as a Result of Unsatisfactory Functioning of Academic Arrangements

In any educational institution, classrooms are the most important provisions from where knowledge is exchanged, transmitted and gained. The main role is played by the teachers in the classrooms. Only the preparation of modernized curriculum can do nothing since the teachers can not automatically become ready to teach unless they are properly trained. The plan gives a good deal of emphasis on teacher training, curriculum development and improvement and development of appropriate teaching techniques. However the situation has not improved much, and with the growing number of students and teachers, the situation may be said to have worsened further.[169]

T.U. Service Commission was arranged for the management of teachers' appointment, promotion etc. and the Dean and campus-chiefs also were given authority to appoint teacher for temporary terms.

Campuses have their own problems. In technical education the problems is more serious because of non-availability of the adequate number of qualified teachers.[170] A study has stressed that one of the basic problems regarding the upgrading of the education standard is the weakness of the teachers. The following table shows the presence of this problems.

Weakness of Teachers[171]

S. No.	Weakness of Teachers	Response in %
1.	Lack of devotion to teaching profession	32.35
2.	Lack of general motivation	29.42
3.	Lack of teaching skill	17.64

The teachers began to give unfair and unreasonable marks in their subject-papers to gain popularity. This brought disappointment among the laborious and qualified students. There was also an arrangement of teachers' evaluation, but it was not brought into practice. Simply the aim of the students is to study and pass the examinations. But most of the courses would not be completed. The model of questions and private-tuition also badly affected the class-room teaching. About 62% of the students are found dissatisfied with the teachers' power given by the New Education System Plan and some other problems were also caused by the decentralization. Due to the environment of fear and threatening, the teachers could not make a fair judgement of the students' quality. So the standard of education declined instead of improving it. The reasons of students' dissatisfaction with the NESP in percentage are as follows:

Reasons for Indiscipline

Q.	Is the absence of discipline in your campus due to	No
(a)	Unsatisfactory Teaching	95
(b)	Undue strictness of the administration	84
(c)	Favouritism by the teachers	73
(d)	Large classes	70
(e)	Incompetent Administration	54
(f)	Favouritism by the administration	50
(g)	Undue laxity in administration	49
(h)	Irresponsible behaviour of student themselves	36
(i)	Interference by outsiders	30[172]

Although new terminologies were invented in the NESP, no working systems were improved, no new methodologies were adopted in teaching. No compulsory presence of the student in classroom, and the presence only in the examination hall without attending classes, the use of unfair means in the examination hall etc. infested the education sector. The educational value diminished with the growing of non-educational atmosphere.

The NESP did not pay attention towards the preparation of appropriate course-books for the students and teachers by designing course-books or curriculum without any consultation with the subject teachers and educationists. The examination system, setting question papers, checking of answer papers, NDS Programmes etc. were used only for experiment. A serious crisis was created by playing fun with the national property and manpower. Moreover, frequent changes of the rules and regulations mentioned in the NESP also created further crisis in the education sector. Within a short period of six years, a great many experiments were made which had little basis of justification. A rough estimate shows that since the introduction of NESP, about 30% of the courses particularly in general education had been changed. This has led to the popular saying that nothing is stable in the university.

Changes introduced without due consideration show the unstable character of NESP, and at the same time the students also feel that any thing can be changed any time in the education system. Because of this, they even dare to demand change, which may directly affect the objectives and policies of the education system. They believe that in the light of frequent changes, NESP can undergo any sort of change.

The following table also shows what the campus administrations feel about the central administration.

View of Campus Chiefs towards Changes in Rules and Regulations

S. No	Views	No	Percentage
1.	The university regulations are frequently changed.	24	80%
2.	Regulations are not made available to the students in time	3	27%
3.	Students are not informed well in time regarding the changes	7	23%
4.	Campus administration is not informed well in time regarding changes.	17	56%[173]

The main feature of the NESP is the semester system. The two terms of examination were taken, in winter and in summer in a year. Internal assessments were taken three times per subject in a semester. One semester of 6 months was not sufficient to complete the scheduled course. Similar problems were in laboratories in the technical education. The rules also were frequently changed. The teachers and the students were feeling uneasy from the changing rules. So the students were compelled to start movement demanding abolition of the NESP. They had to face difficulties related to curriculum, textbooks, question papers, examinations etc. One of the fundamental features of the NESP was correlation between job opportunities and education. The objective was clearly stated: higher education will be organized to meet the manpower requirements of the country based on nation-wide estimates. Its aim will be to maintain a high standard of teaching and study.[174] In the beginning of NESP, a large number of the students used to take part in the classes, libraries, examination hall etc. with great interest. But, later on, as they knew the weaknesses of the NESP that it was only a drama written in the paper to place them in confusion, they began to be disinterested and to criticise it.

In reality, however because of misconceptions on the part of both students and teachers regarding the basic philosophy of this new system of examination, it turned out to be one of the root causes of student unrest. In the internal assessment system, the teachers would check the examination copies. The students who would obtain low marks or fail the assessment would even be ready to attack the teachers or go against them. So the teachers began to feel insure. As the teachers felt their status weak and insecure in the NESP system, disappointment grew in them.[175] The students also lost their interest in study. The trend to pass examination without reading the courses began to grow, along with unfair means in the examination halls for getting high marks. Such disorderly situation compelled the authorities to make a complete change in the education system.

The most important achievement of the NESP is the establishment of Students Welfare Section (SWS). It was established under Rector's office with the units in all the campuses. A teacher in every campus unit used to look after it and the campus chief would help it. Such welfare units had the objective to lead the students to an appropriate direction by developing interest towards extra curricular activities, games, cultural programmes etc. in them. But all the students could not be made to participate in these activities. Some of the students had not even the least knowledge about the students welfare section. The following table clarifies this fact:

Activities of SWS

Knowledge about SWS	No. of Respondents	%
Yes	37	21%
No	141	79%
Total	**178**	**100%**[176]

The above table shows the evidence that the Students Welfare Section had not worked according to its objective. Its work seemed only to send records of students to the T.U. authorities. It was felt to work as CID against the students. It also instigated fighting among the students.[177] Regarding the teachers' responses 75 percent felt that it is there to work as a communicating link between the students and the administration. Actually, the students do not communicate their grievance through this unit, but directly to their campus chief.[178] The only thing the unit did was to keep the records of the students and supply it to the university authority. Specially due to the influence of *Rastravadi Swotantra Vidyarthi Mandal* over it, the general students neither cared nor believed in the propriety of this section.

(d) Students Unrest is a Result of Absence of Feedback Mechanism

The NESP had an aim to make the students participate in T.U. rules and policy making. So, two representatives from the students' side were also to be nominated to the T.U. Council. But it was not appropriately brought into practice. The structure of the T.U. was divided into three main bodies V.C. office, Dean's office and the campus. Not any provision was made for student representative in the institution level. There was no other provision of student representation except to the Student Welfare Section. No common platform of students could be formed. The two representatives did not hear the students' voice; instead they worked as the tools of the T.U. authorities. The student representatives to the T.U. Council did not work for the interest of the student community. The following table shows how grievances were communicated to campus administration.

Communication of Grievances

S. No.	Means	No of Respondents	Percentage
1.	Direct Communication	30	71%
2.	Communication Through teachers	25	60%
3.	Communication through Asst. Campus Chiefs	11	26%
4.	Any other media	12	29%
5.	No response	2	5% [179]

In the NESP, initially there was a provision for students' council which was later replaced by the Sadan system. This system had these benefits-it checked the turning of students organizations into trade unions; provided opportunities for students participation in welfare activities; and it could work as a communication channel. However, the lack of understanding of its values on the part of campus chiefs has resulted in the organizations of Sadan in a very few campuses. The absence of any sort of organization whether Sadan or union of student deprived the administration of any communication channel. Not only this, the absence of students union hindered effective discussion regarding students' problems. One of the basic reasons of the long strike of 1975 is that in the absence of such organization, the university could neither know properly the force behind the strike nor it could find out the bonafide representatives of the students. The same thing happened during the strike of 1978/79 as well.

The following table gives an idea of this problem.

Bodies Negotiating with the Administration

S. No	Description	No. of Respondents	Percentage
1.	Students act as representative	18	53%
2.	By identifying the prime movers	14	41%
3.	At random	6	18%
4.	No response	10	22%[180]

What it makes clear is that in the absence of students organization and proper student representatives to hold discussion on the demands and solve the problems, there arises nation wide complication. So, the government and the T.U. administration became unable to pay attention towards this aspect. As a result the student movement grew on demanding multiparty system, along with the demands for free students union.

(e) Attitude of Administrators

The university is a purely educational institution. Its office holders need to be different from the other offices in nature. Specially they should be able to deal with the teachers and students in a proper manner in the campus levels. There are so many instances of students' excitements due to the administrative weaknesses.

So far the administrations of rules and regulations including academic matters are concerned, only 4 percent of the students regard them as efficient, where as 32 percent think they are inefficient, the rest treating them as moderately efficient. Therefore, they believe that they lack both administrative acumen and administrative skill. With a view to know what-role the students envisage for their union, they were asked if the absence of union had curbed their rights. As much as 82 percent of the student respondents answered in the affirmative. These respondents were further asked about the rights they felt curbed. Their response is presented in the following table:

Student Union

S. No.	Right Curved	No. of Respondents	Percent
1.	The right of forwarding the problems freely	40	27%
2.	Right of participating in extra-curricular activities	36	24%
3.	Right of avoiding unnecessary pressure of teachers and administers	24	16%
4.	Right of pointing the weaknesses of teachers and administers	23	16%
5.	Basic human rights	17	11%
6.	Voting rights	6	4%[181]

This above fact shows that a union is necessary to play the role of communication with the administration and both the works of pointing administrative weaknesses and the presentation of students problems can be done at a time. In most of the campuses *Madal* groups were formed for this objective. But they could not be so effective in its works.

Students Participation

In the absence of student participation, the education sectors and extra curricular activities cannot run and develop in an organized manner. The importance of participation is to make the students understand their duty and activate them organizationally. The NESP could not create any organizational platform of the students. Games and "Sahityik Sadan" departments were a little bit successful to be popular among the students. The participation makes the students realize their rights and duties on the one hand and grant them an opportunity to understand administrative compulsions on the other. This has been clearly seen in Kirtipur Multiple Campus regarding mess administration. After the strike when the management of cafeteria was handed over to the students, in a period of one month, they realized that the reduction in the price of launch and dinner was not possible. After that there has been no trouble regarding the mess. In the absence of participation, students feel deprived, uncared for and ignored.

Student Counselling

Student counselling is of utmost importance to make the students acquainted with the university rules, regulations, facilities and academic requirements. Proper counselling forestalls many confusion which may otherwise become the source of unnecessary troubles.[182] In the Tribhuvan University sub-rules there is a clear provision for appointing[183] teachers as advisors to students with a view to provide the required guidance regarding their academic requirements and help solve their problems from time to time. This is also meant to generate a close support between teachers and students. However, it has been found that it is one of the most neglected aspects of the university programmes which have so many occasions created a number of problems. Student guidance and counselling is a totally neglected aspect. There is no service available in the form of graduate employment exchange.[184]

The NESP had also mentioned that the main task of the Dean in the educational institutions was to teach or suggest or manage job oriented education, so that the students after the completion of their education could get jobs. But this aim could not be achieved. There remained problem for the students of selecting the subjects and reading materials and course books. They were deprived of all the facilities that were provided by the T.U.

Knowledge of Rules

S. No.	Acquaintance with Rules	Yes		No		Total Response
1.	Rules of semester	110	63%	65	37%	175
2.	Calculation of Marks	52	31%	114	69%	166
3.	Code of conduct	50	31%	110	69%	160

In the absence of informative programmes or written materials, many misgivings have arisen. For example, according to a recent amendment, the marks secured by students in internal assessments are added only if they pass the semester examination independently, which differs from the old system of adding the marks of both internal assessment and the semester. Similarly a majority of students do not know what constitutes indiscipline according to the students' code of conduct. Because of all these, many unnecessary misgivings and grumblings have arisen which are the real sources of subsequent major acts which are simply termed as 'student indiscipline'.

(f) The students unrest is a results of intimate linking of the academic institution to the attainment of immediate political ends

The educational institution like the Tribhauvan University is specially the field- of teaching and learning and the center to gain knowledge. In this institution the students gain a special knowledge along with the different events of the world. The educational institutions are the platforms of teaching, learning and doing researches. The scholars remain busy in gaining new knowledge. It is also found that the educational institutions remain effortful to impart new thinking, changes and social development. An academic institution has always to be aware of the changing social values in the context of cardinal traditional values.[185]

The Broad Functions of the University are:

(1) To seek and cultivate new knowledge, to engage vigorously and fearlessly in the pursuit of truth, and to interpret old knowledge and beliefs in the light of new needs and discoveries.

(2) To provide the right kind of leadership in all walks of life, to identify gifted youths and help them develop their potential by cultivating physical fitness, developing the powers of the mind and cultivating right interests, attitudes and moral and intellectual values.

(3) To provide the society with competent men and women trained in agriculture, arts, medicine, science and technology and various other professions.

(4) To strive to promote equality and social justice and to reduce social and cultural differences through diffusion of education and

(5) To foster in the teachers and students, the attitudes, and values for developing 'good life'.

In summary, the university has not only to produce brains for serving the immediate social needs; but it also has to engage itself in the external search for truth. It seeks and cultivates new knowledge and promotes and develops the individuals' faculty of discerning truth. It contributes to the creation of society based on equality and social justice.

Education should not be an allegiance to a system. Its bondage under any political system creates a vacuum once the system undergoes certain changes. Thus broad objectives of education call for a liberal education system independent of any political bias.

The goal of the NESP as started is that it would be the creation of a just dynamic society free from exploitation in conformity with the partyless Panchayat system, possible only through the medium of a healthy and well knit national education system.

The first objective of NESP is:

To produce citizens who are loyal to the nation, monarchy and national independence and who remain ever alert and active toward their rights and duties under the Panchayat System.[186]

This is more clearly laid down in the policy of the NESP which says that, the NESP aims- To supply trained manpower for national development and to generate a deeper faith in the national heritage and the Panachayat system.

Thus the NESP aims not only at making education productive but also at channelizing the educated people towards making the political system of the country a success. Actually, no place was given for the development of individual faculty for knowledge. The implied aim is thus to produce such technocrats who have no more quests than toeing the line prescribed by the Panchayat establishment. The student community is the most conscious and sensitive for changes. This community becomes active and raises voice against injustice. Moreover, in the country like Nepal where the political parties were banned and most of the people are uneducated, the student force is found to be the harbinger of changes. The main media to raise voices for the interests of the intellectuals, political parties, workers, and any international issues became the students forces. In this situation the then government adopted two alternative policies: they were either to make them support the Panchayat system and serve the interest of the government or to suppress them with cruelty. The former effort became impossible, and the later was implemented to disrupt the students movement as for it was possible.[187] The policy that the government adopted to conduct the educational sector with interference was in contrary to the international educational policy.[188] The educational sectors should be left free form political interference; rather it should give priority to the national and people's interests. Indeed, the university is the chief representative of any nation. Moreover, for a developing nation like Nepal, the university is the only main place to produce able and skilled citizens, officers, and technical manpower for the nation. The students who are engaged in finding new knowledge and new thoughts become very conscious in principle.[189] The Nepalese students continued their struggle for political changes and educational development. They began to come to the forefront for political awareness and against injustice even after being divided into two groups as leftists and as democrats after the 1950 revolutionary change.[190] The students' frustration with regard to education within the campus and with regard to the mismanaging of education with opportunities inside the campus is weighted by political ideologies. As Byron Wedge has suggested, restrictions on the behavioural manifestations of discontent may provoke even more vigorous behaviour, ultimately reaching the point of violence.[191] The government had made frequent changes in different acts, rules and regulations as a pretext to get political support from the students. The 1975 amendment of the constitution can be taken, for instance. But the government could not get support of the students. Then a play of 'musical chair' between the leftist and the democratic student groups started. The government adopted a policy of "divide and rule" taking one side to suppress the other in turn. Even then the government could not get success, it resorted to organizing *Rastrabadi Swotantra Viddyarthi Mandal* in favour of the Panchayat government.

The government never tried to associate other groups of students in the mainstream of Panchayat policy but it developed its own group that became the champion of national cause. This led to blocking all the possibilities of an institutionalised political platform for student participation. The students had already taken a way of struggle before the NESP was implemented. After the NESP, the student momentum, the nation wide student movement began in 1971-72. The primary issues were related to the education sectors. Strike started in T.U. and some other campuses. The government and the T.U. administration opposed the strike. The educational institutions became the centers of fulfilling the political interests; the campuses were never taken as education centers and were only taken as the units of the T.U. to fulfil the government's interests. Wherever there was a student strike, the communication hot-line took-place between the local administration and the T.U. The T.U. and government administration did never show any interests towards the student problems. In case the political demands of the students were fulfilled, the other demands remained stocked. The students were also not found to have raised questions for them. The same event was found in question of NDS programme in 1979. Student demands were never considered and reasonable demands were looked upon with suspicion. However, when the establishments' political interest was satisfied, formerly rejected demands of students' were fulfilled even without the students asking for it, as happened in the case of National Development Service programme.

Thus, the students today are divided into several political groups; this is primarily the outcome of the linking of education with the ruling political system. Education was to work as a tool of political gain. Whenever there was strike on an educational issue, this was regarded as a threat to the political system itself. What required was the separation of academic issue from the demands of vested interest groups. But this was not done. When the university gave extraordinary power to a certain group to misuse it against the general students, the other students sought for support in political ideologies.

The government implemented the New Education System plan with the suggestions of some American academicians in 1971. Running of the vocational education sectors with the full-financial aid from the government, implementation of integrated education policy, etc. were some of its positive aspects; however, the education system designed and implemented beyond the social and economic context to Nepal could not be successful since it was imitated from America. It was a kind of neo-colonial education system. It produced dependent and impractical technicians rather than independent intellectuals and skilled manpower which the nation needed. So the students started a nation wide campaign against the anti-people policy of the government in 1971. *Nepal Viddyarthi Sang* (NSU) also had played an active role. Students continued their demonstrations and struggles during the period of 1971 to 1972. The government taking it to be the prestige issue suppressed the students ruthlessly. In the same context, the government opened fire on a rally at Judukuwa in Janakpur in 1972 and Kameswor and Kusheswor, the two students, were killed. The struggle was continued, though the movement could not produce any concrete achievement. Until 1979-80 it went on the same way. In the course of the movement, students went on strike in Dharan and Biratnagar with different demands for two months.

The students had staged nationwide mass meeting, demonstrations and different activities against the annexation of Sikkim by the Indian Government. Nepal government had already imposed ban on the student organizations under the Organizations and Unions Control Act' in 1973. The students rally gave a protest letter to the Indian ambassador in

Kathmandu. The police and 'Mandales' attacked on the rally, many were injured, and many of them were arrested. It provoked the students further.

It was already proved that the so-called new education system plan implemented in 1971 was expensive, unscientific and anti-people. The elections of the campus unions were held since 1973. The students masses were suppressed, making them so weak that they could not even retaliate the vandalism and operation against them. As the country had been made economically destitute, the tyranny of the then "Back to the Village National Campaign" had provoked the *Panchas* themselves and the outlawed political parties were troubled, the students started a movement putting 28 point demands in April, 1975. This movement was anti-imperialist and anti-expansionist on the one hand and apparently directed against the domestic reactionary forces on the other. On 25th April, 1975 the students started strike and demonstration in the Kathmandu valley.[192]

5.5 A Case Study of the Student Strike of 1975

The student movement of 1975 is taken as a nationwide and an important one. In the most recent history of student unrests in Nepal, the strike of 1975 occupies an important place. The preliminaries of this unrest emerged as a protest against the National Development Service (NDS) programme. After the 1960 military event, the students continued their movement for creating democratic atmosphere in the country. They played an important role in the democratic movement against the Panchayat System in the guise of students demanding solutions of different problems including free-student unions. The then government used to suppress all the movements. In such ongoing context, the NESP was implemented, but it became virtually impracticable. It would not do anything for the well-being of Nepal and the Nepalese and the educated community was worried. This factor also contributed to the possibility of the student movement of

1975.[193] The 1975 student movement was launched against the new academic provision of NDS. The third batch of the students of the new education plan was waiting for NDS programme. NDS programme was started in 1973. Its service was used on the voluntary basis. There was no compulsion to be involved in this programme. The first batch of the student were sent to NDS under the 'pilot project'. But there was condition that if any student did into take part in NDS degree, no degree would be awarded to them. So the students began to oppose such a condition. The students were not given prior notice about such provision. Similarly the body which would send the student to "National Development Service" (NDS) also was not clear about this matter and there was confusion. The teaching staffs of the university were also not willing to conduct the orientation programme. First, they were not informed in advance and secondly, there was no provision of granting remuneration for taking additional classes. A faint murmur of disapproval of the university decision by the students was heard by the campus chief.

Government and the T.U. administration began to suppress the student problems by force. As a result, the movement became more tense. The students formed an action committee. They started movement presenting 28 point demands. Among them the main demands are as follows:

- (a) An increase in NDS allowance.
- (b) NDS programme be organized only after the completion of the 4th semester.
- (c) NDS volunteers be provided with transistor radios and other necessary equipment.
- (d) The NDS orientation programme be organized only after the completion of the semester examination.
- (e) Service requirement be reduced to six months.
- (f) Girl students be allowed to serve in their own communities.[194]

The NDS programme could not run regularly as expected.

During the same period the T.U. announced semester examinations and published a notice in the "Gorkhapatra" daily that it had dismissed the demands of the student. This event added the fuel to the fire. The students were more provoked. This was enough initiation to launch a strike which was supported by all other classes of the degree programme. The students including the *Rastravadi* groups agreed to launch the strike. And before the strike was launched the administration arrested some student leaders from Shanker Dev Campus. The students drafted pamphlets, condemning the university and administration, and urging the students to continue the strike. After about a week, the government student body (RSVM) withdraw its support and attempted to break the strike on the pretext that all legitimate demands had been fulfilled in a negotiation which they had conducted with the university authority. Some of them were later beaten by students in Kirtipur. This brought new crises among the students. The action committee with representatives of all the campuses of the Kathmandu valley decided to continue the strike. New demands were added and a valley wide strike was successfully launched. It expanded into a nationwide strike later on. A study of the list of demands reveals that of the 27 demands, 12 were related to the central level, 4 institute level demands comprised of the abolition of entrance examination of private examination up to 1980. The institute level demands asked for repeating the course, exempting fee and re-establish of all academic institutions abolished by NESP. The campuses level demands comprised of the need for adequate number of teachers and an increment in the amount of scholarship, availability of hostel facilities in Tri Chandra and other campuses, provision of remuneration to teachers for checking answer-copies and immediate acceptance of temporary teachers in permanent service.

When the strike was gaining tempo, the detained students were released by the government at their great surprise. But immediately afterwards new arrests were made to dismay of the students. Students did not plead for the release of their friends and continued the strike. When all the measures of wooing the students to attend classes failed, the university ordered the sine die closure of all campuses. In the final phase, the process of negotiation was initiated. In the first round of negotiation the students stuck to their original demands and there was no consideration of the demands on the part of authority as well. The government and the university authority resorted to the classical technique of dividing the students. The process of negotiation continued with different groups of students. Ultimate negotiations were held with the Prime minister but this too failed. A sharp hostility grew between the leftist and the democratic groups of students.

The unrest of 1975 not only harmed the students, it had its repercussions on teachers also. As many as 22 teachers were stripped of their employment on suspicion of their involvement in this unrest.

5.6 A Case Study of the Student Agitation in 1979

The 1979 student movement had been the most successful in taking a decisive step in the history of Nepalese student movement. This movement can be taken as a very crucial historical event. The students came to the forefront raising voice against the political system and demanding for free-students unions for the first time after 1960. The students remained struggling for one or the other cause. The NESP of 1971 angered the students. The 1975 movement taught them that any achievement can be possible by fighting together rather than being divided. The gradual coming back of the opposition political leaders to the country from exile gave an encouragement to the students to reach their goal. The causes of the 1979 student movement had been added for long. The entire situation of the country had widely spread dissatisfaction among the people and the international event also inspired them, to explode the dissatisfaction more than ever before.

The new education system plan was implemented with an objective to make the education vocation oriented and qualitative in 1971. This type of education plan was criticized from every quarter saying that the autonomy of the education was being ended. This dismissal of student unions, entrance examination, comprehensive examination, National Development Service (NDS), compulsory provision of research paper in the master's level, student code of conduct, expulsion of teachers in 1975, price-hike, political coloured arresting etc. had become the causes of student-dissatisfactions. The outlawed ANNFUS, NS U and N.N.S.F. were unanimous in these questions. Restoration of student union had been the main issue. What is very noteworthy here is that the students could form unity against the government since there were no open unions and no envious competitions in the union elections among them would take place. The students demonstrated in a protest rally in Kathmandu valley against the execution of Prime Minister J.A. Bhutto of Pakistan on 7th April., 1979. The rally proceeded towards the Pakistani embassy in Kathmandu to give protest letter chanting slogans against the Pakistani president general Zia Ul Hak. The police batton charged on the rally at Lainchur. The students also retaliated for the interference. The students and police scuffled at the Bir Hospital. A large number of students sustained injury at both the places, many students were arrested. The major causes of the student movements were the police interference in the peaceful demonstrations, injuring and arresting which made the students more excited. The student movement of 1979 took a great turn form minor event to a major one. The then government itself was responsible for the situation.[195]

The T.U. students had made a plan to protest against the execution of the ex-Prime Minister of Pakistan M. Julfikar Ali Bhutto. Some 200 students of T.U. were proceeding peacefully towards the Pakistani Embassy to give a protest letter, the police interfered the rally at Lainchaur and batton-charged on the students, five of them were arrested. The students started strike at T.U. campus Kirtipur and Tri Chandra on 9 April, 1979. The student delegation went to the zonal commissioner and put two demands: the forming of a commission for fair investigation of the 7th April incident and the release of the arrested students. The government did not show any response to the demands, instead it threatened the students. Then the students became more enraged. They formed an action committee to conduct the movement on 10 April, 1979.

5.7 The Student Central Action Committee

The students staged strike in all the campuses of the valley against the oppression of the April 8 and 10 incidents. They boycotted the classes. A nine member central action committee formed on 10 April was as follows:

(1) Bal Bahadur K.C., Benup Prasain and Shiva Bhrutel form Nepal Students Union (NSU)

(2) Sharan Vikram Malla, Bharat Pokherel and Dhruva Gyawali form All Nepal National Free Students Union (ANNFSU)

(3) Kailas Karki, Dhruva Shrestha and Sunil Manandhar form Nepal National Students Federation (NNSF).

Among the nine members, a three-member commanding action committee was also formed comprising of Bal Bahadur K.C., Sharan Vikram Malla and Kailas Karki. This action committee prepared a 24 point demand list. The other students of the other campuses of the valley also began to stage strike putting their own demands. The T.U. had already made a programme of back-paper examinations at that time. But the students did not go to the examination halls despite a strong notice. There were a series of scuffles between the striking students and the *Rastriya Swantra Vidduarthi Mandal* group in the campuses as well as on the streets of Kathmandu. This made the students, more furious and they were determined to continue the strike indefinitely. The university authorities took a number of measures like requesting the guardians for their help in resuming the classes. The senior teachers of the university also made an appeal to the students to be peaceful and to attend the classes. But nothing pacified the students. Even the students of secondary schools went on strike in sympathy of the university students.

On April, 13, 1979 the university decided to close the campuses for a week and circulated a warning notice that if the students did not turn up in the classes, when the campuses will be reopened, it will not hesitate to take severe measure. The students too took a counter-step requesting the guardians and the general public through pamphlets/posters to give them their sympathies in their struggle to achieve the fulfilment of their legitimate academic demands. The twenty four demands of the students were:

(a) Right to form the students union in all the campuses.

(b) Elimination of the comprehensive examination.

(c) Complete withdrawal of the code of conduct for the students.

(d) Elimination of the entrance examination.

(e) Termination of compulsory thesis for the diploma and degree levels, instead it should be made optional.

(f) Raising of the student concession to 50 percent.

(g) Provision of partial examination for the S.L.C. students.

(h) Release of all the students arrested under the Security Act.

(i) Providing an opportunity to complete the in-service training of school teachers.

(j) Security of the students life in the campuses.

(k) Closing of the student welfare section.

(l) Withdraw the regulation concerning the period within which a particular level is to be completed, and the restriction of not admitting to the higher semester on account of the back papers.

(m) Maintaining uniformity in T.U. regulation.

(n) Recognition of the two-year training courses of the forestry, nursing and technical training campuses as certificate level course and elimination of one-year compulsory service.

(o) Elimination of the moderation board.

(p) For the private degree-level students, the service record of their concerning office be recognized as equivalent of NDS service, and the NDS be organized as equivalent of NDS service, and the NDS be organized after the completion of the degree course.

(q) Effective control of inflation.

(r) Student representative be allowed to observe the re-examination of answer-books.

(s) Provision of scholarship to all the students of the technical institutes and to 50 percent of the students of general institutions and a number of beds for students be added in hospital.

(t) Examination fees be reduced and be collected according to the number of papers for private students.

(u) Primary education be made compulsory and the prices of the text books be reduced.

(v) Provisions be made for the provident fund to school teachers; remuneration for the examination of the answer-books; provision for promotion and transfer be made on the basis of the nature of the region.

(w) All the dismissed teachers be reappointed.

(x) The students be taken on study tour once a year.

The students of different campuses under T.U., Biratnagar, Dharan, Rajbiraj, Ilam, Birganj, Janakpur, Palpa and other campuses in the kingdom started strike putting local demands. The campuses in the kingdom started strike putting local demands. The campuses were again opened on 22 April. But the students did not attend the classes. The then State Minister of Education noticed that the authorities of the T.U. and the Ministry of Education were ready for holding dialogue with the students. At the same time, the T.U. student action committee also published a statement that no student shall take part in the dialogue without the decision of the action committee and put three conditions for the dialogue. The three pre-requisites were:

(a) Immediate release of all the students.

(b) Dissolution of *Rastrabadi Swantra Viddyarthi Mandal.*

(c) The T.U. Student Action Committee be officially invited for negotiations.

The action committee decided not to take part in the dialogue until these prerequisites were met by the authorities; the strike would be continued. The students organized a mass meeting at Amrit Campus on 23rd April, 1979[196] A scuffle took place between the police and students. The police searched the hostel and arrested a large number of students. Battons and tear gas were used against the students.

In this scuffle many students and policemen were injured. On the same day T.U. authority published a statement notifying that the T.U. would be closed for an indefinite period and the campus administration also for 7 days. The people showed sympathy for the students. The Bar Association of Nepal protested the police action on the students at Amrit campus and demanded for an investigation commission. Similarly a group of writers published a statement demanding for investigation and action against the culprits of the incident. Though severe steps were taken by the administration, the campuses could not reopen. The same condition was prevailing in all the campuses out of the valley also. Biratnagar campus was totally closed. The students in Hetauda area staged a rally involving workers of the Hetauda industrial state on 27 April, 1979. Police and rally participants seriously scuffled at Karra Bridge. A large number of the ordinary people were injured. Later on, the students trapped the then land reform assistant minister Ramananda Prasad Singh for about 10 hours.[197] The next day, 28 April, the situation turned to a serious mode. The police fired on the students to control the situation. Many were killed, many injured and many arrested. The workers of the Hetauda industrial state also took part in the movement. Then the situation became more tense. Many places of Chitwan like Bharatpur and Naryanghat became tense and the violent situation grew more serious.

The students of Janakpur campus went on strike. A fighting between the agitating students and *Rastra Badi Swotantra Viddyarthi Mandal* took place. The *Rastra Badi Swotantra Viddyarthi Mandal* (Nationalist Free Student Council) was strong in Janakpur campus; moreover, the Janakpur administration was also helping this student group. A fighting between the two student groups took place on 17 April, 1979. Two students were seriously injured. They were taken to Indian Hospital for treatment. A hand of one of them was also broken off. Then the students were provoked and took a violent turn. Even the police could not control them; military was used to bring the situation under control.[198]

The students of Pokhara Campus were also launching movement. On 24th April, the student of the *Rastra Badi Swotantra Viddyarthi Mandal* entered the campus hostel in the mid-night and attacked the students and some of them were seriously injured. Then the students staged protest rally chanting slogans against the *Rastra Badi Swotantra Viddyarthi Mandal*. Pokhara Bazaar remained closed all day long. Scuffles took place between the agitating students and the police. In fact, the local administration was totally responsible for the incident. The students became out of control. It became difficult to maintain law and orders in different part of the kingdom. His Majesty King Birendra announced the formation of the Royal Commission under the Chairmanship of Dhanendra Bhadur Singh, the Judge of the Supreme Court to fairly investigate the situation on May 2, 1979. The members of the commission were Iswori Raj Mishra, Rastriya Panchayat Deputy Chairman Lokendra Bahadur Chand, Surendra Bahadur Basnet and Surya Bahadur Shakya.[199]

The royal commission was assigned to make an impartial inquiry into the circumstances and nature of students strike, various incidents that had occurred at various places in this connection, and to submit a report to HMG along with suggestions for solving the problems. HMG also ordered the release of all students except those who were arrested for criminal cases, the reopening of all education campuses and assured that the demands of the agitating students will be considered sympathetically. In the beginning, some processions were organized by the students to express their protest against the Royal Commission. Later, there were spontaneous responses to the Royal Commission. The Royal Commission collected every information about the incidents that took place in different parts, including Amrit Science Campus, Pokhara, Hetauda, Kalaiya, Janakpur etc. On 22 May, 1979, an agreement was made and signed between the commission and three representatives of the students action committee. The three representatives of the action committee released a joint statement calling off the student strike and appealing the students to attend the classes as usual.[200] The Royal Commission in a statement agreed to implement the following measure to fulfil the demands of the students. The Royal Commission issued the directives to the concerned units:[201]

(a) to allow the students to form free student union at the national level,

(b) to release all the students arrested under the public security Act,

(c) to dissolve the RSVM,

(d) to withdraw the criminal charges levelled against students during the strike,

(e) to make necessary arrangements to reduce the examination fees in proportion to the number of courses offered,

(f) to solve all local problems of the individual campuses and schools at respective levels,

(g) to include a representative of the student union in the committee to be constituted under the student welfare section,

(h) to withdraw the charges based on the code of conduct levelled against students during strike,

(i) to make the dissertation optional and necessary arrangements for term papers of courses in lieu of dissertation for the degree level students,

(j) directive to be issued to the concerned faculty boards to consider sympathetically the application of the student who wanted to get transferred form one institute to another for further study at higher levels,

(k) to allow the students at the medical and engineering institutes to continue further study at 2nd semester with provision for the students to clear up the back papers later,

(l) to make necessary arrangements for the imprisoned students to appear in private examination in prison,

(m) to provide pension to school teachers, and

(n) to fix the maximum period for completing the 3 years courses in 6 years and 2 years courses in 5 years.

The Royal commission in the concluding statement also pledged that it would make impartial inquiry into the loss of life and property caused in various incidents during the students strike and to submit the report to His Majesty the king.[202] The other agitating students did not accept the agreement made and signed by the three student representatives. So the dissatisfied students held a student mass meeting at Amrit Campus on May 23rd, 1979. They had forcefully made the two of he three student representatives, Sharan Vikram Malla and Bal Bahadur K.C. present at the meeting. The angry student did not allow them to speak. Then they trapped the two students and blackened their faces with soot, hung boots round their necks and took them round the city chanting slogans that that two students had played a deceptive role. But the police interfered the rally and snatched Saran Virkram and Bal Bahadur and took them under their own guard for their safety. Then more serious incidents occurred. The angry mass of the students chanted slogans and rallied violently. Some of them entered the RNAC compound, burnt some property ransacked the RNAC building, burnt the Gorkhapatra building and some policemen were injured. A terror spread in the Kathmandu valley, gunshots were heard, law and order situation went beyond control. The army was mobilized to control the situation. Peace was restored only after mid-night. Next day on 24 May, 1979. His Majesty the king announced national referendum. The people could choose one between the reformed Panchayat system or the multiparty system.[203]

The king's address to the nation cooled down all tempers and the situation fast returned to normal in all parts of the country. The student movement did not remain limited to only education sectors and students. It spread all over Nepal starting form Kathmandu. The people who supported the movement belonged to all walks of life. Writers, workers, Bar Association, service holders including different professionals were the most important factors for the success of the movement. Workers' role in that movement was outstanding. The situation compelled the government to think seriously about the political system itself. The students got their rights of free student union and the people could get chance to choose the kind of political system they liked in the referendum. Then the first phase of the student movement was terminated, the next phase began again by which the political leaders came upper ground and the 1990 movement was launched and made successful under their leadership. The democracy movement of 1990 was also started by the students.

When we review and critically examine the student agitation of 1979, we can discern the following characteristics.

a. All the banned political parties were united for a common cause of revolting against the Panchayat system. They made the students a medium to highlight their ideology and to initiate political opposition to Panchayat system. In fact, the students were looking for an excuse for a long time to start an agitation. The peaceful procession organized to make a protest against the execution of Bhutto turned out to be a good excuse.

b. Under NESP, there was no provision for students union. The Sadan-wise student organizations could not work effectively to vindicate the student welfare section; it was also incapable of communicating the legitimate demands of the students. In a way there was a complete break in communication of the grievances of students. So, in the recent students and the law maintaining authorities (including zonal commissioner, CDO and the police) right form the beginning. The university authorities were by-passed and inspite of several requests of the university authorities, the students did not agree to sit at a negotiating table with them.

c. Although most of the demands of the students were academic, the agitation was mainly politically motivated. This will be clear when we examine how the action committee was formed. The action committee consisted of students representing different banned political parties.

d. The local administration and the university authorities were ordered to deal firmly with the student agitation, and so they were not all the beginning. It took a serious turn when the *Rastrabadi Swtantra Viddyarthi Mandal* was used to counter attack the agitating students. The police had to enter the campuses to maintain law and order.

e. It was characterized by nation wide student agitation. First it was started in the Kathmandu valley. Later the students started agitation at Biratnagar, Janakpur, Hetauda, Pokhara, Syangja, Palpa, Bharatpur and other places of the country.

f. RSVM was the government financed student group and had established its branches in almost all districts of the country. It had no support of students in most of the T.U. campuses and was being used frequently by the local administration and the police as a tool to check and threaten the agitating students in campus. It was also a defamed group and was responsible for frequent undesirable incidents in the campuses.[204]

To meet the challenge of the RSVM group and to respond to political challenges, the banned political parties in strong opposition to the Panchayat system, had launched an underground move. This move was launched much earlier to reorganize and strengthen the student organization in different campuses. There were three separate student organization:

(a) Nepal *Biddyarthi Sangh* (Nepal Student Union),

(b) All Nepal National Independent Student Union,

(c) Nepal Student Federation.[205]

These student organizations were getting quite active in organizing their branches in almost all campuses of the Kathmandu valley and in other districts of the country. In fact, they had already set up their organization in 60 districts.

The government in the beginning, grossly under-estimated the strength of the students and could not apprehend the circumstance in which it was initiated and the serious nature of the strike. It was only when the strike became a nation-wide movement that the government was compelled to consider sympathetically the demands of the students.[206]

5.8 Student Unrest and People's Movement of 1990

The 1979 student movement is supposed to be important in different levels. The student community demonstrated their strength and became successful to influence the Nepalese people. The communication media of the world did broadcast the news of the student movement of Nepal in front lines. This proves that Nepalese student movement also influenced the world.[207] The students achieved the rights to organize their Free Student Union for the first time and the Nepalese got their opportunity to take part in the referendum, which was directly related to the political system. This was the consequence of the student movement of 1979.[208] Due to the student movement of 1979 referendum was announced to choose either improved Panchayat system or the multi-party system in the country. Interference and suppression reached the climax under the leadership the Panchayat government.

However, it was 3rd forced to make amendment in the constitution of Nepal in 1980. According to the amended constitution, general election was held in April 1981. In this way the government of the improved Panchayat system proceeded on its own way and the other opposition political parties did not remain silent, rather they inspired teachers, medical-workers, Bank-Service men, industrial and transport workers' to take part in the movements in 1982, 1983 and 1984 respectively. The communist and congress parties led the movement continuously. It was 1979 student movement which created an easy environment for such political movements later on.[209] The non-violent movement led by the Nepali congress in 1985 also brought a new political situation on the country. On 20th of June 1985 several bombs were exploded at different places of the country, including the capital city Kathmandu Ramraja Prasad Singh claimed for the explosions. After the bomb explosions, all kinds of movements, by the students and the non-violent movement of the Nepali congress were suspended.[210] Later on, in April 1986, second general election was held. In the same contest, the students had staged a movement in 1981, expressing dissatisfaction with the management of Kirtipur Campus cafeteria.[211]

The students took an initiative to investigate corruption of millions rupees in T.U. cafeterias. They blamed the T.U. high level authorities to divert the event by allowing police interference for fear of being exposed of the corruption. Then they demanded for an investigation of the police interference in T.U. by an independent commission. The T.U. remained closed on the call of the T.U. union president Balkrishna Khand on 23rd July, 1987. The students held a press conference to inform about the event. They staged group-hunger strike on 27th and 28th July and held a mass meeting on 29th and continued their protest programmes onwards. Then a memorandum about the educational problems was handed over to the then Vice-Chancellor Mahesh Kumar Upadhyaya on 3rd August. The students of different campuses released statements supporting the cafeteria-movement of the T.U.

student union, and finally an agreement was made between the students and T.U. authorities on 5th August.[212]

However, the students did not remain silent, but then continued strikes and protest programmes on different issues time and again. On March 23rd, 1989, India began to block Nepal's trade and transit in excuse of the termination of the treaty. Nepal's economy terrifically declined in 5 or 6 days of the blocking. Nepalese industries and enterprises were paralysed.[213] The weakness of the then government was exposed. The government resorted to nationwide suppression. The people began to demand a united movement against the government. On the other side, the students were conducting different local and national level movements.[214] Again, in connection with launching a nationwide joint movement, ANNFSU (5th) central committee held a second convention of its campus unions in Kathmandu on 30th and 31st July, 1998. This convention orderly defined the student problems and formulated a policy.[215]

In this way an atmosphere of movement grew all over the country ANNFSU council, ANNFSU central committee, NSU coordination committee etc. held their mass meetings in Kathmandu. The campus unions of the Kathmandu valley staged a week long programmes,[216] and in the third week of August, 1989, all the student organizations held talks on different problems of the students and reached an agreement to launch a joint movement for the fulfilment of their demands.[217] As the banned political parties were on the way to a joint movement, it was natural for the student organizations affiliated to them to join hands to start movement.[218] In this context a meeting of nine student organizations including NSU, ANNFSU 10th, Ra. Sa. Pra. Ka. 11th, National Free Student Conference adhoc committee, NNSFN. Revolutionary student organizations, NNSF 7th National convention preparatory committee, ANNFSU 10th, central committee, Nepal Progressive Student Union C.C.O. was held at Kirtipur. The 19 day meeting was represented by

Chandra Bhandary from NSU, Ghanashyam Bhusal form ANNFSU, Puruswottom Neupane form NPSU and others from every organization. This joint convention borough out a nine-point programme on September 12, 1989 in which different demands related to education including restoring of multiparty democratic system were set. As the demands were related to all the Nepalese people, the student representatives unanimously agreed to start nation wide joint struggle from their representatives at different places and also called the Nepalese people to involve in the struggle.[219] The joint statement released by the ninth national student organizations on 5 December is as follows:

It calls on all the student organizations to launch prompt joint movement at every level and increase mutual respect, friendship and cooperation among all the anti-Panchayat organizations of all levels and their members, if any kinds of attacks and interference are made on the interests of any student organization by the Panchayat System or its government,[220] one of the nine organizations, the students organization supporting communist splinter (*Masal*) did not agree with the word "establishment of multiparty democratic system" and insisted on only to mention establishment democratic system and finally two student organizations went away from the nine organizations leaving only seven under one forum.[221] The seven student organizations decided to hold joint mass-meeting in all the five development regions and call on the student-youths to be ready for nationwide people's movement.[222] In the same context the first mass meeting was held in Biratnagar in August, 1998. At the mass meeting Chandra Bhandary form NSU, Ramnath Dhakal from ANNFSU and Prabhunaryan form Marxist gave their speech. After this the administration totally banned mass meetings. But the students continued their activities against the government in different forms.[223]

(a) National Convention of the Nepali Congress

The Nepali Congress held a national convention at

Chhetrapati in the compound of the residence of Ganeshman Singh, on 18th January, 1990 in which three-thousand delegates and observers, leaders of all the anti-Panchayat parties and some Indian leaders were present.[224] It was the first time that the Panchayat government did not interfere the national convention of the outlawed party held in open. The speech given by an Indian leader Chandra Shekhar at the convention was felt to have aroused spirit among the Nepalese. The convention decided to start nation wide movement form 18 February.[225] Two days later, Ganeshman Sing, the Nepali Congress leader, released a statement calling for unity with the left front.[226]

(b) Building of the Mechanism of the Democratic Movement, February 10, 1990

Due to the demand and pressure of the people for the unity between the left front and Nepali Congress, a mechanism of Democratic movement was built on 10th February, 1990. It was jointly declared by the Chairman of left-front Shahana Pradhan and the president of Nepali Congress Krishna Prasad Bhattarai.[227] In this way, the initial works and preparation of joint-leadership for the democratic movement were accomplished.[228]

(c) Joint Student Programme and Police Interference

The student organizations decided to participate in the people's movement according to the phase wise programme of the united student movement as set by themselves.[229] Accordingly seven student organizations issued a joint statements in the last week of December with a joint decision to prepare the atmosphere of people's movement, disseminate, publicise and hold mass meetings in favour of the movement.[230] According to the programme a grand mass meeting was held at Mahendra Morang Campus in Biratnagar on 28 December. Several leaders of different organizations gave speech at the meeting for the united movement against the Panchayat System, similarly a mass meeting was held in Bharatpur on 2

January. The police interfered the mass meeting, clashes between the participants and police ensued and hundreds of students were injured and hundreds were arrested.[231] In the same period, King Birendra was scheduled to visit Pokhara. But the administration terrorised the atmosphere of Pokhara. The Pokhara administration arrested three teachers of Prithivinarayan Campus, Gehendra Koirala, Dharmanath Prashad Shah and Bhupati Dhakal and sent them to prison. Later, on 19th of February Tribhuvan University expelled them from the service. The campus student union launched symbolic strike protesting the arrest of the teachers. They held a mass meeting in connection with the preparation of people's movement on a 12th of February.[232] Different student leaders addressed the meeting. The police attacked them all of a sudden. The students dispersed around the campus, hostel and cafeteria. The event that ensued in the girls hostel is supposed to be most cruel, inhumane and barbaric. Union secretary Laxman Karki was arrested and sent to prison after 30 hours of custody.[233] Many students were arrested and tortured: this event became a matter of national tidings. The political leaders, students and the general people were angered by the incident.[234] An atmosphere of national movement was being prepared. All the professional organizations and classes began to show their solidarity with the student movement. The events and nationwide campus movements became successful to give a decisive mode to the popular movement of 1990.[235] Although political parties, leaders and other professional organization were involved in the movement, the decisive role played by the students with strict discipline and honestly as military men is more important as well as unforgettable.[236]

(d) The Democratic Movement, and Student Adhoc Committee

On the 1st and 12th of February, 1990, Seven student organiztions ANNFSU, NRSO, ANNFSU, C.C.O, NNSF (Manandhar) NNSF (Barma), NPSU and NSU, issued a joint appeal in the name of 'Democratic people's movement student adhoc community'.[237] The appeal was entitled as "A call of national student organizations for making the democratic movement a success". In this appeal a lively exposition of the undemocratic and autocratic character of the Panchayat system was made in the following words:

> *We hereby heartily call all the students and the Nepalese people in the country and aboard for decisively fighting against the autocratic Panchayat system by taking active part in the people's movement sponsored by the united left front and the Nepali congress and to be started on the 19th February for rooting out the autocratic Panchayat system for the establishment of democracy.238*

It appealed to the people to go to *Dharahara* at one o'clock on 18th February, to take part in the nation wide general strike on 19th, to observe as black-day on 25th and to take part in the general strike on 2nd March.

'The students celebrated 18th of February, 1990 by distributing leaflets calling "let's establish democracy or die" let's make the people's movement a success" etc.[239] The government had arrested the leaders of the united left front, the Nepali congress and some of the militants of NSU before 18 February. Despite the interference of the government, the revolutionary students with the coordination of the people became successful to stage a rally on the scheduled day.[240]

In the 1990 popular movement, an agreement was made between NSU and different organizations of ANNFSU. Both the student organizations issued a statement with a decision to take active part in the people's movement. Similarly on 12th of February, a joint statement was released by 7 student organizations in the name of "Democratic people's movement student coordination committee" appealing to all for making the joint democratic movement to be launched for 18th February a success. The movement in which unprecedented participation of the students was seen became successful to root-out the autocratic Panchayat system forever.[241]

In this way, the joint movement initiated by the students continued for fifty days. In this movement Student Coordination Committee, Nepali Congress, United Left Front and their workers, T.U. Teacher's Coordination Committee, Nepal Bar Association, Engineering Association, Nepal National Teachers' organization, Civil Servicemen' Association, Writers' and Artists' Association, Health Workers' Association etc. were involved. In the same way a professional solidarity group was also organized. The movement got more impetus. Later, on 8th of April 1990, King Birendra being forced by the growing movement had to announce multiparty system scraping the Panchayat System. In this movement many revolutionaries got martyrdom. In this way, the movement led by political parties got a momentum due to the unflinching as well as important role played by the students.[242]

References

1 Soorya Lal Amatya, Jagdish Agrawal & Krishna P. Pradhan, A Study of Student-Problem in Tribhuvan University, (Kirtipur: T.U., Rector Office, Research Division, 1980), p. 4.
2 *Ibid.*
3 *Ibid.*, p. 7.
4 *Ibid.*
5 *Ibid.*
6 *Ibid.*
7 *Ibid.*, p. 9.
8 *Ibid.*
9 *Ibid.*
10 *Ibid.*
11 *Ibid.*, p. 10.
12 *Ibid.*
13 *Ibid.*
14 *Ibid.*.
15 *Ibid.*, p. 13.
16 Lok Raj Baral, Oppositional Politics in Nepal, (New Delhi: Abhinav Publication, 1977), p. 146.
17 Amatya, Agrawal & Pradhan, f.n. No. 1., p. 13.
18 Bhuvan Lal Joshi & Leo E. Rose, Democratic Innovation in Nepal, Case Study or Political Acceleration, (California: Berkeley University, California Press, 1976), p. 91.

19 Amatya, Agrawal & Pradhan, f.n. No. 1, p. 14.
20 *Ibid.*
21 *Ibid.*
22 *Ibid.*
23 From an interview with Sher Bahadur Deuba on 1997/2/4, Kathmandu.
24 *Ibid.*
25 From an interview with Janardan Acharaya on 1997/6/14, Kathmandu.
26 *Ibid.*
27 From an interview with Dambar Bir Thapa on 1998/9/13, Kathmandu.
28 From an interview with Birendrabhakta Shrestha on 1997/6/2, Kathmandu.
29 Amatya, Agrawal & Pradhan, f.n. No. 1, p. 16.
30 *Ibid.*
31 *Ibid.*
32 *Ibid.*
33 *Ibid.*
34 From an interview with Dambar Bir Thapa on 1998/9/13, Kathmandu.
35 From an interview with Kamal Chitrakar on 1997/6/3, Kathmandu.
36 Baral, f.n. No. 16, p. 152.
37 *Ibid.*
38 *Ibid.*
39 From an interview with Janardan Acharya on 1997/6/14, Kathmandu.
40 From an interview with Tika Pokharal on 1998/4/1, Kathmandu.
41 From an interview with Balmukunda Kherel on 1998/4/10, Kathmandu.
42 From an interview with Mahesworman Shrestha 1998/9/15, Kathmandu.
43 From an interview with Damber Bir Thapa on 1998/9/13, Kathmandu.
44 From an interview with Maheshworman Shrestha 1998/9/15, Kathmandu.
45 From an interview with Kamal Chitrakar on 1997/6/3, Kathmandu.
46 From an interview with Biswokanta Mainali on 1998/1/19, Kathmandu.
47 From an interview with Birendrabhakta Shrestha on 1997/6/2, Kathmandu.
48 Amatya, Agrawal & Pradhan, f.n. No. 1, p. 17.

49 *Ibid.*
50 *Ibid.*
51 *Ibid.*, p. 18.
52 From an interview with Tekendra Bahadur Karki on 1997/11/20, Kathmandu.
53 From an interview with Pitambar Dahal on 1997/3/11, Kathmandu.
54 From an interview with Kamal Krishna Joshi on 1997/6/20, Lalitpur.
55 From an interview with Devendra Lal Nepali on 1997/11/27, Kathmandu.
56 Amatya, Agrawal & Pradhan, f.n. No. 1, pp. 19-20.
57 From an interview with Marshal Julum Shakya on 1997/3/17, Kathmandu.
58 From an interview with Daman Dhungana on 1997/6/20, Kathmandu.
59 From an interview with Arjun Narsingh K.C. on 1997/7/2, Kathmandu.
60 Amatya, Agrawal & Pradhan, f.n. No. 1, pp. 20-21.
61 *Ibid.*, p. 22.
62 *Ibid.*
63 From an interview with Mukunda Bahadur Shrestha on 1998/9/4, Lalitpur.
64 From an interview with Sher Bahadur Deuba on 1997/2/4, Kathmandu.
65 From an interview with Arjun Narsingh K.C. on 1997/7/2, Kathmandu.
66 From an interview with Birendra Bhakta Shrestha on 1997/6/2, Kathmandu.
67 Form an interview with Pitambar Dahal on 1997/11/22, Kathmandu.
68 Amatya, Agrawal & Pradhan, f.n. No. 1.
69 *Shahid Ko Gatha* (Martyr's Scarifies), (Kathmandu: Published by Madan Asrit Pratisthan, 2052. B.S. (1995), p. 266.
70 From an interview with Birendrabhakta Shrestha on 1997/6/2, Kathmandu.
71 From an interview with Krishna Prashad Pradhan on 1998/3/10, Kathmandu.
72 From an interview with Suryalal Amatya on 1997/11/3, Kathmandu.
73 From an interview with Hari Neupane on 1997/11/10, Kathmandu.
74 From an interview with Yog Prasad Acharya on 1997/11/6.
75 From an interview with Tanka Karki on 1995/5/10, Kathmandu.

76 From an interview with Dilliraman Regmi on 1997/7/20, Kathmandu.
77 From an interview with Kamal Prakash Malla on 1997/7/3, Kathmandu.
78 From an interview with Saranvikram Malla on 1996/1/19, Kathmandu.
79 From an interview with Rabindra Chakarabarti on 1997/10/25, Kathmandu.
80 From an interview with Niranjan Thapa on 1998/3/15, Kathmandu.
81 From an interview with Padam Thakurathi on 1997/1/15, Kathmandu.
82 Amatya, Agrawal & Pradhan, f.n. No. 1, p. 24.
83 *Ibid.*
84 Ministry of Education, HMG/N, National Education System Plan for 1971-76, (Kathmandu: 1971), p. v.
85 *Ibid.*
86 *Ibid.*
87 *Ibid.*, p. 3.
88 Amatya, Agrawal & Pradhan, f.n. No. 1, p. 31.
89 Ministry of Education, HMG/N, f.n. No. 84, p. 1.
90 Amatya, Agrawal & Pradhan, f.n. No. 1, p. 31.
91 *Ibid.*, p. 32.
92 *Ibid.*
93 *Ibid.*
94 Amatya, Agrawal & Pradhan, f.n. 1, p. 32.
95 *Ibid.*, p. 38.
96 *Ibid.*, p. 33-34.
97 *Ibid.*, p. 34.
98 *Ibid.*
99 *Ibid.*, p. 35.
100 *Ibid.*
101 *Ibid.*, p. 36.
102 *Ibid.*
103 *Ibid.*, p. 37.
104 *Ibid.*
105 *Ibid.*, p. 38.
106 *Ibid.*
107 *Ibid.*
108 *Ibid.*
109 *Ibid.*
110 *Ibid.*, p. 39
111 *Ibid.*
112 *Ibid.*
113 *Ibid.*

114 From an interview with Rabindra Chakarabarti on 1997/10/25, Kathmandu.
115 Ministry of Education, f..n. No. 84, p. VII.
116 *Ibid.*, p. 66.
117 Amatya, Agrawal & Pradhan, f.n. No. 1, p. 41.
118 Ministry of Education, HMG/N, f.n. No. 84, p. 23.
119 Amatya, Agrawal & Pradhan, f..n. No. 1, p. 41.
120 Ministry of Education, HMG/N, f.n. No. 84, p. VII.
121 Amatya, Agrawal & Pradhan, f.n. No. 1, p. 42.
122 *Ibid.*
123 *Ibid.*
124 *Ibid.*
125 Ministry of Education, HMG/N, f.n. No. 84, p. 9.
126 Amatya, Agrawal & Pradhan, f.n. No. 1, p. 43.
127 *Ibid.*
128 *Ibid.*
129 *Ibid.*
130 *Ibid.*, p. 44.
131 Ministry of Education, HMG/N, f.n. No. 84, p. 22.
132 *Ibid.*
133 *Ibid.*
134 Amatya, Agrawal & Pradhan, f.n. No. 1, p. 45.
135 *Tribhuvan Biswabidhayalaya Niyamharoo*, (Tribhuvan University Rules and Regulation), (Kirtipur: Tribhuvan University, With Amendments up to 1975, 1979), p. 74.
136 Amatya, Agrawal & Pradhan, f.n. No. 1, p. 45.
137 *Ibid.*, p. 46.
138 Ministry of Education, HMG/N, f.n. No. 84, p. 9-10.
139 Amatya, Agrawal & Pradhan, f.n. No. 1, p. 47.
140 *Ibid.*
141 *Ibid.*
142 *Ibid.*
143 *Tribhuvan Biswabidhayala Niyamharoo*, f.n. No. 135, p. 74.
144 Amatya, Agrawal & Pradhan, f.n. No. 1, p. 47.
145 *Ibid.*
146 *Ibid.*
147 *Ibid.*, p. 50.
148 *Ibid.*, p, 51.
149 From an interview with Bal Mukunda Kharel on 1998/4/10, Kathmandu.
150 Ministry of Education, HMG/N, f.n. No. 84, p. 18
151 Amatya, Agrawal & Pradhan, f.n. No. 1, p. 53.
152 *Ibid.*

153 Tirtha B. Manandhar, Manpower and Education in Nepal a Survey of Education in Nepal, M. Mohsin and Prem Kasaju (ed.), (Kathmandu: National Education Committee, 1974), p. 15.
154 *Ibid.*
155 Kamal P. Malla, "The National Education Plan: Some Problems of Implementation in Higher Education", Vashuda, Vol. XV, No. 8, (Oct.-Nov., 1975), p. 75.
156 Amatya, Agrawal & Pradhan, f.n. No. 1, p. 54
157 *Ibid.*
158 Manandhar, f.n. No. 153, p. 15.
159 Full-Term Evaluation of NESP (Mimeo), 1976, p. 6.
160 Amatya, Agrawal & Pradhan, f.n. No. 1, p. 55.
161 *Ibid.*
162 *Ibid.*
163 *Ibid.*, p. 57.
164 *Ibid.*, p. 58.
165 *Ibid.*
166 *Ibid.*
167 From an interview with Birendra Bhakta Shrestha on 1997/6/2, Kathmandu.
168 *Ibid.*
169 *Ibid.*, p. 59.
170 Full-Term Report, f.n. No. 159, p. 63.
171 Kedar Nath Shrestha, "A study of the problems of Improvement of Instruction: View of Campus Chiefs", Education and Development (Special Issue of Higher Education), Kamal Prakash Malla (eds.), (Kathmandu : National Education Committee, CERID, 1978), pp. 67-78
172 *Ibid.*, p. 68.
173 *Ibid.*
174 Ministry of Education, HMG/N, f.n. No. 84, p. VII.
175 From an interview with Mangal Siddhi Manandhar on 1998/3/7, Kathmandu.
176 Amatiya, Agrawal & Pradhan, f.n. No. 1, p. 85.
177 From an interview with Sharan Vikram Malla on 1996/1/19, Kathmandu.
178 *Ibid.*
179 *Ibid.*
180 *Ibid.*, p. 89.
181 *Ibid.*
182 *Ibid.*
183 Kamal P. Malla, The Role of the Rector, (Mimeo), (Kathmandu: Tribhuvan University, 1979), p. 21.
184 *Ibid.*, p. 21.

185 *Ibid.*, p. 96.
186 Ministry of Education, HMG/N, f.n. No. 84. p. e.
187 From an interview with B.C. Malla on 1996/4/7, Kathmandu.
188 *Ibid.*
189 From an interview with Sharan Vikram Malla on 1998/2/23, Kathmandu.
190 From an interview with Bashudev Dhungana on 1197/3/10, Kathmandu.
191 Byron Wedge, "The Case Study of Students Political Violence: Brazil, 1964 and the Dominican Republic, 1965". World Politics, XXI, (1969), p. 194.
192 Jhalak Prasad Subedi, Nepali Vidyarthi Andolon ko Addha Satabdi 1997-2047 B.S. (Half a Century of Nepal's Students Movement 1940-1990), (Pokhara: Subedi Prakashan 1992).
193 From an interview with Purnaman Shrestha on 1998/7/27, Kathmndu.
194 *Ibid.*, p. 106.
195 *Ibid.*
196 *Ibid.*
197 *Ibid.*
198 *Ibid.*, p. 113.
199 *Ibid.*
200 *Ibid.*, p. 115.
201 *Ibid.*
202 *Ibid.*, p. 116
203 *Ibid.*
204 *Ibid.*, pp. 117-18
205 *Ibid.*, 118.
206 *Ibid.*
207 Form an interview with B.C. Malla on 1996/4/15, Kathmandu.
208 Form an interview with Yagya Prasad Adhikary on 1998/12/3, Kathmandu.
209 Form an interview with Amir Pande on 1997/6/10, Kathmandu.
210 Subedi, f.n. No. 192, p. 78.
211 *Ibid.*
212 Gobhardhan Rana, Prajatantrik Andolan ma Nepal Bidhyarthi Sangha (The Nepal Students' Federation in the Democratic Movement), (Kathmandu: Nepal Student's Federation Western Zones Co-ordination Committee, 1994), p. 622-623.
213 Subedi, f.n. No. 192, p. 79.
214 *Ibid.*
215 *Ibid.*, p. 80.
216 *Ibid.*, p. 83.
217 *Ibid.*

218 Rana, f..n. No. 212, p. 654.
219 Subedi, f.n. No. 192, p. 86.
220 Rana, f.,n. No. 212, p. 655.
221 *Ibid.*
222 *Ibid.*
223 *Ibid.*
224 Subedi, f..n. No. 192, p. 90.
225 *Ibid.*
226 *Ibid.*, p. 91.
227 *Ibid.*
228 *Ibid.*
229 From an interview with Sanker Pokharel on 1998/7/23, Kathmandu.
230 Subedi, f..n. No. 192, p. 86.
231 *Ibid.*, p. 92.
232 From an interview with Rabindra Adhikary on 1998/3/17, Kathmandu.
233 Subedi, f..n. No. 192, p. 93.
234 From an interview with Yougesh Bhattarai on 1998/7/20, Kathmandu.
235 From an interview with Ananda Dev Bhatta on 1998/6/15, Kathmandu.
236 Form an interview with Dr. Druga Prasad Bhandary on 1998/6/17, Kathmandu.
237 Subedi, f..n. No. 192, p. 93.
238 Rana, f..n. No, 212, p. 656.
239 *Ibid.*
240 *Ibid.*
241 *Shahid Ko Gatha* (Martyr's Sacrifices), (Kathmandu: Madan Asrit Pratisthan, 2052 B.S. (1995), p. 267.
242 Subedi, f..n. No. 192, p. 109.

CHAPTER SIX

Young Communist League -Nepal

a. Emergence, Development and Role of Young Communist League(YCL) in the World History

Young Communist League (YCL) is an established name in the World Communist Movement. Communist party and Young Communist League (YCL) are complementary to each other. YCL works according to the ideology, principle, strategy and tactical policy of communist party as its sister organization. Making familiar with the national and international events according to the need for social transformation, the programs of YCL are formulated with the objective to inspire the youths to be dedicated, organized and work dynamically towards the direction of new social structure. Traditionally, YCL is an assisting organization of communist party. The main objective and mission of organizing, YCL, is to produce communist revolutionaries for future by educating the youths with communist ideology. It was the communist ideology that contributed to give an important place to the Russian Revolution in the World History. The Russian Revolution had become successful to take decisive mode due to the communist principle and ideology. In the same course, YCL was organized in Russia according to the joint idea of Lenin and Stalin. Lenin's intimate comrade as well as an associate Kelenin became its Chairperson and Lenin became General Secretary. Kelenin has written a lots of books. His books were included in the courses of study from secondary to university level during the Socialist Government. They were studied as course books. His books have become a subject for special discussions and importance in different regions including Europe.[1]

YCL was called as ComSomal in Russia. Similarly Mao-Tse-Tung also had organized YCL in the People's Republic of China. It was called YCL. In the 21st Century World, the place pride and progress of China has become clear to all.

Sincere mobilization, execution and identification of YCL has proved a milestone for social transformation. Almost all the political parties are mobilizing youths at the forefront as their main sister organization giving it a suitable name. In short, the form of YCL is the same. Traditionally, YCL is the recruitment center of communist party. The main objective and strategy of organizing YCL is to produce competent communists by educating them ideologically and theoretically so that they can lead the country in future. To take appropriate step suitable to the time, situation and events is supposed to be the main duty and responsibility.

b. The Glorious Moments of Young Communist League (YCL) in the History of Nepal:

Young Communist League (YCL) which was founded immediately after the establishment of the Communist Party of Nepal has come all the way through five-decades. It is an important matter that the events, which brought Nepal's image before the world through YCL during the difficult period when Nepal was staggering in transitional politics, staying isolated from the world and was unknown about national and international events, have occupied a remarkable place in the History of Nepal as the glorious moments. The ban imposed on Nepal Communist Party was lifted after Tanka Prashad Achayarya became prime minister. Then Nepal Communist Party took a decision to organize YCL–Nepal with the objective of educating youths with communist ideology, producing communists to lead the future and prepare competent and capable citizens for building the nation.[2] Affiliated to the communist party, YCL has been working as the assisting or sister organization since 1953 A.D.

According to the plan and program, YCL - Nepal was

founded with the efforts of Pushpalal, Mohan Bikram Sing, Keshar Jung Rayamajhi etc. with the objective of giving ideological and organizational education to the youths under 16, make them committed and get them organized with communist ideology. Nirmal Lama was the schooling chief. There was massive participation of young students in YCL. It was compulsory for them to attend Marxist Classes at least six months and work according to the direction given. YCL was organized as per the provision that the youths after receiving ideological education and inspired with political thought and crossing 16 years of age would automatically get membership of communist party on the recommendation of two communist leaders.[3] Left persons or communist party members never remain as single person, they do politics remaining under collective thought and ideology.

Political discipline, dutifulness, collective leadership and commitment are some of the ideals of communist. So, in those days YCL was very popular, attractive and a subject in lime light. The youths organized in YCL attractively, actively and sincerely dedicated themselves in improving and setting Nepal's image in the international arena. YCL occupied a leading position by giving speeches at mass meetings organizing at different places, raising awareness in the people, mobilizing them, exposing injustice and operation, demonstrating protest rallies etc.[4] It was made compulsory for them to live with farmers at least three months a year. During this period they had to make agriculture related working plans and activities, they had to center their special attention to mobilize the farmers towards nation building. YCL cadres used their time in opening public libraries, constructing roads, bridges, health posts etc. They used to do constructive social works as volunteers in villages. The contribution of YCL to bring suppressed communities to the mainstream of the nation has become ever memorable. [5]A meeting of some youths was held in presence of communist party leaders Pushpalal, Mohan Bikram Sing, Dr. Keshar Jung

Rayamajhi etc. in the house of Laxman Rajbansi (the founder principal of Siddhartha Banasthali School) at Wotu, Katmandu. Then YCL was founded according to the decision taken by the same meeting.

The first Chairperson and General Secretary of YCL became Laxman Rajbansi and Hirannyalal Shrestha respectively. Bhagaban Ratna Tuladhar, Maheshlal Pradhan, and Gopal Kayastha became the in charge of Kathmandu, Patan and Bhaktapur respectively. Branches of YCL were expanded and number of YCL members went on gradually increasing. YCL cells were formed in most of the schools. YCL had got responsibility to work in the geographically divided regions such as Uttar Gandak, Koshi etc. YCL cadres were actively working in the campaign for nationwide organization. Thirtha Jyapu and Moti Pahadi were the back bone of YCL. In the situation of then Nepal when no party or person had ventured to be active in politics, student-youths could spontaneously present themselves at the forefront. They would get success to slip, or escape from the hands of police, they would be put in prisons many times and would be released taking them far from their home or villages. Even then they would get organized themselves.

The youths coming from different places, communities and families and getting organized in YCL [6]after being influenced by Marxist Ideology is the nature of YCL.

Whether it was party's decision or only the thought of leaders, it is unknown. However, bringing youths in organizational structure of the communist party is certainly an important idea. This organization of 12 - 15 year old, mostly school students, had its own structural form. The effort made to change the youths- who by thinking different things had desired to be revolutionary, wanted to go against social anomalies and economic exploitations- into an organizational force is certainly an appreciable matter. But the party could not do any special task to give them ideological schooling. Every time programs were made, but they would not be brought in practice or were not pragmatic. However, the party made us grateful to it for three things. They were – a. it made us interested in social politics b. it made us abide by the discipline and made us able to analyze any issue c. it taught us to bear high morality.[7] In those days the leaders or workers whoever we knew used to adhere to the motto 'moral character is the only ideal of a true communist. We were also taught the same. The communist party used to educate and inspire us with moral lessons such as not to gamble, not to drink alcohol, not to go to cinema, not speak lie etc. Those who would commit such mistakes would be given chance for self-criticism, otherwise different types of punishments would be given according the extent of the mistakes.

The Bahal (monastery) located at Basantapur was the party office the same was the YCL office. Meetings would be held in the house of any member according to the situation and convenience. We had no separate office of our own. When demonstration or rallies or mass meeting were to be organized, we would tear our copies and write posters, paste them at different places, walls or posts and make flags taking-off our clothes. Many of the comrades who did such works are still alive. We would earn a little amount as commission for selling party bulletin 'Mashal'. We would give even such amount to the party as donation. Except the donation amount collected at different times, we would not have any other amount.[8]

In those days YCL had gained popularity, people were highly influenced by it. It had become very useful organization for the communist party. The youths and students organized in YCL contributed significant help to the communist party in the first election held in 1958. The sincere role played by them was highly appreciable. They learnt the art of propagation, method of working as volunteers, chance for getting acquainted themselves with the positive or negative activities done at voting centers. Although the task of raising revolutionary slogans, gather people for mass meetings, giving them political views educating them with political ideology was very difficult, we would do such works cheerfully and enthusiastically. Such experience proved to be useful in the coming days on the one hand and necessary manpower became available to the party on the other. [9]

YCL conducted mock-up election in Darbhanga during Party Plenum and got majority in favor of Constitution Assembly. It also strongly protested import of vegetable ghee (Dalda Ghee) and Gandak Agreement signed between Nepal and India. YCL was involved in the campaign of social transformation, creating public opinion for systematic as well as people oriented political structure keeping in view of different national and international events. On the other, the political parties and government were entangled in political strife and bickering. Conspiracies and serious events began to take place one after another. The 3rd Congress (General Convention) of the Communist Party of Nepal was successfully concluded at Prabha Cinema Hall Lainchaur, Katmandu in 1957.

The political views of the leaders such as Pushpalal, MohanBikram Sing, Kesherjung Rayamajhi etc. contradicted or differed on political resolution, difference went on growing among them. The same thing was repeated at Darbhanga Plenum. In principle, or virtually the communist party had already got split. The leaders put forth the slogan for General Elections abandoning the demand for the election of Constitution Assembly. At the time when king Mahendra took over the power in 1960, the leaders of communist party were not here, they were visiting in Russia, in China or in India. Some leaders who were living within the country were arrested and kept in prisons and the rest ones went underground. Then YCL cadres became helpless and lonely like "chickens after their mother-hen is taken away by an eagle". They were compelled to suffer psychological infliction, many were arrested and given physical and mental tortures. Then YCL cadres became disappointed and frustrated resulting in disappearance or disintegration of the organization of Young Communist League- Nepal, YCL- Nepal. [10]

Following the 1960 coup d'état by king Mahendra, communist party was banned second time. Political confusion overshadowed the country. Some of us, militant YCL cadres began to meet or keep contact with the underground communist leaders with the determination to fight against the unwanted change brought in the country through military force. We also went to prisons, foreign country to meet and take advice of the leaders. But not any of them, neither Pushpalal nor Mohan Bilram Sing, or Kesharjung or Manmohan Adhikary or others agreed to our proposal. Then, a kind of regret and frustration came up to the mentality of YCL cadres. They took their own way according to their understanding, thought and decision. Finally, the organization 'Yong Communist League–Nepal,' disappeared before getting itself young.[11]

Founder of YCL-Nepal and Katmandu in charge Bhagaban Ratna Tuladhar says," Now, if YCL has been established anywhere and done anything by it, that may be under the protection or patronage of different communist splinters. But the unified single organization of YCL-Nepal founded before 1960 has remained limited only in history. While looking back on past YCL in today's context, an important influence of that organization is felt on our life. Whatever question mark has been put on the utility of Marxism in the present capitalist age, how can the ideals such as good sentiment , good- wishes and morality upheld by the communist party for social equality, justice and against exploitations be criticized ? Even the youths who could not stay within the party structure after the 1960 event, the influence of the then YCL-Nepal shall remain fresh in them for ever" [12]

c. 'Young Communist League–Nepal'-Organized by Nepal Communist Party (Maoist): The Campaigner for a Prosperous Nation, Age making Change and Challenges

At present, the Communist Party of Nepal has got divided in dozens of communist parties. Each of them seem to have organized and mobilized youths as their sister organization under their own patronage. But no noticeable organized activities can be seen. It is clearly seen that the parties are maintaining their policy to mobilize youths giving first priority to party interest rather than making them truthful and capable citizens of the country by developing the immature minds of youths. Now it is seen crystal clear that the youths just crossed 16 have been dragged into politics at once.[13]

In 1981 All Nepal Youth Organization was established under the leadership of Com. Pushpa Kamal Dahal (Prachanda), the present Chairperson of CPN (Maoist). Under his leadership, a strong militant team of youths started ideological struggle against the rightist narrow minded groupist trend. In the same course, YCL was organized under the leadership (Chairmanship) of Com. Top Bahadur Rayamajhi. Then YCL began to learn Marxism, Leninism and Maoism, get schooling on political matters and implement party policy and programs. At the same time, it also marched ahead through ideological and physical fighting towards preparation of People's War. YCL played an important role in mobilizing youths electoral struggle, people's struggle and rural class struggle as per the party policy and in conducting resistance programs such as building of People's Army and launching of People's War. [14]

In course of boycotting the mid-term election of 1994, YCL became successful to capture voting booths and hound out the police administration in different place including Rolpa district. During the period when the government resorted to suppress, arrest, torture, kill or cause disappearance of many, the youths were organized under the flag of YCL facing all such insidious acts of the government. YCL implemented party policies and plans. It played a significant role in making people's struggle and rural class struggle a militant.

After the start of 'People's War', it was not necessary nor was such situation to handle YCL from central command. Most of the YCL cadres were recruited in security squad, combatant- guerrilla squad, people's militia and people's liberation army (Red army).

During the period of 10 Years 'People's War', the youths marched ahead under the guidance of the dynamic as well as scientific policy and direction of the communist party of Nepal (Maoist) maintaining honestly the sentiment of sacrifice and dedication. During the last phase, the youths actively worked to raise the people's movement to the climax on the basis of 12-point understanding and conducted mobile -war, urban attack, sabotage etc. according to the urban- focused operational policy of the party. The conscious youth community which was interfering and continuing military attacks on the old state-power under the apt leadership of the party has now become greatly successful to interfere politically and organizationally in all sectors. Various social works such as campaigns for raising people' awareness, controlling crimes, maintaining peace and security including resistance movement, cleaning and sanitation, relief oriented people's services, reform oriented works etc. have been conducted from capital city to remote villages by the youths under the command of the CPN (Maoist).[15]

It will be helpful to make future plans and programs if presented the summery and preliminary evaluation of the works done after the first meeting of the Central Committee of YCL-Nepal held on December 2, 2006. At that meeting, party Chairperson and the supreme commander of People's Army, Com. Prachanda gave instruction and schooling to the YCL cadres. This made clearer the theoretical concept of YCL and its role in the present developed situation and created new understanding, spirit, enthusiasm, courage and seriousness in the youths by eliminating the old confusing situation. As present YCL is the sister organization of militant youths developing under the guidance and patronage of Nepal Communist Party (Maoist), it is resisting organization and directly implements the idea, thoughts, policy, direction , strategy, operational/tactical policy, programs etc. of the same party.

Some theoretical aspects of YCL-Nepal are as follows-

a. Marxism, Leninism and Maoism and Prachanda Path shall be the guiding principle of YCL-Nepal.

b. In the beginning ' Long-term People's War', but in the context of Nepal it was started paired with people's movement and with the objective reality and political initiative. The strategic connotation (definition) relating to building of base- areas made by the Fourth Plenary Meeting qualitatively raised the People's War high. The dialectical relationship between political and military attacks has got a synthesized shape as a new guide-line from the Second National Conference.

c. To build or develop the youths as the backbone of the revolution of 21st century by transforming struggle and unity.

d. To use the integrated developed guideline creatively in the present situation by realizing the Marxist belief of armed struggle and long-term people's war.

e. The program with ultimate goal to reach socialism and communism will also be our program going through completion of new democratic revolution by establishing people's democratic republic for the time being.

f. To give emphasis to build and develop Young Communist League as a militant organization affirming revolutionary thought and leadership.

g. Young Communist League–Nepal shall perform the role as propagandist or indoctrinator, organizer, agitator and producer (4 actors) with integration and proper coordination.

About the future works

The future works such as ideological, political, organizational, struggle related works, production and economic - physical works,- sports, creative works, social and cultural etc. will be completed as a total package through phase-wise campaigns. Major and minor works, regular works, campaign oriented works or programs etc. should be implemented in a coordinated way according to necessity with intense pace, wider size and militant manner.[16]

Young Communist League – Nepal is a common organization of anti-feudalist and anti- imperialist youths. The guiding principle of this organization is Marxism, Leninism and Maoism (MLM) and Prachanda Path. This organization shall remain as the assisting sister organization of Nepal Communist Party (Maoist). YCL feels both its responsibility and duty to use the development made in the political structure by CPM (Maoist) protecting it. So, realizing the need of revolution the Statute of Young Communist League- Nepal has been prepared to encompass all the youths belonging different regions, classes, races or casts, languages, religions , cultures and genders. The Statute passed by the National Convention of YCL-Nepal contains 9 Chapters and 18 Sections (Articles). It is said in it that the youths affiliated with YCL means the cadres (members) from 16 to 40 years of age.

The statement of the Chairperson of CPN (Maoist), Com.Prachanda , about the formation of YCL Nepal is as follows:

"Y CL itself is the established name in the world communist movement since long, and its character or nature is found different depending upon the fact who brings it out in what form and at what time and which party brings it out under what type of leadership. The YCL founded by Lenin in Russia , the YCL founded by Mao in China and the YCL founded by us in Nepal years ago and the YCL formed by us now are not same in every thing. The main purpose of forming YCL is to organize youths, make them agitate, struggle and mobilize them for social transformation. But the theme under what particular thought / ideology and under what particular strategy is this done ? makes at least some difference in its nature, quality, or it has been found different both qualitatively and quantitavely, this is the first thing. The second is that in the present situation we have already entered into peace process after signing 12–point, understanding, YCL- Nepal came into existence in the context of developing absolutely new strategy, new process of thinking and most exceptionally using both flexibility and rigidity of tactical policy. Moreover, it came into existence at such time when there was a doubt and danger whether the party would gradually move towards reformism.

The tactical policy adopted by the party during the last phase, there increased the danger of rightist opportunism automatically. That tactical policy is that. The tactical policy like coming to cities, going to parliament, participating in government is such a tactical policy from which there always remains danger of dominance of rightist opportunism over the party. If looked into the concrete situation of Nepal, YCL has been brought into existence at such a time when the party has been adopting a very challenging tactical policy; hence with the objective of preventing danger of rightist opportunism in the party and to make the party leadership uphold and boost up revolutionary thought more carefully, collect and organize the revolutionary forces. So, I say that it is also a thought. The essence of saying that YCL is not only in system, organization, struggle or so is that. Because in the first decade of 21st century we have started pushing forward the revolution adopting a very challenging tactical policy and the lately adopted tactical policy may cause to increase the danger of rightist opportunism while there was already its danger.

In this situation, there must be a strong assisting force and ideology to prevent the party from the danger during the time we have adopted such tactical policy. Only then, the party can be prevented from sliding towards rightist opportunism. For the same purpose and thought YCL was formed. At this very sensitive phase of revolution, the technique of structure which we have adopted to organize YCL from lower to the upper level placing the commanders and commissars of Peoples' Army at the leadership level is not anywhere in the world. Anywhere in the world I have not seen such technique of keeping the regular part of People's Army at cantonments and bringing out the other regular part of combatants to control command of youths. It is exceptional, if there is any party anywhere to use the technique like ours. As organizationally and in a well planned way, we have applied the method to organize youths under the command of the commanders and commissars of People's Army to prepare a huge mass of militant youths is an idiosyncratic matter. I call, it is a technique and also a tactical policy. Or it is called a technique and fundamental of organization. To talk about strategy and tactical policy, when our People's Army was in the process of going to cantonment, at that time all the anti people forces such as imperialists, expansionists, reactionaries including revisionists were thinking that after the People's Army would be living in cantonment, only then they would chase away the Maoists from everywhere by baton (Lathi) charges. This was their strategy. So, YCL is also the counter of their strategy. It is a counter strategy expressed through YCL saying " If you try to do so against the proletarian revolutionary thought , try to interfere it, it does not differ even if our People's Army remains at cantonment. We have also our another army outside the cantonment." This has proved true now.

Considering from this point of view, YCL has come forth as a technique, a strategy in the course of development of MLM-ism in the first decade of the 21st century. It does not mean that there is no need of improvement of YCL, or there are no weaknesses in it. But if you look it on the whole, any politically conscious and a revolutionary person deeply looks into it, there is no difficulty to understand that the intrinsic sentiment, thought , strategy and tactical policy are great. Yes, due to our limitations, lack of resources and means, we have not been able to make it as we have thought to make and it should be. The national and international reactionaries used to protest Maoist Party in the past and are protesting YCL at present, that has been so because of thought and strategy. They openly blame that Maoist affiliated YCL breached the rules and regulations, extorted, attacked, used force and so on. This may be or may not be so on one side, however we don't assert that YCL has not committed any mistake or it is totally right.

The trend of mistake may be of three natures. After we have come into peace process, the method which should have been used to win the heart of people, has not been used satisfactorily as it should have been and some sporadic mistakes have taken place on some issues. Unnecessary force has been used and prejudiced or subjective analysis has been done. Such mistakes and the behavior of the organization and comrades can be gradually corrected. But it is also found that some immoral persons by penetrating from enemy camps stage inadmissible acts in the name of YCL to blur the image of YCL or discredit it.

I want to say a very surprising thing about it. Some days ago we held a big gathering of industry and business entrepreneurs at Thamel, Katmandu. All the entrepreneurs requested in a same voice to provide help of YCL against different swindlers including ruffian , gangsters who would come to collect money in the name of weekly-taxes. This proves that they expect protection from YCL against hooligans and thugs. That means they believe that YCL does good for the society and takes actions on criminals. People also believe that YCL builds roads, bridges, including many other sanitary and constructive works. They seek YCL for protection from different types of criminals, the other they speak against YCL. This is a dual character, we should strongly expose it.

Whether speak about yesterdays People's Army or today's cantonment based People's Army and present YCL, the essence of both the organizations is that they are organizations of youths mobilized for achievement of the objective as determined by the party. Now YCL has become like the army of peace–phase, it is doing so.

Because of YCL's resistance, protest and exposure of the wickedness, evil deeds, oppression of the reactionaries and revisionists, they are making futile attempt to discredit it. Nepal's history is moving towards a very decisive, age making mode. The responsibility that comes once after hundreds of years has now come on the shoulder of the youths. It is historical necessity to resolutely march ahead from their own places. I want to call all the youths for the same."[17]

The view of the senior leader of CPN (Maoist) Dr. Baburam Bhattarai on YCL is as follows- " As for the question of YCL, in the Nepalese history, perhaps, it has become an established as well as popular organization both at national and international level within a shorter time.

Traditionally, YCL is a sister organization of a communist party. But YCL – Nepal was reorganized in February, 2007. Its role and character is different and developed from the traditional YCL. On the one YCL has traditional ideological as well as political character, on the other it is a changed form of People's Militia which were not encompassed in peace agreement. So, YCL is both political and military organization at a time. As it is an organization of both political and military characters, it has become an unprecedented , widened and established organization within a shorter time. There are also many wrong attitudes, thinking, confusions and curiosity about YCL -Nepal. As an organization of youths educated with communist thought and ideology, YCL has established itself among the people as a reliable friend and helper. It is its main part / side, the YCL comrades should feel proud of it. They should continuously devote themselves to the service of the people and revolution more resolutely. On the other, as the military aspect of YCL is a new and unexpected, unprecedented, it is not unnatural to have some confusion and raise doubts about it. First, despite great effort of CPN (Maoist), thousands of People's Militia could not be included in security mechanism in the process of entering into Comprehensive Peace - Agreement. But it was also indispensable to involve such high spirited, trained youth-force in people's service and security even during the interim period. Keeping in view the same fact, YCL got established nationwide with two in–one roles. YCL has become popular established force among the people, especially among the people who have been feeling nausea and bothered from senseless and corrupt character of the formally recognized police force of the state. But, since YCL could not get legitimate status by the Peace Agreement and Interim Constitution, there appeared a situation to raise questions on some activities of YCL and will remain the same further on.

In such situation, as the entire security sector is in the process of restructure, it will be much better to adjust those YCL leaders and cadres who have more military character in the security mechanism of the country and the rest in the traditional political works and regular party activities."[18]

d. In the present situation , 'Young Communist League-Nepal' – a subject of thought and curiosity among general people

Historically Young Communist League- is itself is world famous organization of high spirited youths. It has already got success to set its name and fame in the world history. In the present age of 21st century, the reemergence or reorganization of YCL in Nepal can not be helped taking it as a proud historical event. The credit for this goes to CPN (Maoist).

Needless to say that the activities of CPN (Maoist) guided YCL have become more effective, but much more complains or comments have been made on it than that. On the one, penetrated gangsters or may be agents of reactionaries are effortful to discredit YCL by committing immoral, criminal acts in the name of YCL and on the other, a feeling of fear, anarchy and terror has been created in the mind of people.

Expressions of dissatisfactions and complaint against YCL activities even by the power sharing parties and other political leaders is certainly not a good sign for the smooth politics of Nepal. So, it is felt that CPN (Maoist) needs to improve, develop, sharpen its policy, plans, programs, mobilization and implementation more responsibly.

It is imperative to harmonize and coordinate political objective, social activities, policy and programs with one another into real situation. If any person is made a victim or sufferer without any crime, one day the party itself shall have to pay the price of such mistakes. The trend of committing or causing to commit mistakes one after another and begging pardon every time for every mistake may not certainly include in responsible politics. On the whole as for YCL, it got very short time to be transformed from war time to peace process, it could not get opportunity to be acquainted with the people and influence them, it could not make proper time-schedule according to the time and situation, it legged behind to make effort to maintain good image in the national and international context, it could not be able to adapt itself with the national and international events, it could not study down to the earth reality, it legged behind to have education, patience and strict discipline including many other things. All such imperfections have stood as challenges and serious problems before YCL. So, only after achieving perfection and victory over such challenges and problems, YCL –Nepal will certainly get success o discharge its noble duty of rebuilding new Nepal and making the people free from suppression, oppression and exploitation gradually leading the nation towards everlasting peace and prosperity.

References

1 A part of the discussion with the founder General Secretary of Young Communist League-Nepal and former Nepalese Ambassador to Russia Hirannya Lal Shrestha on November 17 2007.

2 A part of discussion with the founder chairperson of YCL-Nepal and the founder principal of Siddyartha Institute Banastahli, held on November 20, 2007.

3 Ibid

4 A part of the discussion with the active member of YCL-Nepal, Prf. Giriraj Shankar Rajbans held on June 2, 2007.

5 A part of discussion with the founder General Secretary of YCL-

Nepal Hirannya Lal Shrestha

6 A part of discussion with the then active member of YCL-Nepal and present Chairperson of Nepal Majdoor Kisan Party and MP,Narayanman Bijukchhe held on March 3, 2007.

7 A part of discussion with YCL- Kathmandu in charge Pr. Bhaganban Ratna Tuladhar held on December 3, 2007.

8 Ibid

9 Ibid

10 A part of the discussion with the YCL-Nepal Founder Chairperson, Laxman Rajbamsi

11 Ibid, Discussion with Bhagaban Ratna Tuladhar

12 The Communist, 1998, Vol. 9 Year ii, p.24

13 A per of discussion with founder Chairperson of YCL-Nepal , Laxman Rajbansi,

14 Report and Statute passed by the first convention of YCL- Nepal (February 2-3, 2007.Kathmandu.

15 Excerpt from Report and Statute passed by the first National convention of YCL-Nepal, (Feb.2- 3, 2007, Katmandu, p.15.

16 Ibid, p. 31.

17 Bulletin, (mouth peace) of YCL- Nepal , year1,Issue 1 Octbur, 2007, P. 8-14.

18 Bulletin, (Mouth peace) Young Communist League- Nepal, Year 1, issue 1, October 2007, P 22.

Conclusion

Youths are the main basis or the backbone of any country. Moreover, the educated youth force can bring a total change in a country. The voice raised by the students for their own nation and against any injustice, oppression and exploitations cannot be less strong than the modern weapons, and it would not be any exaggeration to say that the role of students in the process of development and building a nation in the modern world is most important. Leaving some exceptions, the student movements are found to have played positive role. Some students movements are also found misused in some cases, and in some others, the reactionaries also are found to have used the student force against the popular government. In Burma, the student movement became the cause to topple the socialist government of UNU and bring the military rule of General Newin in power. Similarly in Indonesia, student movement did topple the government of Sukarno and placed Suharto in power. So, the students despite being a force to bring age making changes, in some cases this force is found to have been used by reactionaries to serve their vested interests. The student community does not like to write a history of any authoritarian order, rather it likes to remain a fertile-land of or research and investigation. There is no possibility of any progress nor peace nor revolt in a country where slackness and idleness takes place in the spirit if the students.

Nepal also has been successful in making itself a democratic country in the globe. Nepal had to struggle to achieve democracy since the Rana period. The Rana regime came in to existence as the result of *Kotparba* which took place due to dissension among the courtiers in the palace on September 14, 1846 and revolts against the rulers had began since then. Consciousness also had begun to grow among the people through different means. A foundation of modern education was laid along with the Rana autocratic rule, however, it was in the beginning limited within the Rana family. People's attraction towards education also began to grow. The educated youths began to criticize the policies of the Rana regime through circulation of literature, social, religious and economic reformation. Such events implanted a national sentiment in the people for the first time and, at the same time, policies to suppress these national sentiments also were adopted by the governments. The role of students in such events against the authoritarian government could be very effective.

The episodes like, *Makaiko Kheti,* the *Pustakalaya Parba* and the *Arya Samaj* movement were very effective in developing political consciousness in Nepal. Here the role of students was paramount. In fact, the Nepalese student continued movement both from inside and outside the country since the founding of *Paraja Parisad.*

The students of *Tindhara Paksala* (Sanskrit Hostel) also could not remain without being influenced by the sweeping wave of national awakening throughout the country. These students also were suffering from suppression, exploitation and oppression of the autocratic Rana government. Anti-Rana sentiment had already been rooted in the students. They used to express their dissatisfaction with the Rana government through different ways. The Rana government itself had created a discordant atmosphere between the students of English education and Sanskrit education, making the Sanskrit students feel inferior. The Sanskrit students took initiative to have the Sanskrit education improved by being inspired by the new awakening taking place among the students studying English. A new atmosphere had automatically developed among the students of English schools and colleges to think about the situation in the country in an organized way. They were acquainted with the 'Free India movement' of Indian people when they had to go to India for academic examinations. A large number of them had actively taken part in founding the Nepali National Congress and its conventions. In this way, a political culture began to develop in them. The same students led the student strike which started on the 5th of June, 1947, putting different educational demands. This strike had a great effect on the people to get their support and sympathy. This strike took a shape of student movement. The *Sanskrit* students of *Tindhara Pakshala* started the strike on the 15th of June putting four point demands for admission of 210 students in the Sanskrit hostel as usual, inclusion of geography, history, civics, social science etc. in the courses of study, establishment of a Sanskrit university and arrangement of examination in Nepal. This historical movement was the first-organized student movement of Nepal. It was not only the first student movement but also was the first to reflect the democratic spirit taking a very important place in the history of Nepal. It implanted a sense of awareness and consciousness among the people in their fight for their civil and political rights against the autocratic family rule of the Ranas. So *Jayatu Sanskritam* has a special place in the history of democratic movement of Nepal. The then Rana government was compelled to be positive towards the demands of the students by declaring a constitution for the people. It was the first constitution of Nepal (1947) which was declared by Padma Shumsher J.B.R. the then Prime Minister. Students who had taken part in the *Jayatu Sanskritam* movement facilitated the process.

Organizations are also one of the main agents to create democratic system of culture. Their main goals are to be aware for their profession and professional rights with duty of national development and thoughts. The role of students is very important in the development of modern democratic system and culture. In the beginning, the students who were studying in India worked in the Indian student organizations. Later on, the Nepalese students also realized the need of their own organization, role and importance. In the same context, the students founded Banaras Student Union following the foundation of Nepali National Congress, glorifying the dignity of students. Similarly, the Nepalese students were involved in 'Himanchal Student Union' in Calcutta. Later on, All Nepalese Indian Student Union came to exist. In this way, the Nepalese students studying in India developed a democratic culture in different ways. Before 1960, All Nepal Student Federation, Student Union, Nepal student union, Sanskrit student union as common holding all thoughts, were working as main student organizations. After the 1960 military event, an atmosphere of indecision' prevailed. All the political parties were banned, the leaders went underground. In such a situation the students had to play a role of political leaders. So, it became necessary for the students to launch struggle. In such a perilous situation, they were compelled to start movement demanding 'Free Student Union' to achieve democratic culture with free environment. In this process All Nepal National Free Student Union, Nationalist Free Student Council, and Nepal Student Union were founded. Gradually there appeared division in the left political groups as a result of to which separate student organizations also came to exist. The objectives of these student organizations were to solve the student problems by themselves, to work and remain effortful to achieve student-rights and protect them, to struggle against economic, political, and social exploitations, strengthen and promote nationality along with the creation of democratic environment and show solidarity to the international democratic movements and objectives. On the basis of the same objectives different programmes were conducted. The nature of the student force is not only to remain confined to educational problems but also to be responsible for solving every national issue. In the context of Nepal, the works that have been successful due to the active role of the students are taken to be very important. The student community does not only remain limited to the educational problems but also struggles against social, economic political and other several problems. This fact has been proved by innumerable events in the world. The current student movement of Indonesia of 1998 is an example of it.

The role of students in the democratic movement in Nepal really took off after the *Jayutu Sanskritum* Movement. During the 60's, 70s and 80s it was the campuses of Nepal that kept alive the torch of dissenting voice in Nepal; and occasionally took politics into the streets- all culminating into the revolution of 1990. The 1950 democratic revolution is taken as the result of students initiative. After the military take over in 1960, the political situation became confusing, all the political parties were banned, the leaders went underground or into exile. In such a difficult condition, the students had to play the role of political parties and leaders. So the students took initiative to create a democratic environment putting the demands for 'Free Student Union'. The students strongly protested the New Education System plan 1971 since it was not suitable to the nation. They demanded dismissal of this plan. The student movements of 1972, 1975 and 1979 have their own importance. They achieved Free Student Union through 1979 movement and changes in the new education system plan and the people got the opportunity to choose between multiparty system and reformed Panchayat system by voting in the referendum. In this, the reformed Panchayat system was declared victorious. After this event, the students did continue their movement for democracy chanting political slogans including "down with the Panchayat system," which culminated into the 1990 democracy movement for which the students had played the most important role.

Once the ban on political parties was lifted after the revolution of 1990 the campuses of Nepal ceased to be the center of political activities. There was a time when almost all the political leaders were recruited from the student front. But after 1990 the political importance of the student organization declined. Yet it did not diminish altogether. All political parties in Nepal today have their student wings; and all use the students to take politics to the streets when the need arises.

Appendices

APPENDIX - I

Questionnaires

(1) How do you define students and what do you mean by student movement?

(2) What role did the students play in the student's movement?

(3) What influence did the country's situation had on student movement?

(4) What influence did the external events have on the movement?

(5) Was there any organization/association opened by Nepalese students outside the country? How do you evaluate the cause and effect of it?

(6) When did the history of the student organizations begin?

(7) The credit to *Jayatu Sanskritam* movement goes to renaissance. Do you agree with it?

(8) *Jayatu Sanskritam* Movement is the leading and decisive point in developing solidarity, organization and student interest. Give your opinion on it.

(9) Political parties have used students as tool to serve their political interests. Students organizations are the major recruitment centre of political parties. Give your views about it.

(10) Are student organizations directed or sponsored by political parties? What reasons do you give to support your contention?

(11) In which environment and how were students organized?

(12) How did Nepalese students advance on the national and international issues?

(13) What were the demands and slogans of the students?

(14) Is there equal gender participation in the Nepalese student movement? Explain it clearly.

(15) Is there any separate struggle launched for women education, liberty and equality. How did students advance the cause of gender participation?

(16) What were the stands of students for fulfilling their rights and interests?

(17) How far is the National Guidance Act 1961 responsible for the formation of student organization?

(18) Give your comments on the New Education Plan 19&1.

(19) Whether there were other students organizations than those undermentioned.

- Chhatra Sangha (Benaras)
- All India Nepal Students Union
- Himanchal Chhatra Sngha (Calcutta)
- Sanskrit Chhatra Sngha
- All Nepal Students Federation
- Nepal Chhatra Sangha
- Student Union
- Trichandra College Union
- TU Union
- Gaurishankar Chhatra Samiti
- Gandaki Chhatra Samiti
- All Nepal Independent Students Union
  (a) ANNISU (Fifth)
  (b) ANNISU (Sixth)
  (c) Nepal Revolutionary Student Union
  (d) Nepal National Student Federation (Verma)
  (e) Nepal National Student Federation (Manandhar)
  (f) Nepal Progressive Student Union

Nepal Student Union

- Nationalist Independent Student Mandal

(20) Give details of the student organization you were involved in including name, objectives, constraints and achievements

(21) What was relations between the Government of HMG? What do you think the relationship should be like?

(22) Do you agree with the following classification of over half a century long of students movements in?
- Before 1950
- From 1960 to 1970
- From 1971 to 1975
- From 1976 to 1978
- From 1979 to 1990
- What was the relationship among the student organizations?
- What type of relations maintained between factions within a student organization?

(25) Do you appreciate the role of students in the democratic movement of Nepal? If you agree with it, give your comments in brief.

(26) If you have any other personal views.

APPENDIX - II

One day in July 1905, Madhab Raj Joshi, follower of Aryasamaj and father of Sukra Raj Shastri, was called to the court of King Prithvi Bir Bikram Shah and Maharaja Chandra Shamsher for a discourse. During the courst of discourse, he called the sun 'a watch' and the Pashupatinath Temple 'a stone.' The royal priest beat him until he had bruises all over his body and his tunic was tained with blood. He then had him taken round the city and imprisoned. Shukra Raj Shastri was studying in class five then. In the pretext that the family members of an imprisoned person lost caste, all the students of the Durbar high school stopped drinking water touched by Shukra Raj Shastri and his brother.

They were not even allowed to touch water touched by Shukra Raj Shastri and his brother. They were not even allowed to touch the water jars filled with drinking water. They continued to study in the school enduring the insult. But Head Master Batuk Krishna expelled them from school after some time.

A Panjabi teacher called Gurudayal Singh was also present at the court to listen to the discourse. He was banished from Nepal for his support to Madhab Raj Joshi in the discourse. But he could not reach Punjab.

Soruce: Bhuvan Lal Pradhan, Kathmandu.

APPENDIX - III

"The reason of my presence at this function is that it is the anniversary of my august father Commander In-Chief Dhir Shamsher Jung Bahadur Rana and that I also once was a student of this school. When we studied here the school was just opened for ordinary people. The founder of this school was my father. It was not easy at that time to find teachers. Even the pilgrims of *Shivratri* had to be requested to work as teachers. It is well known to all how my father made Master Kalinath and Swami Purnananda Giri to work as teachers in this school. We have seen it grow into adulthood from the time when it was established in our own house and class rooms had been built in the eastern court yard of our palace.

It is appreciable that our education department has been emphasizing industrial education realizing the inadequacy of the higher education. ... it will be realized if we keep on trying. Rome was not built in a day.

The value of mother tongue is great. it is a pleasure to see that the people's interest is growing towards it. In order to reward those who write good books in vernacular language, I have sanctioned three thousand rupees to be disbursed in the director general's discretion.

The ten thousand rupees I have given earlier and the ... annual contribution of Rs. 500 each year seems adequate for the English language lbirary.

The arrangement for health check-up for the students has also produced good result ... I will also allocate necessary funds for the provision of food to those students who do not get adequate food in their houses ... and to buy books for those who cannot afford to buy them.

I am happy to know that the arrangement to provide six hundred rupees as a reward to talented students each year has also produced good result.

In view of the growing crowd of students, separate schools were opened in Patan and Bhaktapur. Sections were also added to the classes of this school also ... has given approval to private school. It is expected to lessen the pressure of the students.

I am happy that Major General Mrigendra Shamsher has run the affairs of the education department satisfactorily. I am happy to hear the satisfactory performance of the employees of this department. As the type of training students receive effects them throughout their lives, I hope that all the professors, teachers, and pundits teaching in this school have been shouldering their responsibility of leading the students to a right path.

Dear, student! I have to say something to you also. You students of this school shall be citizens of this country tomorrow. You should not forget the service of the country letting yourself to become proud of the skill and education you have received. The skill you have learnt is not only for you. It is also for the betterment of your country. Do not ever think that once you have learnt foreign language and skill through it, you have to follow the ways of a understands the dignity, situation and practices of this country ...

Source: Bhuvan Lal Pradhan, Kathmandu.

APPENDIX - IV

B.p.'s Appeal As Published In The Search Light

India won independence from British colonial rule in August 1947. Perceiving an imminent change in India B.P. thought that it was now possible to do something for his country also. He, therefore, published an appeal in the Search Light on October 4, 1946. It reads: "The British rule is coming to an end in India soon. The Rana regime which has existed in its support shall be weakened a little. It will therefore not be so difficult for us to overthrow it. For this, let us organize and form a party to facilitate our march ahead. The wave of time waits for no one. I appeal to all the brothers and sisters of our country to do something listening to the voice of the time."

Source: Bhuvan Lal Pradhan, Kathmandu.

APPENDIX - V

28 March, 1960

At 6.45 this morning, Bishweswor Prasad Koirala gave a thirty minutes interview to the representatives of *Himanchal Chhatra Sangh*. The delegatio of the *Himanchal Chhatra Sangh* was as follows:

Mr. J.P. Ale, President; Mr. Prithvi Raj Giri, General Secretary; Mr. Renu Kumar thapa, Cashier, Ms. Kanti Pakhrin, Vice-president; Ms. Sundhara Thapa, Assistant Secretary; Ms Indira Pradhan, Women member of the executive committee and Mr. nabindra Prasad Bantawa.

The interview took place at Kanak building at appointed time. There were many other people waiting for interview. But we were given the first priority. As soon as we entered, the Prime Minister showed his curiosity to learn about the background of the Himanchal *Chhatra Sangh*. The chief secretary of the Sangh Prithvi Raj Giri gave a short description of its background and said that the association was not new. It was established 31 years ago and was not sectarian. It had worked for the promotion of brotherhood in association with other social organization.

After that Mr. Giri asked the first question with the Prime Minister on behalf of the association. Mr. Prime Minister can the Nepalese government give us any facilities so that we Nepalese in India, who are in the minority, may get some opportunity to acquire higher education?

The Prime Minister replied that he could not give any assurance on this right now because the Nepalese living in Nepal would be the first claimants of such facilities. On this question Mr. Giri further said that since Nepal was also their motherland, they had the rights to expect these facilities. "If we were no Nepalese we would not have come to Nepal to moan about our plight. We therefore hope that you will think about it seriously," he said. The Prime Minister kept quiet on this.

Mr. Giri asked another question to the Prime Minister. He said that the educated Nepalese people were not getting job even after acquiring good education and asked if the Nepalese government could give them an opportunity for moral and material development by giving employment.

The Prime Minister asked him to send a list of those looking for employment but reminded that these people should have the desire to serve the motherland and should have high sense of renunciation and sacrifice. He also said that Nepal was a poor country and it could not afford to pay according to their qualification.

Mr. Giri asked the third question. Would you please, Prime Minister pay an official visit to the places where overseas Nepalese are staying? It would provide you an opportunity to hear the entreaty of those people.

The Prime Minister assured that he would try to do so.

Mr. Thapa asked the fourth question on behalf of the Sangh Mr. Prime Minister, What is the Nepalese government's view to the overseas Nepalese people?

Nepal looks at them sympathetically, He replied-

Mr. Giri asked the fifth question on behalf of the Sangh. Mr. Prime Minister the Young Gorkha Association in its petition, had demanded a Nepali medium school. This is a genuine demand of almost all the Nepalese. I also want to reiterate this demand on behalf of the Sangh. We hope that honourable Prime Minister will take appropriate steps to fulfill this demand.

He gave a positive reply to this question.

Mr. Thapa asked the sixth question on behalf of the Sangh. Mr. prime Minister a number of non-Nepalese are reported to be winning scholarship under the Colombo Plan. But the overseas Nepalese are being deprived of the facilities though they are bonafide Nepalese.

In reply to this question he said that the state of affairs of the country was not being run properly. As a result such flaws could appear now and then. With the introduction of a new change these anomalies would be corrected.

After that Mr. Giri demanded with the Prime Minister that the Nepalese language should be included in the list of major languages included in the Indian constitution. Mr. Giri also said that the Nepalese would make progress if students from Darjeeling would be allotted quota for study of engineering course as they were being allotted to study medical course. He also sought the Prime Minister's advice on the issue.

The Prime Minister said that he would think about it if they would make a petition in writing.

Finally Mr. Giri requested the Prime Minister for a felicitation message for the upcoming issue of Himanchal magazine.

The Prime Minister promptly wrote a felicitation for the magazine. We asked leave with the Prime Minister highly satisfied with our interview.

Source: Annual Himanchal Magazine from 1964-65.

APPENDIX - VI

Constitution of Nepal National Students' Federation

Clause-1

Name: The name of this organization shall be Nepal National Students' Federation. In short it shall be called NNSF. Unless the subject or context requires otherwise, the NNFS may be referred to as federation in other parts of the constitution.

Clause-2

Central Office: Generally, the office of the Federation shall be in Kathmandu. It may, however, be shifted to other places if need be.

Clause-3

(a) The flag of the Federation shall be as follows: There shall be an open book on the map of Nepal drawn in the red background and a heptagonal star at the north-west corner of the flag. The colour of countour of the map, book and the star shall be white.

(b) The measurement of the flag shall be 2 ′ 3.

© Definition of the flag: The red colour of the flag indicates revolutionary progressive character of the federation. White colour symbolizes peace. The book symbolizes knowledge and the star symbolizes peace, democracy and social progress.

Clause-4

Objective:

(a) To instill the students with a sense of world peace, democracy, social progress and patriotism.

(b) To propagate the ideals of national independence and sovereignty and to try to translate these ideals into practice.

(c) To struggle for the achievement of cheap, accessible, scientific and democratic educational system.

(d) To struggle for the basic rights of the students and mobilize them for the safeguard of these rights.

(e) To orient the students' movement toward national democracy linking it with the movement of the Nepalese people for democratic restoration.

(f) To fight against sectarianism parochialism, religious fanaticism, class superiority and all kinds of privileges that obstruct the development and progress of the society.

(g) To struggle for the preservation of national culture and arts.

(h) To foster a healthy and close relationship among the teachers and the students.

(i) To inspire the Nepalese students to foster the friendly solidarity with the youths and students of the world against imperialism, colonialism, neocolonialism, apartheid and racism.

Clause-5

(a) Membership: All the students studying in colleges and schools who subscribe to the constitution, objectives, policies and programmes irrespective of religion, race and sex.

(b) Every person willing to be its member shall have to fill up a form which shall be as follows: I fully subscribe to the objectives and programmes of NNFS and I want to be a member of this organization. I will fully abide by the constitution of the organization.

(c) A member of the Federation shall have to pay a sum of three rupees annually as a levy of 25 pice per month.

(d) The membership is subject to renewal each year.

(e) The membership shall expire after two years a student ceases his studies.

(f) A member of the Federation shall not be permitted to become a member of other students' organization.

(g) A student shall have to be 12 years a class six student to acquire the membership of the Federation.

Clause-6

Rights and duties of a member:

Sub-clause-1, duties:

(a) To a abide by the constitution and programme of the Federation.

(b) To discharge the duties as assigned by the Federation.

(c) To be prepared at all times to discharge the duty assigned with the best interest of the Federation in mind.

(d) The instruction of higher committees and majority decisions shall have to be carried out.

Sub-clause-2, rights:

(a) Right for candidacy at all level of committees of the Federation.

(b) Right to be or elect representative for all level of conferences of the Federation.

(c) Right to give his opinion in forming the tactics, goals and programmes of the Federation.

(d) Right to discuss on documents, decisions and circulars and to give suggestions.

(e) Right to participate in delegations of the Federation and the discussions and seminars held by the Federation.

Clause-7

Structure of the organization:

Sub-clause-1, National conference:

(a) The national conference of the Federation shall be generally held once in two years. The national conference shall be the highest and most powerful agency. Its decision on policies and programmes shall be final.

(b) The national assembly shall be composed of the members of the central committee, district representatives, observers and guests. The district representatives shall be designated by the central committee.

(c) Observers and guests shall have the right to participate in discussion, give suggestions and offer amendment. But they will have no right to vote.

(d) The national assembly shall elect the members of the central committee as required.

(e) A special national conference may also be held if the central committee thinks it necessary.

Sub-clause-2, Central Committee

(a) The central committee shall be the highest level of the Federation in the intervening period of two national conferences. During this period, the decisions of the central committee shall be final.

(b) The main responsibility of executing the policies, instructions and programmes endorsed by the National congress shall rest on the Central committee.

(c) This committee shall organize the national congress, fix the number of representatives and date of the congress. This committee shall also be responsible for drafting and presenting documents in the national congress.

(d) If need be, this committee shall have the right to nominate one fourth of the members of the central committee from among ordinary members.

(e) This committee shall have the right to establish international relation and send representatives. The central committee shall elect the central office bearers and central secretariat.

(f) The Central committee shall have to hold its meeting once in six months.

(g) If need be, the central committee shall have the right to hold an extended meeting of the central committee and fix its numbers.

Sub-clause-3

(a) The district assembly shall elect the district committee.

(b) The district committee shall work according to the condition of the district under the decisions of the central agencies and the decisions of the district council.

(c) The district committee should hold its district congress at least once in a year.

(d) The district committee shall have to elect the district secretariat and the representatives for the national congress.

(e) The meeting of the district committee should be held once in two months.

Sub-clause-4, Regional committee

(a) In order to expand organization in a certain place the central committee shall have the necessary office bearers.

(b) The regional congress shall have the rights to form the regional committee with necessary office bearers.

(c) The regional committee shall have to work in accordance with the decision of the central body and the instruction of the regional congress.

(d) The Central committee shall define the rights and functions of the regional committee.

Sub-clauses-5, Branch and branch committee

(a) All the members in an educational institution shall be members of a branch.

(b) A branch shall propagate all the higher level decisions among the students and try to bring as many students as possible under the banner of the Federation.

(c) The general assembly of entire members shall have to take place twice a year.

(d) It shall have the responsibility to propagate all the decisions, objectives and programmes of the Federation among the students.

(e) If need be, each branch shall have the rights to form as many branch committees under it as possible.

(f) The branch committee shall have the rights of renewing membership and raise levey.

(g) A branch committee shall be the basic and primary committee of the Federation.

Clause-8

Office bearers, duties and functions;

Sub-clause-1, Office bearers

(a) The central committee shall elect from among itself office bearers such as chair person, general secretary, secretary and cashier.

(b) The chairperson shall chair the meeting of the committee.

(c) The chairperson, general secretary shall be the chief spokesman and spokesman of the federation.

(d) The chairperson shall have to present report on the tactic of the Federation by making an evaluation of national and international situation.

(e) The vice-president shall discharge all the functions of the president at his absence.

(f) The general secretary shall call the meeting in consultation with the president. He can, however, call the meeting himself if situation does not permit consultation with the president.

(g) The general secretary shall be entirely responsible for organizational activities.

(h) The secretary shall discharge all the functions of the general secretary at his absence.

(i) The cashier shall control the central funds of the party. He shall be responsible for maintaining the balance sheet.

Sub-clause-2, Central secretariat

(a) The central committee shall elect a central secretariat from among itself. It may include the central president, general secretary, cashier and other central members as needed.

It is responsible for conducting day to day functions and other activities under the guidance of the central committee when it is not in session.

Sub-clause-3, District secretariat

(a) The district committee shall elect the members of the district secretariat from among itself. it may include the district chairman, vice-chairman, secretary, deputy-secretary, cashier and the secretary of the concerned department it need be. The district committee shall define the duties and functions of each of the members.

(b) The district chairman shall chair the meeting.

(c) The vice-chairman shall be responsible for discharging all the functions of the chairman at his absence.

(d) The secretary shall call the meeting in consultation with the chairman. he has to submit an organizational report at the meeting.

(e) The chairman shall be responsible for creating district funds and maintaining the balance sheet.

Clause-9

Quorum

(a) A simple majority of the committee members shall be required to establish quorum at all levels.

(b) The decisions taken by the majority required by the quorum shall be valid decisions of the Federation.

Clause-10

Disciplinary action and expulsion

Sub-clause-1, disciplinary action

(a) Any member of the committee shall be subject to clarification, criticism, reprimand and expulsion if they are found guilty of the following conduct.

(b) If they act against the constitution, policies, programmes and objectives of the federation.

(c) If they keep passive and fail to assist the federation.

(d) If he or she is found to be corrupt and immoral.

(e) If he or she is found to be undisciplined.

A simple majority of a committee concerned shall have the right to take disciplinary action against the defaulting member of the committee. The action against the district committee and as office bearers shall be subject to the approval of the central secretariat.

Sub-clause-2, Expulsion

The members of the committees shall be subject to expulsion in the following situation:

(a) If found to be guilty of the act mentioned in Clause-5 (a).

(b) If the motion for expulsion of a member is approved by a simple majority of a committee.

(c) If the resignation given by a member of a committee is approved by the majority of the committee. The expelled or suspended members, however, shall have the right to defend themselves.

(d) If a member is absent in consecutive three meetings of the committee in which he is a member.

Clause-11

Vacancy and fulfillment of a post

If a post of the Federation falls vacant for any reason, it has to be filled by a simple majority of the committee concerned.

Clause-12

Funds

(a) A fund shall be created out of the fees, donation, and the amount raised from cultural and sports programmes.

(b) The fund shall be operated by the cashier or the person specified by the concerned committee at the absence of the former.

(c) If discrepancies are found in the income and expenditure, the responsible person shall be reprimanded, suspended or expelled. But the action shall be taken only by a competent authority.

Clause-13

Rule

Apart from this constitution, the central committee shall enact rules and regulation in the subjects deemed necessary.

Clause-14

Amendment

The central committee shall have the right to amend, repeal or suspend any clause of this constitution by a simple majority. It will be subject to approval by the national assembly.

Clause-15

Enforcement of the constitution

The constitution shall have immediate effect

It is compulsory for the district committees to keep a copy of this constitution

The Central Secretariat
NNSF

Soruce: Nepal National Students' Federation, Kathmandu.

APPENDIX - VII

Nepal Revolutionary Student Union

(Reports and Constitution endorsed by the 4th National Conference, 1990)

The wave of democratic changes that took place in the socialist countries made necessary to have improvement in socialism. This new trend has forced the socialist countries and socialism itself to think in a new way.

This conference of the union has further heightened its glorious history at the present world situation in which the socialist movement is weakening and the capitalist movement is overpowering.

1. **Name:**

   Name of this organization shall be "Nepal Revolutionary Student Union." In short it shall be called "Mekra. VI. Sang." In English 'Nepal Revolutionary Student Union (NRSU).

2. **Flag:**

   A map of Nepal with white border lies slanted at the south east corner on red background and it the west-north corner lies five conned white star, and an open pen lies pointing north-west from south-east.

3. **Objective:**

   (a) To achieve rights and interests of the student community and remain effortful to project them.

   (b) To move the students, genuine citizens, of the nation by implanting scientific and democratic sentiment in them campaigning against the superstitions, racial discrimination, social evils, the feudal culture and backwardness.

   (c) To take part in the struggle for the protection of freedom and sovereignty of the nation.

   (d) To help in the justiceable struggle of the people of different class and community.

(e) To give moral support to the just struggle of outside suppression of the people of other nations upholding the sentiment of proletariat internationalism.

(f) To institutionalize the multiparty system achieved through the historic democracy movement.

(g) To remain struggling to achieve socialism, and to uphold the Marxism, Leninism, and Mao Tes Tung thought as guidelines for such struggle.

4. Membership:

(a) Any left and progressive Nepalese student studying in educational institutions either inside or outside the country can take membership of the this union only accepting the union's constitution and programme and paying Rs. 1.

Generally, the student's membership shall be valid up to one year more after his final examination finishes.

(b) The primary union committee shall provide membership after necessary investigation.

(c) The membership shall be renewed once every year.

(d) In the case of being arrested or imprisoned for any charges while in the course of struggle for the rights and interests of the student community, the membership shall remain valid.

5. Rights and Duties:

(a) Ordinary member of the union shall have the rights to elect leadership and be elected obeying the principle and policy of the organization.

(b) All the members shall be effortful to implement the programmes and objectives mentioned in the constitution.

(c) All the members shall have to follow the policy of democratic centralism within the organization.

(d) All the members shall have to abide by the discipline and responsibility of the organization.

6. Disqualifications:

(a) The students who do not fulfill the conditions

mentioned under the clause 4 and 5 shall not be qualified for membership.

7. Organizational Policy:

(a) The minority shall have to abide by the majority decisions. But the minority side shall have rights to put forth the views in the meetings.

(b) Lower organizations shall be subjected to the higher organizations.

(c) Individual shall be subjected to the organization.

(d) The upper organization shall notify about policies, decisions and give direction to the lower organizations.

(e) Any committee or any member of the committees shall have the rights to suggest to and comment on the organization of any member of any committee.

8. Local Committee:

(a) The union's primary committee shall be the lower unit of the organization.

(b) The units of schools, campuses, university, or any ward or village shall be the primary committees.

(c) Primary committee can be formed in any place where there are at least 5 members.

(d) Ward committee shall be organized by a gathering of all the units of the total ward area.

(e) Ward committee shall be formed comprising at least 5 members not exceeding to 10.

(f) Under the guidance and knowledge of the district level committee, separate conventions of ward units and primary committees shall reorganize the committee once a year.

(g) Meeting of the primary committees and ward units shall have to be held at least once a month. If needed, it can be held at any time and more than once.

The primary committee shall have to send its report to the ward unit every month, and the ward units shall have to send monthly report to the village or city unit committee every month.

(h) Every ward or primary committee shall have to send 50% levy collected from the members to the village or city committee.

9. Village or City Committee:

(a) The upper level committee to command the ward unit shall be the city or village committee.

(b) In any village or city area, if there are not more than 9 members, village or city preparatory committee can be formed.

(c) The village or city committee shall be formed by a conference of the representatives of schools, colleges, and primary committees of the city or village area.

(d) There shall be 10-15 members in the village or city committee.

(e) A chairman, a deputy chairman, a secretary, an assistant secretary and a treasurer shall be elected from among the members of the village or city committee to conduct, supervise and lead all the works.

(f) Meeting of the village or city committee must be held once a month, if needed the meetings can be called for more than once.

(g) The village or city committees must send reports with suggestions once every two months.

(h) 50% of the collected membership levy and donation must be sent to the district committee regularly

9. Duties of the local Organizations:

(a) All the decisions made by district, village or city committees must be implemented.

(b) 50% of the collected amount (levy) and progress report must be sent to the upper level committees regularly.

(c) An intimate relation with different classes and communities must be kept and made them understand the unions policy and principle.

(d) Studying and teaching of Marxism, Leninism and Mao Tse Tung thought and learning of different new changes and current development must be carried on.

(e) All the student problems must be analyzed on the basis of Marxist and Leninist approach and be solved.

10. District Committee:

(a) The upper committee of the village or city committee shall be the district committee.

(b) In any district where there are less than 50 members, a temporary district committee shall be formed.

(c) Secretary:

(i) To call committees meetings, conduct meetings and hold daily responsibilities of the office works according to the direction for the chairman.

(ii) To keep all the records of works of the executive committee and present reports at the session on behalf of the committee.

(iii) To deal in writing from the part of the committee.

(d) Co-secretary:

Co-secretary shall work in the absence of secretary.

(e) Treasurer:

(i) Treasury of the union shall remain under the control of treasurer including the president (chairman).

(ii) All the account must be kept fair.

(iii) The treasurer can spend certain amount of the union's fund for necessary works of the union, on condition approved by the concerned committee.

(f) Members:

The members shall have to do or make do any work assigned by the executive committee.

16. Delegates and Observers:

(a) Except the primary convention of the union, in all the conventions delegates and observers shall be called to take part.

(b) The observers shall have the equal rights to the delegates to take part in discussions on any issue or subject, but the observers shall not have the rights of voting.

(c) The central committee has the rights to the numbers of delegates and observers for any conference.

17. Disciplinary Action:

The members of the "Nepal Revolutionary Student Union" shall have to work favour of the people and the nation strictly abiding the limit of discipline, honesty and loyalty to the union. If any member of the union exhibits his character as mentioned below shall be subjected to disciplinary action or be expelled by the decision of the two third majority of the central committee or concerned committee.

(a) If constitution, rules and programmes are violated.

(b) If opposed to the organization, opened paralel organization, and leaked the secrecy.

(c) In other cases than mentioned above if committed minor mistakes against the organization, the organization shall take clarification, suspension of membership and warning shall be given.

(d) But the concerned members of member shall not be deprived of the rights to give clarification to the upper level committee.

17. Vacancy and Filling up the Posts:

(a) The posts shall be vacant in case of resignation.

(b) One year after passing the examination of the intended level, the membership shall automatically expire.

(c) If expelled by the organization as punishment or in case of death.

(d) The vacant position shall be filled by the upper levelf committee picking up any of the lower level committee post holders on the basis of activeness, and efficiency.

19. Quorum:

(a) The presence of 51% of the total number of members is compulsory for any ordinary meeting. If the necessary number of the members are not present at the first meeting, second meeting shall have to be called, if the quorum is not met in the second, meeting shall be counted as quorum number.

(b) If any decision is to be made, simple majority can pass it.

20. Accounts:

(a) All the committees of the unions shall have to clear the account once three months and annual clearance once a year.

(b) The fund of all the committees shall be audited by upper level committee every year.

21. Amendment of Constitution:

Two third majority of national conference can change, add or remove any clause of the constitution.

22. Coat of the Office of the Union:

The official coat of NRSU shall be full double-circled and the outer circle is the simple line circle and the inner circle shall be curbline circle. On the upper side of the half circle lies Nepal Revolutionary Student Union' in Nepali and on the lower half of the circle "Nepal Revolutionary Student Union lies in English. There lies a five conned stars on each side in between the Nepali and English name and at the center of the coat, there lies the flag in the design as mentioned in the constitution.

Source: Nepal Revolutionary Student Union, Kathmandu.

APPENDIX - VIII

A Protest Rally At The Embassy of Pakistan in Kathmandu

Nepal Progressive Student Union (NPSU) staged a protest rally against the ruthless suppression of democratic movement of Pakistani people and students by the military dictator Zia Ul Hak at the Pakistan Embassy in Kathmandu chanting the slogans, "down with the military dictator!, Pakistanese people must be granted civil rights!, restore democracy in Pakistani students!." In support of Pakistani people, for the restoration of democracy, the Nepalese students organized protest programmes in different campuses including protest campaigns.

Protesters towards Pak Embassy

NPSU

Honorable Ambassador

Embassy of Pakistan, Kathmandu

Honorable Ambassador

The Protest Letter is as follows:

Embassy of Pakistan, Kathmandu

To Your Honour,

We, the Nepalese students wish to make your honour know that we have come to streets protesting against the cruel acts of killing of the popularly elected prime minister of Pakistan, J.A. Bhutto by the military dictator Zia Ul Hak in July 1977 taking over the constitutional and democratically elected government, snatching all the civil rights of the Pakistani people and imposition of military dictatorship on them; and we show our profound solidarity to the Pakistani people who are suffering the crelty of the military dictatorship.

The glorious descriptions of the brave and difficult struggles of the Pakistani people for the achievement of democratic rights have remained in golden letters in the history of the world. We are confident that the Pakistani people do not like to live in the fetters under the Zia Ul Hak's barbarous rule of middle age in the name of Islam. The "People's movement for the restoration of civil rights" currently going on in Pakistan has represented the just and sacred wish of the Pakistani people, we, the Nepalese students offer hearty congratulation to the initiator of this movement, the Pakistani students and the people, we reiterate our profound support.

It is very regretable to inhumanly suppress the movement of the Pakistani people and students for the civil rights and civil government instead of restoring tfeir civil rights in Pakistan.

Arresting of agitating students, thousands of ordinary people political workers and leaders including Miss Benazir Bhutto and Khan Abdul Gafar, firing on the peaceful mass rally, killing hundreds of peaceful students and general people, ae the cruelest actions which are more than the Nazi regime and have made the human beings feel shame the world over.

We strongly protest and condemn the suppression and oppression led by the military dictator of Pakistan.

Military dictatorship is the thing which has been already unaccepted many times by the Pakistani people. It is not anything more than an adventurism to impose this kind of rule on the Pakistani people again. So, we strongly demand for the restoration of democracy and civil rights and freedom by immediately scraping the military rule.

On behalf of all the Nepalese Students
Porna Bahadur Karki
President
Nepal Progressive Student Union
Central Committee

Source: Nepal Progressive Student Union, Central Committee, Mul Prabaha, Bulletin No. 5,

APPENDIX - IX

The Historical Material

The constitution of the Sanskrit Student Union is an important historical matter. It clarifies the reality of Sanskrit Student Union.

Sanskrit Student Union (Nepal)

Constitution-

(Approved by the first historical congress held in Kathmandu in 1955)

Publisher:

Sanskrit Student union, Central Office, 11/765, Tyod, Kathmandu, Nepal

Constitution of Sanskrit Student Union (Nepal)

Clause-1

This organization shall bear the name 'Nepal Sanskrit Student Union (Nepal).' Its central office shall locate in Kathmandu.

Clause-2

Its symbol shall be a hexagon on green background.

Clause-3 Objectives:

(a) Its objective shall be to try to change the existing education system to be useful to the nation and to make the Sanskrit education contextual to the time and modernize it.

(b) To try to produce patriotic students by developing a positive and common sentiment in them along with promotion of their physical, mental, intellectual, social, political and economic condition.

(c) To discharge the duties of the Nepalese students without forgetting the responsibilities along with the creative works as far as they are possible to be done.

(d) To raise appropriate steps and strengthen democratic principle at the time when the independence of the country get at danger and the civil rights of the people are being confiscated.

Clause-4 (Membership):

(a) Any student completing the qualification of primary education and studying in any Sanskrit school, university or privately learning Sanskrit loving student or girl student can obtain membership of this organization.

(b) To obtain membership of the organization, 50 paisa NR, or 20 Paisa I.C. shall have to be paid every year.

(c) The students who have completed education or passed last examination of their intended level also shall be qualified to obtain membership for this organization for two years.

Clause-5 (General Assembly, Parliament):

(a) An executive committee and a general assembly (parliament) shall be created to conduct this organization.

(b) Members of the general assembly (Parliament) shall be elected representing all the sectors or departments by a congress.

(c) The number of the members of the parliament (assembly) shall be from 25 to 100.

(d) The session of the assembly shall take place once a year, and if necessary, it may be called many times.

(e) Chairman of the assembly shall be elected by the members of the assembly.

(f) The central executive committee shall be responsible to the assembly.

(g) President of the executive committee also shall be elected by the assembly.

(h) In extraordinary situation, in case the chairman does not call the session of the assembly, one-third of the assembly members can call the session giving reasons, stating the subject with their signature.

(i) The assembly (Parliament) shall appoint three-member account committee to inspect the annual record of income and expenditure of the organization.

Clause-5

(a) (Central Executive Committee):

(a) Central executive committee shall be formed by the president elected by the assembly picking from every sector as far as practicable and possible.

(b) The members of the central executive committee shall be appointed every year.

(c) The president shall departmentalize works of the central committee members taking suggestions from them.

(d) The members of the departments can be the members only of the central assembly.

(e) The members of the executive committee shall consist of up to 15 from 7 including executive committee chairman, deputy chairman, general secretary treasurer and department secretaries.

(f) The meeting of the executive committee shall be held once every four months, and it needed, it can be held at any time.

(g) The executive committee can make necessary rules and regulation under the constitution at the time even when there is no assembly session.

(h) The central Committee shall have the full rights to take reasonable disciplinary action on any member whoever goes against the organization.

(i) If deputies are to be sent anywhere representing this organization, the central committee shall take decision on the matter.

(b) President:

(a) The president (chairman) elected by the assembly shall be responsible to the assembly.

(b) The president (chairman) shall have the rights to vote only if there appeared equal votes between any two sides as deciding vote.

(c) The president (chairman) suggests to secretary general to call central executive meeting.

(d) He shall supervise all the works and affairs of the central committee.

Vice-President

(e) To conduct works of president in the absence of president.

(f) To help president in his work.

General Secretary

(g) To call assembly meeting at required times taking provision from president.

(h) To prepare reports of the organization.

(i) To exchange letters on behalf of the organization and supervise works and procedures of different departments shall be the duty of the general secretary.

Treasurer

(j) To keep clear account of income and expenditure of the organization.

(k) If there is more than 200 rupees, to keep this amount in bank in his own name or in the name of the president on behalf of the organization.

(l) To give expense for any work of the organization not acceding more than 100 rupees according to the permission of the president or the general secretary.

(m) The treasurer shall have the rights to spend up to NRs. or I.C. 25 if needed for the works of the organization.

Clause-6, Departments

(a) Units or (departments) of the Sanskrit Student Union can locate at anywhere in the Kingdom of Nepal.

(b) Every unit shall have the rights to formulate local rules and regulations, but these shall not be contrary to the objective, policy, constitution and principle of the organization.

(c) In every region (the chief district officer's unit), there shall be unit office and under the direction of this unit other sub-units may be established in necessary locations.

(d) All the units and sub-units shall have to send half of the total amount of the levy and one fourth of the sub-levy to the central office of the organization.

(e) All the Units and sub-units shall have to accept any decision of the central committee in a disciplined way, and should not go against the decisions, any dissatisfactions should be filled or presented to the council's session.

(f) The central committee should be notified about the establishment of units or sub-units and get certificate from the central committee.

(g) All the units or sub-units shall have to show any account, or bills if the deputies of the central committee sent to supervise annual account want to look any.

(h) All the units or sub-units shall have the rights to hold district level conventions, demand solution of any local problems, to convice for demands, to organize and to stage struggle.

(i) The central committee shall give appropriate help and decision if there appear difficulties and dissension in the units or sub-units.

(j) The unit's organizational shape and procedure shall be in consonance with the central committee and the district level conference shall be held once a year.

(k) All the units or sub-units shall have to present their annual report at every annual session of the council or conference and at any time if the central committee asks for.

Clause-7, Congress

(a) Deputies for the congress shall be selected from every region of the kingdom on the proportional basis of the number of the members of the organization.

(b) The congress can be held if two thirds of the deputies of the members of Sanskrit Student Union are present.

(c) The congress shall elect council's members representing all regions for 3 years.

(d) The congress shall be held once every in three years, and if needed it can be held at any and many times.

(e) The meeting of the congress can be held in the central office or anywhere in the unit's office as needed.

(f) Notice for congress should be disseminated to all the members of the central committee and units before 2 months of the scheduled date as far as practicable.

(g) The objective and policy of the 'Sanskrit Student Union' shall be adopted by the congress, apart from this, the council session shall have the rights to formulate all the practical programmes, rules and regulations.

(h) The congress meeting shall be called by the central executive committee at appropriate time.

(i) The units also can call the congress taking permission of the central committee.

(j) To call for holding congress without the approval of central committee, permission of more than half of the total number of the units.

(k) In case any seat or any member of the assembly falls vacant, the seat shall be fulfilled by election in the same region the elected members shall be nominated as member of the assembly by the assembly chairman.

Clause-8, Rights and Duties of the Ordinary Members

(a) All the ordinary members of the organization shall have the duty to obey every direction and order of the central committee.

(b) All the ordinary members shall have the rights to elect representative or be elected from their respective region.

(c) Any member of the organization shall not have the right to disseminate or propagate against the organization or to the loss of the organization.

Clause-9, Constitution Amendment

(a) If more than half of the number of the assembly members bring forth a written proposal for the amendment of any clauses of the constitution, wide discussion shall be held on it, and if more than two-third of the assembly members support it, the clauses shall get amendment.

(b) If proposal for amendment of any clause of the constitution is put forth in the assembly by more than half of the units of the 'Sanskrit Student Union' and the proposal is supported by more than half of the assembly members, the clause shall be amended.

(c) Any member of the assembly who remains absent without any reason for three sessions consecutively, the member shall be automatically expelled.

(d) One-third of the assembly members can file no confidence motion against the assembly chairman, if the motion is supported by two third of assembly members, the chairman loses guides the post.

(e) One third of the assembly members shall be considered simple majority, and simple majority for executive committee shall be working quorum.

(f) The members of the Sanskrit Student Union shall not be allowed to get membership of any other student organizations.

(g) Any complains of the sub-units shall be looked by unit, if the unit does not accept, central committee shall look it.

The rules related to the units endorsed by the Ist conference of the central committee of the Sanskrit Student Union, held since 20th of July.

(a) The elections for the district level-convention of all the district units shall be handled by a commissner appointed by the central committee, and all the units shall have to notify the central committee about the district convention one month previously.

(b) The unit of the district in which the central committee office is located shall be fully commanded by the central committee and in this unit, two central members shall be included.

(c) If there are atleast 25 members of the 'Sanskrit Student Union' in any area and at the differences of one 'Koshi' length, a sub-unit can be founded.

(d) Such sub-units shall work under the command of local unit.

- From the Constitution of the Sanskrit Student Union.

Source: Bhupahari Poudel, Historical Matters of the Sanskrit Student Hostel, Kathmandu Purna Prakash Nepal 'Yatri,' 1991 A.D.

APPENDIX - X

NEPAL STUDENTS UNION 1970

AMENDED CONSTITUTION - 1991

Constitution of the Nepal Students Union

(Amended by the Sixth Convention 1991)

Clause 1: Name

(a) This organization shall bear the name "Nepal Students Union-1970"

(b) This shall be abbreviated as NSU.

(c) The headquarters of the Union shall be based in Kathmandu.

Clause 2: Symbol

(a) The flag of the Nepal Students Union shall include a pen and a fire torch inside a white circle on red background.

(b)

(i) The green coloured pen shall face left wards from right.

(ii) The torch with a red flame and a green stick shall face rightwards from left.

Clause 3:

The central committee shall have the right to formulate laws and by laws so far as they do not contradict with this constitution of the union.

Clause 4: Ideals

The ideals of the Nepal Students Union are student unity, nationalism and socialism.

Clause 5: Objectives

With an objective of resolving the student's problems themselves, they shall be

(a) To make aware and active towards their rights and duty.

(b) To developed true nationalism.

(c) To inspire for the preservation, promotion and development of democratic and fundamental rights.

(d) To enable them to make efforts for the promotion and consolidation of the multiparty democratic system reinstated by a popular movement.

(e) To encourage militancy against economic and social exploitations existing in the society.

(f) To maintain relations with various organizations that represent similar objectives, concepts and beliefs.

(g) To inspire the students who have faith in the objectives and principles of the NSU and are studying abroad, to form an organization of Nepalese students in accordance with the ideals of NSU.

(h) To make efforts in bringing about an environment that enables exercising of human rights and freedom for all menkind for the sovereignty and independence of all the countries of the world.

Clause 6: Membership

(a) All the Nepalese students of educational institutions all over the kingdom of Nepal who have faith in the ideals, objectives and working system shall be eligible for its membership.

(b) Nepalese students who are studying in educational institutions in foreign countries shall also be eligible for the membership.

(c) The membership of a member shall remain valid even after two years of completion of regular studies.

(d) The members shall have to renew their membership every two years by paying a membership fee of Rs. 1.

(e) The maximum limit of age for the membership of Nepal

Students Union shall be 35. No membership shall be issued to a person of more than 35 years of age.

(f) Every unit shall be liable to submitting its number of members in their respective districts and membership papers at the central office two months before the central convention.

Clause7: Formation

(a) The NSU units shall be district, university, campus and constituency level. For example, NSU Kathmandu (unit), NSU, TU (unit), Kathmandu constituency No. 1 (unit). The district unit shall act as district branch of NSU, T.U. unit as T.U. committee, campus unit as campus level NSU unit and constituency unit as constituency sub-branch.

(b)

(1) NSU foreign sector central branch shall be established in countries where Nepalese students are studying.
The central branch shall form municipality and university units of NSU which shall act as NSU branch and unit.

(2) A NSU foreign sector gathering shall be organized in a national level represented by four each from branches and two each from sub-branches. The gathering shall elect representatives to participate in the National Convention.

(c) Five Development Regions

(1) A development regional level coordiantion committee of NSU shall be constituted. The office of the committee shall be based in the concerned region.

(2) The coordinator of the regional coordination committee shall be the central vice-chairman representing the region and the members shall be all the central members, district chairmen and campus unit chairmen of the region.

(d) Fourteen Zones

(1) A NSU zonal level coordination committee shall be constituted in each of the zones.

(2) The coordinator of the committee shall be the NSU central member representing the concerned zone and the members shall be the central members, district chairmen and campus unit chairmen of the zone.

(d) The coordination committees mentioned in the sub-clause 'c' and 'd' of clause 7 shall consolidate the NSU by coordinating the branches and sub-branches in the regions and zones.

Clause 8: Convention

(a) The national convention of the NSU shall be organized every two years.

(b) The national convention shall be participated in by the following No. of representatives.

(1) From each of the district branches - 4

(2) From each university committee - 4

(3) From each campus unit - 2

(4) From each constituency sub-branch - 2

(5) From free student unions where NSE has been elected - 2

(6) Foreign sectors

(a) From countries with 4 sub-branches - 2

(b) From countries with 8 sub-branches - 4

(c) From countries with more than 8 sub-branches - 8

(c) Each of the units and sub-branches can send their observers for the convention as fixed by the central working committee, who shall not have voting rights.

(1) The office bearers and members of the central working committee shall automatically be members of the convention general assembly, who shall have voting rights.

(2) The chairmen of all the branches, sub-branches

and units representing the convention shall have the right to participate as representatives.

(3) While selecting other representatives and observers other than those participating automatically, at least 25% shall have to be selected from among girl students.

Clause 9: General Assembly

(a) The central general assembly of NSU shall be constituted on the basis of all the representatives participating in the National Convention.

(b) The general assembly shall elect the NSU central committee. Generally, the National assembly shall be concluded together with the National convention.

(c) One third of the members of central general assembly can file a no-confidence motion against any of the central committee office bearer pointing out reasons in writing. A separate general assembly shall have to be called in special circumstances.

(d) The working committee shall have to call central general assembly within one month of filing of the motion as per clause 9, c.

(e) The motion pertaining to clause 9.c shall have to be addressed to the Vice Chairman, if the motion is against the chairman and to the chairman, if the motion is against other members of the working committee.

(f) The motion under clause 9.c can only be passed by two thirds of all the members of the central general assembly.

(g) Fifty one percent of the total number of members is compulsory to conduct the central general assembly meeting.

Clause 10: Formation of Central Working Committee

The 35 member central working committee shall be constituted as follows:

(a) All the voters of the central general assembly can be candidates to the chairman and the general secretary and all the representatives can elect them.

(b) Five vice-chairmen can be elected from Eastern, Central, Western, Mid-Western and Far Western region, for which only the representatives to the central general assembly from the concerned region can be the candidates as well as the voters.

(c) Fourteen members one each from 14 zones shall be elected for which only the district representatives of the concerned area can be candidates as well as the voters.

(d) Five members, one each from all the five development regions in such a way that only the voters from campus units under various universities can stand as candidates and be the voters.

(e) Five central members to be nominated by the chairman.

(f) While nominating, the chairman shall have to nominate one central member compulsorily from the district where the convention is held at the time.

(g) The girl student representatives participating in the national convention shall elect two girl student representatives as central members.

(h) All the representatives coming from foreign sectors shall elect one central member from among themselves.

(i) A NSU university committee shall be formed in each of the centre of excellency of each university. There shall be one central member from among the representatives of university committees. Presently, it shall be noted that this clause shall denote T.U. Kirtipur and Mahendra Sanskrit University, Dang, Belghundi.

(j) The area of the regions mentioned in sub-clause (b) and (d) shall be as fixed in the annex.

Notes:

(1) Region and zone indicates the region and zone where the unit represented is located.

(2) While allocating portfolios the chairman shall do it from among themselves including assistant general secretary, treasurer and other departmental secretaries.

(3) The term of office for all the office bearers and members of the central working committee shall be generally two years.

(4) An eleven member secretariat shall be constituted under the chairmanship of the central working committee chairman and it can carry out all the works of the central working committee.

(5) The chairman, general secretary, vice-chairman, assistant general secretary and treasurer shall be ex-officio where as other two members shall be as elected by the working committee.

Clause 11: Responsibilities of the Central Working Committee

(a) The central working committee shall implement policies outlined by the central general assembly and shall undertake day to day business of the NSU.

(b) Shall give directives to its units, control them and supervise their works.

(c) A 51 percent of attendance is compulsory for the meeting of the central working committee.

(d) The decisions reached by the simple majority of the number of members attending shall be valid to all.

(e) Generally, the central committee meeting shall be held once in three months.

(f) The procedures for the meeting of the secretariat shall be according to the regulations formulated under the mutual understanding of the secretariat members.

(g) The right to formulate all the rules and regulations mentioned in the clause 3 shall be with the central working committee.

(h) In case any complaint are received from any of the NSU units if any dispute arises, the central working committee can form a tribunal with one member three members to solve the dispute.

Clause 12: Rights and Duties of the Chairman

(a) To chair the meeting of the central working committee.

(b) To provide leadership and guidance.

(c) To spend up to Rs. 12,000 within a year in his own discretion for the running of works from the funds of the NSU.

(d) To give a decisive vote in case the votes of the members present in the meeting of the central working committee opposing each others in any topic comes to a draw.

(e)

(1) to nominate representatives to other organizations from the NSU in accordance with the recommendations of the central committee members.

(2) to provide leadership on behalf of the NSU in any meetings and conferences and other organizations.

(f) In case the chairman is absent, he can designate one of the five vice-chairmen to hold his portfolio.

(g) While tendering resignation, the chairman shall submit his resignation to the central working committee through the group of vice-chairmen.

(h) The right whether to accept or reject the resignation lies with the central working committee.

(i) In case the post of the chairman comes to be vacant, the working committee shall nominate acting chairman from among the vice-chairmen.

Clause 13: Rights and Duties of the Vice-Chairman

(a) A designated vice-chairman shall perform the duty of the chairman in his absence.

(b) The vice chairman shall act as a regional incharge while undertaking special activities for the organization in the specified region under the directives of the central working committee.

(c) The vice-chairman shall have to tender his resignation addressed to the chairman if he desires so. The resignation shall be passed by the central working committee.

Clause 14: Rights and Duties of the Secretary General

(a) The secretary general shall keep all the documents of

the NSU, carry on correspondence and the day to day business.

(b) To call the meeting of the working committee in accordance with the directives of the chairman.

(c) The working committee can approve the resignation tendered by the secretary general to the chairman.

(d) In case the post of the secretary general remains vacant, the chairman shall appoint one secretary general from among the working committee members in accordance with the suggestions made by the secretariat.

Clause 15: Assistant Secretary General

(a) The assistant secretary general shall undertake all the works according to the clause 14 sub-clause (a) and (b) during the absence of the secretary general.

(b) The central working committee can approve the resignation tendered by the assistant secretary general throught he chairman.

Clause 16: Rights and Duties of the Treasurer

(a) The treasurer— keep the records of income and expenditure of the NSU and shall spend in urgent works as fixed by the working committee.

(b) The treasurer can keep an amount not exceeding Rs. 500 belonging to the union.

(c) The accounts of the NSU shall be opened in the bank in the name of the chairman and the treasurer.

(d) The treasurer shall have to submit his resignation in the name of the chairman and the working committee can approve it.

(e) In case the post of the treasurer lies vacent, the chairman shall on the suggestions of the secretariat nominate one of the members of the working committee to the post of the treasurer.

Clause 17: Disciplinary Action

(a) Any of the members who acts against the unity, interest, principles and objectives of the NSU can be warned in written, his membership can be suspended or terminated.

(b) The majority of the central working committee shall take the disciplinary action against any member of the district branch, university committee, campus unit, constituency sub-branch, all the committees of the foreign sector unit or the working committee.

(c) The concerned member can appeal to the central working committee within 35 days against any disciplinary action taken to general member by the district working committee.

(d) The concerned person or the committee can appeal to the judicial and disciplinary committee within 35 days against any disciplinary action taken to them.

(e) The decision to be taken by the judicial and disciplinary committee shall be final.

Clause 18: General Judicial and Disciplinary committee

(a) A judicial and disciplinary committee shall be constituted to make final decisions on the disciplinary action taken by the central working committee in order to maintain total discipline within the NSU.

(b) The central working committee (CWC) shall constitute outside CWC a three member judicial and disciplinary committee within one month of formation of the central working committee of the NSU.

(c) There shall be departmental secretaries in various departments such as organization, sports, cultural, literary, publicity, and foreign departments. The working committee shall take decisions regarding departmental functions.

(d) All the members of the working committee shall have to assist in the day to day functioning of the NSU.

(e) Amendment of the constitution-

(1) One third of the total number of central general assembly members can submit a proposal for amendment of the NSU constitution to the central working committee and the CWC to the central general assembly.

(2) Such a proposal can only be passed by a two third majority of all the members of central general assembly.

(f) Delineation of the regions-

(1) The delination of regions as per the clause 10, sub-clause 1 shall be as follows:

- Eastern region (Mechi, Koshi and Sagarmatha)
- Central region (Janakpur, Bagmati and Narayani)
- Western region (Lumbini, Gandaki and Dhawalagiri)
- Mid-western (Rapti, Bheri and Karnali)
- Far-western (Seti and Mahakali) zones.

(3) "Generally" in clause 10, sub-clause 3 shall have to be understood as the condition when there is no serious crisis upon NSU and when the convention has not been held. Generally, the term of office of the central office bearers of NSU shall be of two years.

(g) Additional duties of the vice chairman.

The vice chairman shall have to visit campuses and districts within his area of operation twice during his tenure.

(h) Additional duties of zonal members:

They shall have to visit the districts within their area of operation three times during their tenure.

(j) Additional duties of regional campus representatives:

(1) They shall have to visit each campus once in their tenure.

(2) The representative to the general convention shall have to be from among students of the concerned campus.

(k) The foreign section, university committee and provision of university assembly and its formation in the foreign section shall be as per the regulations formulated by the central committee.

(l) The setting up of the NSU regional office and the foreign department formed in order to extend its relations with international student's organizations shall be as defined by the central committee.

District regulations

(Amended by the meeting of CWC)

Procedures of formation of district working committee

(a) The district working committee shall have 15 members.

(b) There shall be four representatives and observers each from each campus units in the district participating as district convention, two each from secondary school units, four each from town committees and two each from Village Development Committees (VDCs), but the observers shall have no voting rights.

(c) The office bearers of the present district working committee shall automatically be the representatives to the district convention.

(d) The constituency sub-branch chairman shall be ex-officio member of the District Working Committee (DWC).

(e) There shall be three women while forming the DWC.

(f) The term of office of the DWC shall be of one year.

(g) The meeting of the district working committee shall be held at least six times a year.

(h) The district convention shall be observed by central representative.

District Assembly

(a) All the representatives to the district convention shall be members of the NSU district assembly.

(b) The district assembly shall elect a district working committee.

(c) The quorum for the holding of the district assembly shall be 51 percent of the total members.

Responsibilities of the district working committee

(a) To implement the policies and programmes formulated

by the district assembly as well as to run day to day business.

(b) To control and direct sub-branches and units within the district.

(c) Take necessary measures for the organizational consolidation.

(d) The DWC shall forward disciplinary action to the CWC against any member and office bearer who violates the principles, objectives and norms of NSU.

Rights and duties

(a) Chairman:

(1) The chairman shall provide leadership to the organization and give directives as well as chair the working committee meeting, the chairman shall give a decisive vote in case the members present at the meeting are equally divided in their opinion.

(2) To nominate representatives to meetings, conferences and other organizations on behalf of the NSU.

(3) The chairman can spend up to Rs. 3,000 a year for organizational activities in his own discretion.

(b) Vice-Chairman

The vice chairman shall act on the directives of the chairman in organizational works and shall chair the working committee meeting in absence of the chairman.

(c) Secretary

To call the working committee meeting on the orders of the chairman and to run day to day works along with to keep all the office documents.

(d) Joint Secretary

To work on behalf of the secretary in his absence.

(c) Treasurer

1) The treasurer shall keep the income and

expenditure and spend as directed by the working committee in casual expenses. The bank account shall be conducted by the joint signature of the NSU chairman and treasurer.

2) If any office bearer of the working committee is to resign, he shall have to submit it to the chairman and the working committee meeting shall approve it. The filling of the post thus vacated shall be done by the chairman on the advice of the working committee.

3) The chairman of the district working committee shall submit his resignation before the central chairman.

4) Constituency sub-branch

(a) Formation of the constituency sub-branch

(1) The constituency sub-branch shall have thirteen members.

(2) Four representatives and observers each from each of the secondary schools and town committees and two each from the VDCs can take part in the constituency sub-branch convention, but the observers shall have no voting rights.

(3) If the municipality is divided into two or more areas, it shall have two representatives each from each of the areas.

(4) Three women shall have to be included while forming the constituency committee.

(5) The term of office of this committee shall be of one year.

(6) If there is only one constituency in any of the district, there shall be no constituency committee.

(7) There shall be compulsory observation by the representative of the district working committee in the convention of the constituency committee.

(8) All the representatives to the constituency convention shall be members of the constituency assembly, and the assembly shall elect a constituency committee.

(9) The quorum for the constituency assembly shall be 51 percent of the members.

(10) Implementation of the organizational works formulated by the constituency assembly.

(11) Carrying out organizational consolidation works under the directives and control of the district working committee.

(12) The district working committee, constituency sub-branch, the campus unit and the town and village committees shall have fixed number of members as well as chairman, vice chairman, secretary, joint secretary and treasurer.

(13) Anything unclear in the district regulations shall be as directed by the central constitution.

Source: Nepal Student Union, Kathmandu.

APPENDIX - XI

All the Progressive, democratic and Patriotic Students of all over the country, unite

Constitution of the All Nepal National Free Students Union

Amended and revised by the Eighth National Conference

1983

Part - 1

Name

This organization shall be named as All Nepal National Free Students Union. It shall be called ANNFSU in abbreviated form.

Commencement

This constitution shall be effective to all the members of this organization after being passed by the Eighth National Conference of ANNFSU.

Flag

The flag of ANNFSU shall be of right-angled rectangular in shape with red background. The length and breadth shall be in the ratio of 3.2. There shall be a white star with five corners on the upper left corner and there shall be a white pen with its lead opened and inclined towards the star in 30 degrees.

Party - 2

Membership

1. Anyone who agrees to the ANNFSU programmes and its constitution.
   a. Anyone who is a regular student of any academic institution.
   b. Anyone who is giving private educational examination.
   c. Any one who has not spent two years after passing an educational level in any school or college.
   d. Any Nepali student who has passed two years after being cleared if he is expelled with or without any charges or on false charges by any academic institution can be an ordinary member of this organization.
2. The preliminary committee, special preliminary committee and liaison committees within their area of

operation and the town, *ilaka* and district level committees in absence of the former can provide within their area of operation, ordinary membership of ANNFSU by charging Rupees one.

3. Each member shall have to renew his membership once a year by paying rupee one.

Organization

1. The supreme leading institution of ANNFSU is the National Conference. A 20-member central committee is elected from the national conference. Central committee members shall elect the following office-bearers from among themselves, such as president, vice-president, general secretary, secretary, treasurer. The supreme leading institution of ANNFSU shall be the central committee itself unless a National Conferences is held.
2. The following regional committees shall be formed by the regional level conference, (Mechi, (b) Koshi, (c) Sagarmatha, (d) Narayani, Dhanusha, Sindhuli, Sarlahi and Mahottari, (e) Bagmati, Dolakha and Ramechhap, (f) Gandaki, (g) Dhawalagiri, (h) Lumbini, (i) Rapti, (j) Behri, (k) Far western (Seti and Mahakali zones) regional committees.

The regional committees shall have 7 to 15 members. These committee shall have a Chairman. Vice-Chairman, Secretary, Joint Secretary and a Treasure. The regional committee shall take the leadership f the works of the ANNFSU until another regional conference is held.

3. The regional committees shall have 7 to 15 members as required by the works of the organization. The committee shall have a chairman vice chairman, secretary joint secretary and a treasurer. The committee shall take the leadership of the ANNFSU until another district conference is held.
4. The district committee shall form *ilaka* and town committees by organizing conferences in the area of operation level from among the representatives of the preliminary committees after grouping them in *ilakas*

as deemed necessary in order to make effective the functioning of ANNFSU.

5. Minimum of five member preliminary committee shall be formed in the name of the educational institution from among the general members of the ANNFSU studying in those institutions. The concerned upper level committees can form a special preliminary committee from among the general members living at certain places and mentioned in part 2 clause 4.1. b, c and d or general members living at certain places and mentioned in part 2 clause 4.1. b, c and d or general members studying in any of the educational institutions or if necessary members from both the criterion are sufficient.

6. The preliminary committees shall, considering the number of members and the facilities for running the organization, form joint preliminary committees under themselves.

7. The members of ANNFSU from different regions and districts studying in the Kathmandu valley can form regional liaison committees with five to eleven members according to the regions mentioned in article 4 clause 2.

   Except for the area of operation of the Bagmati regional committee, the regional Liaison committees from various regions and districts of those studying in the Kathmandu valley shall remain under the central committee.

   Other regional Liaison committees can form district Liaison committees with permission from the central committee except for the Bagmati regional Liaison committee. The status of the regional Liaison committee shall be equal to the district committee and the status of district Liaison committee equal to the preliminary committee.

8. The committees under the district committee shall have five to eleven members.

9. All the committees can form an efficient secretariat involving responsible committee members for their smooth functioning.

Part - 3

Conference, general members, assembly and meetings

1. Normally, the National Conference shall be held every two years, the regional conference in every one and a half years and the district and town conference every year.

   On special occasions, the respective conferences shall be called before the fixed date if two third of the members elected by the conference demand.

2. The central chairman or the secretariat shall have to call the National Conference within six months, if the majority district members or the majority central committee members demand for the same. Otherwise, the majority district committees or the central committee members can themselves call the national Conference by forming an organizing committee. The conference which is not represented by majority districts having district committees shall not be regarded a National Conference.

3. The representatives for the National conference shall be arranged as given below:

   (a) All members of the central Committee

   (b) One from the regional committee

   (c) One from the regional liaison committee

   (d) Representatives can be sent with approval from the district committee.

   (i) One from the district committee and additional one from the *ilaka* committee or school preliminary committee by the district committee which has 500 general members except for those studying in the campuses. One additional representative can be sent from the *ilaka* committee or school preliminary committee if they have 1000 or more general members.

   (ii) One from the preliminary committee of campus level and additional one from the preliminary committee which has more than 15 joint preliminary committees.

4. The district committee can send two representatives, those district committees which have upto 15 school preliminary committees can send additional one and those district committees which have more than 15 school preliminary committees can send one representative to the regional conference.

   One representative from each campus preliminary committee with the consent from the district committee and one each from the town school committee and *ilaka* or town committee can be sent to the regional conference.

   The regional liaison committees can send one each representative to the Bagmati regional conference.

5.
   a The regional committee secretariat or the chairman and secretary shall have to call regional conference within three months if the majority committees representing in the regional conference, demand so. Otherwise, the majority committees demanding the conference can call the regional conference by forming a regional conference organizing committee. This can also be done by a upper level committee if demand is made from the majority committees to dissolve the regional committee and to form regional conference organizing committee.

   b. The district committee secretariat or chairman and secretary shall have to call the district conference within one and a half month if the majority preliminary committees, special preliminary committees, town schools committee and *ilaka* or town committee within the district demand so. Otherwise, the majority committees demanding the conference can call the district conference by forming district conference organizing committee. This can also be done by the upper level committee if demand is made by the majority committees to form a district conference organizing committee by dissolving the district committee.

6.

a Representatives can be sent to the district conference two each from each of the *ilaka* and town committees, one each from each preliminary committees or special preliminary committees, additional one representative from each PC which has upto five joint preliminary committees, three representatives from PCs which have upto ten joint preliminary committees and representatives not more than five for whatever more number of joint preliminary committees than that.

b. The district committee can increase the number of required representatives with the approval of the upper level committee by considering the necessity if the educational institutions or the number of students is less than required as per clause 6.6(a) in any given district. The upper level committee shall make arrangements for the same where there is no district committee.

c. Representatives can be sent to the town school conference one each from each of the school preliminary committees, additional one from the preliminary committees which have upto two joint preliminary committees, three representatives from preliminary committees which have upto five joint preliminary committees, thereafter not more than five representatives for whatever more number of joint preliminary committee.

7. The formation of the liaison committee, preliminary committee, special PC, and joint PC shall be done from the assembly of all general members within their own area of operation. The formation shall be undertaken through democratic discussion and through secret voting system if necessary. In the case of voting, the victorious candidate shall have to receive simple majority of votes.

8.

a In special circumstances, the right to alter the number of representatives to the conference of any level shall rest with the upper level committee. Similarly, in the case of National conference, this right shall rest with the central committee.

b. Committees of any level can form organizing committees to hold conference of their own level. In the case of conference of central level, the central committee can form National Conference organizing committee. Thus the secretariat meeting can form the conference organizing committee in case there is lack of quorum for consecutive three times to form a conference organizing committee by the concerned committee.

9.

a Generally, the central committee meeting shall have to be held every six months, that of regional committee every three months, that of district committee every one and a half months and of the town school committee, the *ilaka* committee, the district contact committee, preliminary committee, the special PCs and joint PCs in each month.

b. In certain circumstances, the secretary of the concerned committee can call a meeting any time with advice from the chairman.

c. Generally, there shall have to be majority in holding each meetings. Meetings of all committees shall have to be held regularly.

Part-4

Rights and duties and discipline

1. The Supreme institution of ANNFSU shall be its National Conference. This shall possess the right to supervise the works of the central committee. This shall

formulate future programmes of the ANNFSU and form its central committee.

2. The supreme organ during the period between two National Conferences shall be the central committee itself. This shall implement programmes passed by the National Conference, maintain lively contact with the lower committees, give directives and suggestions on important issues and supervise their works while working as per the constitution, programmes and objectives of the ANNFSU.
3. The district and regional committees shall carry out mass programmes and objectives and directives of upper level committees within this own area of operation. While doing so, the upper level committee shall be contacted if it has an impact on other areas and if assistance is needed.
4. In special circumstances, the district or higher level committees can call an extensive meeting of their own level by including representatives from the lower level committees. Likewise, the central committee shall have to call an extensive meeting if majority of the district committees demand for the same.
5. The running of the organizational principles and the committee business shall be on the basis of democratic centralism. A person remains under the organization, minority under majority, lower level committee under the higher level committee and all the members under the central committee and that all the committees shall abide by the principles of discipline.
6. Each committee can strongly criticize, or suspend or dissolve or give warning or suspend the membership or expel any committee or member within or under itself who act against the objectives or organizational discipline of ANNFSU and violate it time to time with an intent or remain inactive in its works.

   The committee or member thus dissolved, expelled, or suspended can appeal to the upper level committee. The issue can be taken to the central committee whenever necessary.

7. Any of the committee members shall be demanded written clarification or the concerned persons can be denied information on the committee decisions if they don't fulfill their responsibility and remain inactive for two months despite frequent suggestions and directives from the committee. Any of the member who remains absent for three consecutive meetings without any appropriate reasons can be removed from the committee.
8. Any of the committee shall have to use two third majority of the plenary meeting of the concerned committee while taking disciplinary action. The disciplinary action on a central committee member shall be undertaken by the central secretariat and that it shall have to be approved by the central committee meeting. But as regards expulsion, prior consent shall have to be taken from the district committee in the case of committees and members under the district committee and that of the central secretariat in the case of higher than that.

   The central committee shall have to approve the expulsion of its own members from the next national conference.

   Functions and duties of the office bearers and members:

   (a) Chairman

   (1) The chairman shall preside over the committee meeting.

   (2) Shall take care and supervise the works of the committee members.

   (3) Shall use his decisive vote in case of equal votes.

   (4) The chairman of the central committee can in his discretion spend upto Rs. 500, the chairman of the regional committee Rs. 150 and chairman of the district committee Rs. 100. The expenditure shall have to be approved by the next meeting of the committee or the secretariat.

(b) Vice Chairman

(1) Shall do the works of the chairman in his absence.

(2) Shall cooperate with the chairman in his works.

(c) Secretary general

(1) Shall prepare reports for the meeting and call meetings by consulting with the chairman.

(2) Shall run day to day business of the committee.

(3) Shall collect, preserve and promote committee documents and movable and immovable properties as well as give advice to the chairman.

(4) If necessary the secretary general can spend upto Rs. 200 in his discretion which shall have to be approved in the next meeting of the central committee secretariat.

(i) Secretary

(ii) Shall assist the secretary general in the case of central committee and shall do the works mentioned in clause 9(c) 1, 2, 3 in the case of other committees.

(e) Joint Secretary

(1) Shall assist in the works of secretary when necessary

(2) Shall undertake the works of secretary in his absence

(i) Treasurer

(ii) Shall keep accounts of income and expenditure.

(3) Shall prepare the budget under the directives of the chairman and present it in the meetings.

(4) Shall provide economic leadership by formulating various plans and programmes in order to make ANNFSU economically strong.

(i) Members of all the committees can supervise and inspect their committee works and take the full leadership of ANNFSU in their area.

(ii) Other members of the committee shall have to strongly hold the committee spirit and general members the spirit of organization. They shall have to work in line with the ANNFSU programmes and to involve firmly in protecting and promoting the struggle, selflessness of our foreurnners and the ideal of self-sacrifice for the country and the people.

(iii) The chairman of each committee shall have to take oath of office from the office bearer or member of the higher level committee and other office bearers and members shall have to take oath of office from their own committee chairman.

Part - 5

Resignation, vacancy and filling of vacancy:

1. Resignation- any of the committee members and the office bearers can submit their resignation to the chairman of the concerned committee and in the case of the chairman of the lower committees, the resignation should he submitted to the chairman of the higher committee and in the case of the central committee chairman the resignation shall have to be presented before the central committee vice chairman. The vice chairman shall have to present the resignation to the central committee. Two thirds majority of the concerned committee can accept the resignation.
2. Vacancy- any post is regarded as vacant if the membership of any of the committee members or office bearers is expired or abolished or expelled from the committee in a disciplinary action and if the resignation from the post is formally accepted.
3. Filling of vacancy- The filling of such vacancies can be approved by two thirds majority of the concerned committee and the approval of the higher committee.

Part - 6

Financial management

1. Each of the committee shall have to send monthly regular

levy fixed by the higher committee to the higher committees by assessing the condition of the lower committees. Any of the committee can spend the amount raised for certain works in such works partially or wholly.

2. The lower committee shall have to consult the higher level committee while collecting special funds.
3. Committees of each level shall have to present their fiscal account to the higher committee every three moths. The central committee shall have to send its fiscal account upto the district committee every six month.
4. Each of the committee shall have to make itself or the ANNFSU financially strong.
5. The economic resources shall be the amount received from the membership fees, donations, amount received from various programmes and other sources.
6. A member of ANNFSU from the campus level shall have to pay a regular levy of Rs. 1.00 and the secondary level student shall have to pay Rs. 0.50 paisa per month to their committees.
7. Each of the members or the committee office bearers shall have to strictly abide by economic discipline.

Part - 7

Office

The central office of ANNFSU shall be based in a place fixed by the central committee.

Amendments

If this constitution is required to be amended or revamped, it can be done by two thirds majority of the members present in the National conference.

Right to formulate regulations

Each of the committees can formulate regulations for their functioning without contradicting to the constitution.

Miscellaneous

a. The central committee can form special committees at home and abroad on the basis of requirement.

b. The provision for the secretary general shall be only in the central committee.

c. The central committee can provide guest membership of the ANNFSU to any of the students studying in any of the educational institution in Nepal. These guest members are authorized to exercise all the rights of the general members except for the right to elect or be elected.

d. Considering the requirement, the central committee can alter the regions mentioned in part 2 clause 5 sub-clause 2.

Source: All Nepal National Free Students Union, Kathmandu.

APPENDIX - XII

Let All the Leftist, Progressive,
Patriotic and Democratic
Students, Unite !

Constitution and Report Of the All Nepal National Students Union (Sixth) 1996, January

[Passed by the historical thirteenth
National Conference of the
A.N.N.F.S. (Sixth) held of Pokhara
(January 1996)

Part - 1

Preliminary

Article -1

This organization shall be named as All Nepal National Free Students Union (Sixth).

In abbreviated form it shall be called A.Ne.Ra.Swa.bi.u. (Sixth) in Nepali and ANNFSU (Sixth) in English. In this constitution both the full name and the abbreviation shall be represented by the word "Union."

Article - 2

Commencement:- This constitution shall be fully effective after being passed by the 13th National Conference of the Union.

Article - 3

Explanation:- Only the central committee shall make explanation if anything is unclear in this constitution.

Article - 4

Amendment:- The right to amend, revamp and alter this constitution shall rest only with the National Conference.

Article - 5

Working out regulations:- All the committees can work out regulations and by-laws under this constitution and implement them if necessary for the implementation of the objectives or the constitution of the union.

Article - 6

Flag:-

The flag of the union shall be rectangular in shape and with red background. The measurement of the length and breadth shall be 3:2(1 ′ 1.5). On the left side near the stand at the upper corner, there shall be a five cornered star and a white pen with its lead opened pointing towards it at an angle of 30 degrees.

Part - 2

Article- 7, Objectives and Programmes

1 It shall always be struggling for the safeguarding of rights of all the student community.

2 It shall be effortful in developing mental, intellectual, physical capabilities and confidence of all the students.

3 It shall emphasize on the building of progressive culture in all the students.

4 It shall condemn the indecent, unruly, western oriented and anti-people art, culture and literature based on blind faith and shall publicize progressive art, culture and literature.

5 It shall always fight for the acquisition of new democratic education by struggling to free education from commercialization and power politics.

6 It shall struggle for the implementation of policies for making primary education compulsory and for making secondary education free of charges.

7 It shall struggle for maintaining academic values in universities and for protection of autonomy of the educational institutions and for vocational education and employment.

8 It shall build an atmosphere so that students from the backward classes, nationalities and from remote areas shall have an opportunity to acquire higher education.

9 It shall struggle for a practical, scientific, inexpensive, democratic and employment-oriented education system by denouncing existing unscientific education system.

10 It shall emphasize on the free education to the people of oppressed classes.

11 It shall emphasize on the teaching of all the students of all castes and nationalities and language groups in their mother tongue up to primary level.

12 It shall give extensive support and help to the just struggle of all the oppressed Nepalese people at home and abroad for their rights and interests.

13 It shall support and cooperate to the struggles aimed against social, lingual and cultural exploitation by all the nationalities and language groups of the country.

14 It shall fight against unequal and anti-national treaties by standing firm in support of nationalism, national independence, sovereignty and territorial integrity of the nation and shall raise voice for a relation based on the principles of *panchasheel*.

15 It shall launch struggles for the restoration of New Democratic System by preserving the limited democratic rights achieved by the Nepali people and by emphasizing on the struggle against reaction arise and condemnation of opportunism.

16 It shall mobilize the student community in the establishment of New democratic system by cooperating and supporting various struggles launched against domestic feudalism, comparador beaurocratic bourgeoisie, expansionism, imperialism, social imperialism, colonialism, new colonialism and their exploitation, repression, and injustice and extremism.

17 It shall launch programmes under the policy of combined struggle on common issues by forging a lively contact with various organizations of the people.

18 It shall expand international friendly relations by forging lively contact with progressive organizations of the world.

19 It shall make efforts to develop a morality and character befitting Marxism, Leninism and Maoist thought by extending a moral support to it.

20 It shall launch struggles for restoring equal opportunities in education and equal rights for property to women.

21 It shall lay emphasis on the preservation and development of national industries by freeing the national economy from the monopolistic control of the beaurocratic capital.

22 It shall extend solidarity to the just struggles launched against casteism, apartheid gender discrimination and

untouchability in support of patriotic struggles launched in the country or anywhere in the world.

Part - 3

Article - 8, membership

1 The students with the following qualification can acquire membership who unconditionally agree to the constitution, report and programme of this union.

a. Nepali students who have joined any educational institution or is sitting in any private examination in the country or abroad.

b. Such a student shall have to be able to abide by or having a leftist, progressive, patriotic and democratic ideology.

2 Rs. 1 shall have to be paid while taking membership or renewing it. The membership shall have to be renewed each year.

3 One is considered a student in the cause of a student who has given an examination of any educational level in any school or college and for upto two years after being expelled from an educational institution on a charge or a baseless charge while participating in a struggle of students or in pro-people activities.

4 The central committee can provide guest membership to any foreign student studying in a Nepalese educational institution with a membership fee of Rs. 2. The guest members can exercise all the rights of a general member except for the right to elect or be elected.

5 The primary record of a member who has membership shall have to be kept at the concerned unit committee.

6 Principal responsibilities of the members:

(a) They shall have to adopt the ideals of martyrs by supporting the rights and interests of the students and exploited and oppressed people.

(b) They shall have to publicize the policies and programmes of the union by forging a relation with the student community and community of the people through a progressive spirit.

(c) They shall have to strongly abide by the discipline of the union and have to behave in a progressive discipline and manners with other members.

(d) They shall have to be committed to implement and help implement the programmes of the union and directives of the upper level committee.

(e) They shall have to inform the concerned level committee in time, in order to resolve the non-organizational behaviour arising among the members of the union.

(f) They shall have to look for and study progressive journals, bulletins and books published by the union or from elsewhere.

(g) They shall have to develop an ability not to repeat one's mistake by making self criticism and to promptly criticize other's mistakes organizationally.

7 Rights of the members:-

(a) Right to elect a leader for the union or be elected.

(b) Right to discuss, criticize and argue within the union's discipline.

(c) They can freely express their idea or opinion in the central committee or national gathering or National Conference even if it is disagreed by other members or not passed in any concerned committee under the union.

(d) They can demand a decision from the concerned committee on any petition and appeal presented to any concerned committee of the union or a higher committee.

8 Condition for termination of membership:-

(a) If one is involved in activities contrasting to the provision under Part 2 of this constitution, or

(b) If membership is not acquired duely under the provisions of article 8.1 and 8.2 of Part 3 of this constitution, or

(c) If one is considered immoral without progressive morality of the union.

(d) If one breaches the secrecy of the union frequently. But this criteria is effective even for the first time judging by the seriousness of secrecy.

(e) If one is found to be intruding by establishing a direct or indirect relation with the reactionary and opposing organizaitons, or

(f) If one dies, or

(g) If one loses mental stability, or

(h) If a tendered resignation is accepted.

Part - 4

Organs of the union

Article - 8, National Conference:-

(a) The supreme body of the union shall be the National Conference.

(b) The central committee or the central organization committee or the National Conference organizing committee shall call the National Conference.

(c) The majority of district committees of the union can demand for a National Conference, if it is needed for the consolidation of the union or for any fundamental matters.

In such a condition, the National Conference can be called within six months by forming a central organization committee in a National gathering or National Council meeting by the central committee.

If the six month period is elapsed without calling the national conference, the majority of district committees can call the national conference by forming a National Conference organizing committee.

Article-10, National Council

1 A National Council shall be constituted by the Nationala Cofnerence or a National gathering. The number of

members of this council shall be fixed by the National Conference or the National gathering.

2 The members of the central committee and co-members shall be the ex-officio members of the National Council.

The National Conference or gathering shall elect all other remaining members so as to be called by the central committee 25 percent of the total number of National Council members temporarily at the time of meeting.

3 The chairman and general secretary of the central committee shall be the ex-officio chairman and secretary of the council.

4 All the members shall have eq2ual rights in voting.

5 The meeting of the National Council shall normally be held once a year.

Article 11, Central Committee

A central committee shall be constituted by the National Conference.

1 The executive members of the central committee shall elect office bearers and constitute secretariat.

2 Generally, there shall be the following five permanent departments under the central committee:-

a. Educational and statistics department.

b. Publication and publicity department.

c. Cultural department.

d. Sports department.

e. Women's department.

3 The central committee shall constitute the departments under the chairmanship of department secretaries by including various level committee members as is necessary.

4 The central committee can also constitute other departments, if necessary.

5 The central committee itself shall be regarded as the supreme body of the union during the period between two national conferences.

6 The chairman of each of the regional coordination committees shall be the ex-officio co-member for the central committee. The co-members shall have all the rights exercised by the central members except for voting and being elected as the central office bearer.

7 The central committee shall be automatically dissolved if the majority members elected from the National Conference tender their resignation or violate the policies and objectives of the organization or remain out of the central committee for other reasons.

8 In such a situation, the remaining central members can take an initiative to call National gathering or National Council meeting and form the central organization committee in order to run union businesses for an interim period. But if the National Conference is very near, a central organizaiton committee shall be formed after calling a meeting of the National gathering or National Council.

9 The temporary central committee or the central organization committee thus constituted shall have to hold National Conference within six Months.

Article-12, Regional Co-ordination Committee:-

1 The central committee shall, with a view to bring about efficiency in its performance and to make lively understanding between the centre and the districts, constitute regional co-ordination committees by delineating regions with certain districts udner them.

2 The forming of regional co-ordination committee shall be done by calling a gathering of the districts as necessary on the basis of the dineated region or by the central committee directly.

3 The co-ordination committee elected by the gathering shall elect the office bearers.

Article -13, District Committee:-

1 The election fo district committee shall be held each year by organizing district conference in the presence of a

central representative and as called by the district committee or district organization committee.

2 The committee elected by the conference shall elect office bearers and constitute a secretariat.

Article-14, Preliminary bodies:

1 Area Committee

a. An area committee is constituted by organizing area level gathering on the initiative of the district committee after dividing areas.

Which include certain Village Development Committee, schools, campuses and hostels of the district.

b. The town committee constituted under the municipality shall be equal to the areas committee.

c. The area committee shall coordinate unit committees within its area, shall follow up and mobilize them effectively.

2 Unit Committee:-

a. A gathering of the general members under a school, campus, hostel and VDCs shall constitute a unit committee in its area.

b. The unit committee shall form joint unit committees in different levels of the schools and campuses, in different faculties, shifts, villages and localities from a gathering of the general members of the concerned sectors under it with view to systematize the works in its area. In the localities and wards of a municipality, unit committees shall be constituted and the joint unit committee shall be formed under them.

Article -15, Special bodies:-

1 Advisory Committee:- The central and district committees can constitute an advisory committee with upto five members, from among the former office bearer members of the union or those who are close to the policies of the union with a view to receive suggestions

and recommendations. The members of the advisor committee can attend the working committee meeting and give suggestions. But the working committee shall have the right not to implement the suggestions.

2 Special Committee:- Committees of all levels of the union can form a special committee if they consider it necessary so as to perform their special works. The committee while forming a special committee shall have to give necessary directives on the level, works, area of operation, procedures and the term of office of the special committee. The term of office of such a committee shall not exceed six months.

3 Liaison Committee:- A liaison committee shall be constituted for establishing contact with various zones, regions, district, campus, school or community. These committees shall be constituted on the directives or presence from the upper level committee. The liaison committee or its member shall have to make regular contact and reporting to the upper level committee.

Part - 5

Article-16, Office bearers and members of the union

In committees of each level of the union, there shall be the following office bearers and members:-

a. Chairman

b. Vice chairman (upto two individuals in the central committee)

c. General secretary (Only in the central committee)

d. Secretary (In central committee as necessary)

e. Joint secretary (except in the central committee)

f. Treasurer

g. ffice secretary (The central, regional and district committee can appoint one office secretaryf rom among the executive, if necessary)

h. Convenor (In the case if there is no need of other office bearers, and

i. Members (In all levels as necessary).

Part - 6

Article -17, Organizational Policies,

The procedures for running of the organization and organizational policies shall be as follows:-

1 All the members shall remain under the union constitution, report and the regulations and democratic centralism shall be applied.

2 The lower committees of this union shall be under the upper committees, all the committees under central committee and all the members under the union.

3 The minority shall have to accept the majority decision as union decision. But the majority shall have to prove the issues and ideas of the minority as meaningless with appropriate reasons. If an appropriate reason is not mentioned, the minority issue shall have to be recognized.

4 The committee business shall be performed according to the policy of collective leadership and personal responsibility.

5 All the organs and bodies of the union shall have to compulsorily abide by the upper level directives of the union.

6 The upper level committee shall have regularly dispatch union programmes to the lower committee in time through appropriate procedure. Redirections have to be made after inspecting and evaluating whether or not works have been done according to the directives. The lower level committees shall have to dispatch their reports of performance compulsorily and without delay to the upper committees.

7 Committees of any level can formulate and implement regulations, by-laws, plans and programmes without contradicting to the union constitution, report and decisions for the implementation of the policies and programmes. The report of this shall have to be dispatched to the upper committee. In the case of central committee, it shall have to be presented at the National Conference.

8 Any committee or a member can present any theoretical and practical suggestions through an organizational medium. Similarly, a healthy criticism can be made according to organizational procedures and internal debate can be made within the union.

Part - 7

Article -18, Rights and duties:-

1 Organizational:-

a. The national conference organized after calling representatives and observers from various district committees and district organization committees shall constitute central committee and the meeting of the National gathering or National Council shall constitute central organization committee.

The National Conference regarded as the supreme body shall formulate overall programems, objectives and strategies of the organization and shall evaluate the past actions.

b. The central committee shall mobilize the organization according to the programmes, objectives and strategies forwarded by the national Conference and shall implement the central programmes and policies. The decisions or actions taken by the central office or central secretariat at a time when the central committee meeting is not held shall have to be approved at the next meeting of the central committee.

c. Any of the lower committees shall work on the action plan, leadership and implementation in their area of operation as per the directives of the upper committee, the union objectives and programmes.

d. The regional, district and area committees can organize workers, gatherings in their own level whenever necessary.

2 As per the post:

a. Chairman:-

(1) Chairing of the meeting

(2) Supervise, direct and inspect committee office bearers and their work

(3) Using decisive vote in case of equal votes in the committee

b. Vice-chairman:-

(1) Assisting the chairman in his works

(2) Performing all the works to be done by the chairman in his absence.

c. General Secretary:-

(1) Preparing reports and programmes for the meeting by consulting with the chairman and calling of meetings.

(2) Running of day today committee business.

(3) Preserving and promoting committee documents and properties.

(4) Giving necessary advice to the chairman, and

(5) Coordinating departmental works.

d. Secretary:-

(1) Leading one's department in the case of secretary of the central committee, assisting the general secretary, performing the works of the general secretary in his absence, presenting action plan to the office or secretariat or the committee after preparing it on the advice of the chairman.

(2) In the case of lower committee secretary, performing works as mentioned in part-7, article 18.2(c).

e. Joint-secretary:-

(1) Assisting in the works of the secretary

(2) Performing all the works of secretary in his absence

f. Treasurer:-

(1) Preparing various economic plans and programmes

(2) Presenting budget at the meeting after preparing it as directed by the chairman

(3) Keeping accounts of income and expenditure.

g. Member:-

(1) Take full leadership of the union in one's area

(2) Reviewing and supervising committees' works

(3) Assisting in the works of office bearers.

h. Office secretary:-

(1) Running day to day business of the office

(2) Making contacts and correspondence and other necessary works on behalf of the office under the directives of the chairman, general secretary and secretary.

(3) Receiving notices, reports, newspapers and magazines and other materials for the office and union and prepare its record and file and present it at the meeting.

Part - 8

Article-19, Conference, Gathering and Meeting

1 Generally, the national Conference shall be held once in every two years, regional gathering, district conference area and unit gathering shall be held every year. In extra-ordinary situation, it can be held sooner or later.

2 If conference is demanded by two thirds members of any committee formed through a conference in special situations before its due time, it shall have to be called in its own level.

3 The national gathering shall be organized once between two conferences. It can be held sooner or later in special situations.

4 Representatives and observers shall be called for the National Conference or National gathering from the district committees and district organization committees.

The central committee can invite observers, or audiences from other districts and special places. The right to decide representatives and observers lies with the central committee.

5 The Organizers of the concerned conference or gathering shall automatically be the representatives for the conference.

6 Observers can also be called from the special committees, coordination committees and liaison committees which are constituted in the presence of central representative. But these committees shall have to be from the area or upper level.

7 The full meeting of the central committee shall be held twice a year in normal situations and can be held any time in extraordinary and necessary situations or when demanded by one third members.

8 The regional co-ordinating committees meeting shall be held once in four months, the district committee meeting in three months, the area committee meeting once a month. But it can be shifted sooner or later in extraordinary situations.

9 The quorium of the meeting of any level committees shall be regarded a simple majority or 51% of the total number of members.

10 The majority of a concerned committee can appoint another person on acting basis and run the business if any executive member is jailed or is unable to perform the responsibilities of the organizaiton for other reasons.

11 The decision making is done in an committees through discussion, understanding and secret voting. This system is also applicable for the election. But in times of secret voting, two persons for proposing and two for supporting for the candidate shall have to be from among the representatives.

Part - 9

Article-20, Discipline and action:-

Action and punishment can be applied to members who act against the part 2 of this constitution or according to the part 3 article 8 and clause 8 or attempts to open a parallel organization and violates the discipline on the basis of his mistake and seriousness of the act. (As per the theory applied to save a sick person from the illness).

Article-21

The following procedure shall be applied while taking disciplinary action:

a. asking for clarification,

b. giving from the post,

c. removing from the post,

d. suspending from the membership and

e. removing from even the general membership.

Considering the gravity of the mistake, severest action can also be applied in the beginning.

Article - 22

Generally, no person shall be convicted without trial. No action shall be taken to him without giving an opportunity to defend.

Part - 10

Vacancy and Fulfillment

Article - 23

The seat is regarded as lying vacant if resignation tendered on one's own will is accepted, or if he dies or has his mental condition deteriorated or if his membership is quashed or if he is removed from his post upon being taken disciplinary action.

Article -24

The resignation shall have to be represented by any member or office bearer of a committee before the chairman, of the concerned committee and in the case of lower level committee chairman, it shall have to be presented before upper level committee. In the case of central committee chairman, it shall have to be presented at the central committee meeting. The resignation shall be either approved or rejected by the majority of the concerned committee.

Article - 25

The filling of vacancies can also be done from among the general members. The upper level committees' approval is compulsory while filling posts in the lower committees.

Part - 1

Article-26, Financial Condition

1 The accounts of financial income and expenditure of all the committees under this union shall be under the responsibility of the treasurer. While spending any amount, approval of the committee chairman, or office or secretariat shall have to be sought.

2 The income and expenditure of any level committee shall have to be audited compulsorily once in six months or twice a year. The auditing shall be done by serially upper level. In the case of central committee, the secretariat shall have to audit and present the report in the National Council meeting or National gathering or National Conference.

3 The sources of the fund shall be union's regular income as directed by the central committee and the union's financial sources shall also be the sources defined by the local committee or the district committee.

4 Separate arrangements shall have to be made in every level for spending and keeping a fund.

Article -27

The sharing of income percentage shall be made as follows:

1 The whole of the membership fees shall go to the centre.

2 The unit shall get 50%, the area 10% and the district 40% from among all the accounts raised in the unit. Fifty percent shall go to the district committee if there is no area committee.

3 Of all the accounts raised in the district, 50% shall go to the district, 20% to the regional co-ordination committee and 30% to the central committee.

4 From among the accounts raised by the area committee and the regional committee in their own initiative, the area committee shall have to keep 75% itself and 25% to the district and that the regional co-ordination committee shall have to allot 75% for itself and 25% for the centre.

5 While raising donation, the lower committees shall have to give a share percentage to the upper committee.

But the percentage of the lower committee shall remain with the committee, which coLlects the donation. According to this, 50 percent shall remain in the district itself which also includes that of the local committee if the district collects any donation, and 20% shall go to the regional co-ordination committee and 30% to the centre. If the donation is raised by the regional co-ordination committee, it shall take 75% and the rest 25% shall go to the centre.

6 Any donations or assistance raised for a certain task shall have to be utilized in the same task. But the amount that remains without being spend wholly shall be divided as per the above articles of 27.2, 27.3 and 27.4.

7 But the 50% of entrance fees raised during district or regional level conference, gathering and campus shall have to be dispatched to the center and the 50% of the entrance fees raised in the preliminary level gathering and camp shall have to be dispatched to the district.

8 On the accounts of publication, all the amount shall have to be dispatched to the concerned committee except for the lower committees taking specied percentage as their share.

Part -12

Miscellaneous

28. The central office of the union shall be based in Kathmandu. The offices of other committees shall remain in the places specified by the concerned committee.

29. The chairman and general secretary can make decision on behalf of the office by consulting with other available executives. The decision shall have to be approved at the meeting of the concerned committee.

30. The central committee can designate certain persons as central representatives for a certain period of time in connection with organizational works.

31. All the members shall be called at the unit committee gathering of this union and representatives and observers shall be called to participate on behalf of the organization in any other gatherings and conferences. The right to vote in any issue shall be only with the representative. The observers can discuss and give suggestions.

32. Mutual co-operation shall be extended with any brotherly student organization of this union working in foreign countries which has common objectives by maintaining brotherly relations, but the central committee can open liaison committee of this union in a country where no such organization exist.

Source: All Nepal National Students Union (Sixth), Kathmandu.

APPENDIX - XIII

Constitution of Nepal National Students' Federation

Clause-1, Name

The name of this organization shall by Nepal national Students' Federation. In short it shall be called NNSF. Unless the subject or context requires otherwise, the NNSF may be referred to as federation in other parts of the constitution.

Clause -2, Central Office:-

Generally, the office of the Federation shall be in Kathmandu. It may, however, be shifted to other places if need be.

Clause-3, Flag:-

(a) The flag of the Federation shall be as follows: There shall be an open book on the map of Nepal drawn in the red background and a heptagonal star at the north-west corner of the flag. The colour of contour of the map, book and the star shall be white.

(b) The measurement of the flag shall be 2 ′ 3.

(c) Definition of the flag:- The red colour fo the flag indicates revolutionary progressive character of the federation. White colour symbolizes peace. The book symbolizes knowledge and the star symbolizes peace, democracy and social progress.

Clause -4, Objective:-

(a) To instill the students with a sense of world peace, democracy, social progress and patriotism.

(b) To propagate the ideals of national independence and sovereignty and to try to translate these ideals into practice.

(c) To struggle for the achievement of cheap, accessible, scientific and democratic education system.

(d) To struggle for the basic rights of the students and mobilize them for the safeguard of these rights.

(e) To orient the students' movement toward national democracy linking it with the movement of the Nepalese people for democratic restoration.

(f) To fight against sectarianism, parochialims, religious fanaticism, class superiority and all kinds of privileges that obstruct the development and progress of the society.

(g) To struggle for the preservation of national culture and arts.

(h) To foster a healthy and close relationship among the teachers and the students.

(i) To struggle for the achievement of those facilities which are necessary for the all-round development of students.

(j) To inspire the Nepalese students to foster the friendly solidarity with the youths and students of the world against imperialism, colonialism, neocolonialism, apartheid and racism.

Clause -5

(a) Membership: All the students studying in colleges and schools who subscribe to the constitution, objectives, policies and programems irrespective of religion, race and sex.

(b) Every person willing to be its member shall have to fill up a form which shall be as follows: I fully subscribe to the objectives and programmes of NNFS and I want to be a member of this organization. I will fully abide by the constitution of the organization.

(c) A member of the Federation shall have to pay a sum of three rupees annually and a levy of 25 piece per months.

(d) The membership is subject to renewal each year.

(e) The membership shall expire after two years a student ceases his studies.

(f) A member of the Federation shall not be permitted to become a member of other students' organization.

(g) A student shall have to be 12 years a class six student to acquire the membership of the Federation.

Clause -6

Rights and duties of a member:

Sub-clause-1, Duties:

(a) To abide by the constitution and programmme of the Federation

(b) To discharge the duties as assigned by the Federation.

(c) To be prepared at all times to discharge the duty assigned with the best interest of the Federation in mind.

(d) The instruction of higher committees and majority decisions shall have to be carried out.

Sub-clause-2, Rights:

(a) Right for candidacy at all level of committees of the Federation.

(b) Right to be or elect representative for all level of conferences of the Federation.

(c) Right to give his opinion in forming the tactics, goals and programmes of the Federation.

(d) Right to discuss on documents, decisions and circulars and to give suggestions.

(e) Right to participate in delegations of the Federation and the discussions and seminars held by the Federation.

Clause-7

Structure of the organization:

Sub-clause-1, National conference:

(a) The national conference of the Federation shall be generally held once in two years. The national conference shall be the highest and most powerful agency. Its decision on policies and programmes shall be final.

(b) The national assembly shall be composed of the members of the central committee. District representatives, observers and guests. The district representatives shall be designated by the central committee.

(c) Observers and guests shall have the right to participate in discussion, give suggestions and offer amendment. But they will have no right to vote.

(d) The national assembly shall elect the members of the central committee as required.

(e) A special national conference may also be held if the central committee thinks it necessary.

Sub-clause-2, Central Committee

(a) The central committee shall be the highest level of the Federation in the intervening period of two national conference. During this period, the decisions of the central committee shall be final.

(b) The main responsibility of executing the policies, instructions and programmes endorsed by the National congress shall rest on the Central committee.

(c) This committee shall organize the national congress, fix the number of representatives and date of the congress. This committee shall also be responsible for drafting and presenting documents in the national congress.

(d) If need be, this committee shall have the right to nominate one fourth of the members of the central committee from among ordinary members.

(e) This committee shall have the right to establish international relation and send representatives. The central committee shall elect the central office bearers and central secretariat.

(f) The Central committee shall have to hold its meeting once in six months.

(g) If need be, the central committee shall have the right to hold an extended meeting of the central committee and fix its numbers.

Sub-clause-3, District Committees:

(a) The district assembly shall elect the district committee.

(b) The district committee shall work according to the condition of the district under the decisions of the central agencies and the decisions of the district council.

(c) The district committee should hold its district congress at least once in a year.

(d) The district committee shall have to elect the district secretariat and the representatives for the national congress.

(e) The meeting of the district committee should be held once in two months.

Sub-clause-4, Regional committee:

(a) In order to expand organization in a certain place the central committee shall have the rights to convene a regional congress if needed.

(b) The regional congress shall have the rights to form the regional committee with necessary office bearers.

(c) The regional committee shall have to work in accordance with the decision of the central body and the instruction of the regional congress.

(d) The Central committee shall define the rights and functions of the regional committee.

Sub-clauses-5, Branch and branch committee

(a) All the members in an educational institutions shall be members of a branch.

(b) A branch shall propagate all the higher level decisions among the students and try to bring as many students as possible under the banner of the Federation.

(c) The general assembly of entire members shall have to take place twice a year.

(d) It shall have the responsibility to propagate all the decisions, objectives and programmes of the Federation among the students.

(e) If need be, each branch shall have the rights to form as many branch committees under it as possible.

(f) The branch committee shall have the rights of renewing membership and raise levy.

(g) A branch committee shall be the basic and primary committee of the Federation.

Clause-8, Office bearers, duties and functions:

Sub-clause-1, Office bearers

(a) The central committee shall elect from among itself office bearers such as chair person, general secretary, secretary and cashier.

(b) The chair person shall chair the meeting of the committee.

(c) The chair person general secretary shall be the chief spokesman and spokesman of the federation.

(d) The chair person, shall have to present report on the tactic of the Federation by making an evaluation of national and international situation.

(e) The vice-president shall discharge all the functions of the president at his absence.

(f) The general secretary shall call the meeting in consultation with the president. He can, however, call the meeting himself if situation does not permit consultation with the president.

(g) The general secretary shall be entirely responsible for organizational activities.

(h) The secretary shall discharge all the functions of the general secretary at his absence.

(i) The cashier shall control the central funds of the party. He shall be responsible for maintaining the balance sheet.

Sub-clause-2, Central secretariat

(a) The central committee shall elect a central secretariat from among itself. It may include the central president, general secretary, cashier and other central members as needed.

It is responsible for conducting day to day functions and other activities under the guidance of the central committee when it is not in session.

Sub-clause-3, District secretariat

(a) The district committee shall elect the members of the

district secretariat from among itself. It may include the district chairman, vice-chairman, secretary, deputy-secretary, cashier and the secretary of the concerned department in need be. The district committee shall define the duties and functions of each of the members.

(b) The district chairman shall chair the meeting.

(c) The vice-chairman shall be responsible for discharging all the functions of the chairman at his absence.

(d) The secretary shall call the meeting in consultation with the chairman. He has to submit an organizational report at the meeting.

(e) The chairman shall be responsible for creating district funds and maintaining the balance sheet.

Clause-9, Quorum

(a) A simple majority of the committee members shall be required to establish quorum at all levels.

(b) The decisions taken by the majority required by the quorum shall be valid decisions of the Federation.

Clause-10, Disciplinary action and expulsion

Sub-clause-1, Disciplinary action

(a) Any member or the committee shall be subject to clarification, criticism, repaimand of expulsion if they are found guilty of the following conduct.

(b) If they act against the constitution, policies, programmes and objectives of the federation.

(c) If they keep passive and fail to assist the federation.

(d) If he or she is found to be corrupt and immoral.

(e) If he or she is found to be undisciplined.

A simple majority of a committee concerned shall have the right to take disciplinary action against the defaulting member of the committee. The action against the district committee and its office bearers shall be subject to the approval of the central secretariat.

Sub-clause-2, Expulsion

The members of the committees shall be subject to expulsion in the following situation:

(a) If found to be guilty of the act mentioned in Clause-5 (a).

(b) If the motion for expulsion of a member is approved by a simple majority of a committee.

(c) If the resignation given by a member of a committee is approved by the majority of the committee. The expelled or suspended members, however, shall have the right to defend themselves.

(d) If a member is absent in consecutive three meetings of the committee in which he is a member.

Clause-11, Vacancy and fulfillment of a post

If a post of the Federation falls vacant for any reason, it has to be filled by a simple majority of the committee concerned.

Clause-12, Funds

(a) A fund shall be created out of the fees, donation, and the amount raised from cultural and sports programmes.

(b) The fund shall be operated by the cashier or the person specified by the concerned committee at the absence of the former.

(c) If discrepancies are found in the income and expenditure, the responsible person shall be reprimanded, suspended or expelled. But the action shall be taken only by a competent authority.

Clause-13, Rule

Apart from this constitution, the central committee shall enact rules and regulation in the subjects deemed necessary.

Clause-14, Amendment

The central committee shall have the right to amend, repeal or suspend any clause of this constitution by a simple majority. It will be subject to approval by the national assembly.

Clause-15, Enforcement of the constitution

The constitution shall have immediate effect.

It is compulsory for the district committees to keep a copy of this constitution.

The Central Secretariat

NNSF

Source: Nepal National Students' Federation, Kathmandu.

APPENDIX - XIV

A Note on Student Demands

In the year 1973-1974

In the year 1973-74 there was a student strike in Thapathali Campus. The main demand was for hostel facility to the students. In Hetauda also the students went on strike demanding drinking water, electricity and lavatory facilities and these demands were met immediately. This was followed by the strike in Patan Campus which demanded for increased sports facilities. Instead of resolving the problem locally it was forwarded to the central office. In the same year student unrest engulfed Mahendra Morang Campus demanding adequate physical facilities for the increased number of student applicants. In this case the demand was fulfilled. Underlining dissatisfaction over the examination system and the types of questions asked in the semester examination, the students of Janta (Sanskrit) Campus, Dang, Saraswati Campus Kathmandu and Prithvi Narayan Campus also went on strike. In Janata Campus the question papers had typing mistakes and a few questions were asked from outside the course. The questions were changed. In Sanothimi Campus a strike was launched focussing on the bus problem. The strike in Pokhara Campus was a protest against the shortage of teachers and also the incompetency of the available teachers additional teachers were appointed but the incompetent teachers were allowed to continue.

In the Years 1974-75

In the year 1974-75, the students' strike was characterized by clashes among the students of different groups. Their major demand was the release of the detained students and fulfillment of all their demands. There was also a strike in Tansen (ANM) Campus) demanding change in the educational programme. The problems were resolved by mutual discussions. In Janta Campus (Dang) also there was a strike demanding higher ration allowance and proper management of mess. The students were not ready to manage the mess themselves. Hence they demanded ration allowance in cash. Demanding adequate physical facilities for the Campus for the increased number of students, the students of Mahendra Morang Campus, Biratnagar went on strike for a week. A strike was launched in Saraswati Campus protesting against difficult examination questions. In Hetauda, the students of Forestry went on a strike for one week demanding the administrative status in the service after the completion of the study. The students of Mahendra Campus, Dharan also went on strike for one day in the year 1974 in protest against India's occupation of Sikkim.

In the Year 1975-76

The students' agitation in 1975-76 is considered to be one of the most important student's unrests in Nepal. This unrest continued for about 4 months all over the country. But this strike was not successful. On the contrary, the students lost the facilities and rights which had been acquired in the past. The strike put up some 27 demands of all kinds. The students should have the chance of attending class without any fee, re-establishment of campus and academic institution abolished by NESP. The campus level demands which were 11 in number were as follows; fulfilment of shortage of teachers in all the campuses, increase in the number of books in the library in the campuses, transport facility, arrangement of necessary expenditure for writing thesis in degree level programme, transfer of students to suitable place from Man Bhawan, Patan payment of full salary to the inservice teachers and increment in the amount of scholarship, hostel facility of Tri-Chandra and other campuses and payment of remuneration to the teachers for examining answer copies. Tehre were altogether 27 students' demands. In the year 1975-76, the strikes were recorded in 16 different campuses. Being a national level strike, all of the campuses in Nepal were involved in the strike. The strike lasted for 4 months with more or less similar demands.

In the Year 1976-77

In the year 1976-77, student unrest was recorded in 7 different campuses. The numbers of demand were central level 1, institute level 7 and campus level 6. The central level demand was related to the abolition of the comprehensive examination. Provision of trained and experienced teachers and continuation of scholarships to students from remote areas even if they fails characterized the institute level demand. In the more or less similar fashion the campus level demand highlighted the need for timely result, selection of questions from within evaluation. In Balmiki Campus, Kathmandu, the students showed dissatisfaction over the insufficiency of the vegetables served in the hostel mess. To fulfil this demand the amount of allowance was increased. In Kritipur Campus also there was a students unrest due to the dissatisfaction in the hostel mess. Later the hostel mess was properly organized. In Ratna Rajya Laxmi Campus, Kathmandu the students who were not admitted showed dissatisfaction and went on a strike in the same year. The main strike in the year 1976-77 was the strike at Sanothimi Campus, which was mainly concerned with the academic improvement and welfare of the students. Due to the conflicts among the students of two groups, strike were welfare of the students. Due to the conflicts among the students of two groups, strike were recorded in Thakurram Campus, Birganj and R.R. Campus, Janakpur. Similarly in Shanker Dev Campus students went on strike with the academic and physical demands.

In the Year 1977-78

In the year 1977-78, the student's unrest was recorded in 7 different campuses. The strike of Mahrajgunj Campus was notewrorthly. In that strike there were 2 central level demands, 3 institute level demands and 15 campus level demands. The institute level demands include increament in the amount of scholarship, reduction in semester fees and payment of scholarship in advance. The campus level demands, consisted of hostel facility to the students of the first semester, clinic facility, sports facility, improvement in cafeteria, transport and library, that was a strike in Mahottari Campus for the improvement in the quality of the food served in the hostel mess. In Sanothimi Campus, there was a strike arising out of a volley ball competition. The other participant campuses protested that one of the player was not a regular student. Similarly in Janta Campus, Dang, there was a strike relating to sports. In Hetauda, the students of forestry were involved in strike for the administrative status in service equivalent to other certificate level. Similarly in engineering campus also there was a strike demanding uniform facility to the students. In Mahabaudha Nursing Campus also there was a strike for an increment in the amount of the stipend.

In the Year 1978-79

In this year no strike was recorded except one in Pokhara. The main demand of that strike was regarding the smooth running of the hostel mess.

In the Year 1979-80

The students' agitation in 1979-80 was one of the greatest student movement in Nepal. The movement was started with a simple issue of beating of the students by the police who took part in a peaceful protest demonstration over the execution of Mr. Bhutto in Pakistan. The movement was started by the students of Kirtipur multiple campus, and it affected all the campuses in the country within 15 days.

All of the campuses were closed for indifinite period and led to many adhoc decisions on the part of the authority. It violently challenged the political system of the country as well.

This movement continued for 4 months and paved the way for referendum to decide on the political system. Hence, this movement should be considered as the fruitful one. In this strike there were 24 demands, of which 7 of central level, 2 of institute level and 2 of campus level were noteworthy. Besides these 24 demands, there were also demand put forth by the students of different campuses of the country. Out of these 24, important demands were the thesis for degree student should be made optional, freeship should be provided to 20% students, the students of forestry should get the status of certificate level, provision of fees according to subject for private students, abolition of the limit of 5 years for completing the course etc. Notworthy institute level demands were abolition of pre-requisite course and provision of timely result. The campus level demands included administrative reform library facility, sports, drinking water, health clinic etc.

In the year 1979, the demands of the students covered all the fields, academic, administrative, scholarship, students welfare, and physical facilities. In the academic demands 11 were of the central level, 19 were of institute level and the rest 9 were of the campus level. In the demands related to the TU Administration 3 were of the central level, 5 of institute level and 13 of campus level. Similarly, out of the total demands relating to the physical facilities 1 demand was of the institute level and 27 of campus level.

In Nepal, the role of strikes in the improvement of the existing situation is very important. The students want to have more faciliteis and the university cannot fulfill them as demanded by the students and this leads to confrontation between the university authorities and the students. After the introduction of NESP the university seems to have lost its autonomy. Even simple decisions have to be approved by the outside authorities. This escalates the tension between the students and the university. Most of the strikes seem to have been prolonged because of the distrust and utter neglect meted out by the University authority and the government towards the students community. An environment where both the striking party and the university can co-exist and trust one another will mitigate the need for violent strike and pave the way for the peaceful settlement of the disputes arising between them.

Source: Sorya L. Amatya, Jagadish Agrawal, Krishna P. Pradhan, A Study in the Nature of Student Problem in Tribhuvan University, Tribhuvan University, Rector's Office, Research Division, Kirtipur, 1980.

APPENDIX - XV

Some Views on Present Student Problems

Background:

The present student problem was started on April, 1979 when a few hundred students were badly beaten up by the police as they were marching in a peaceful procession to handover a protest note to Pakistan Embassy. Five students were arrested. April, T.U. students constituted a committee at a meeting held at Kirtipur Campus. A student delegation met a high official at the Zonal Commissioner's Office and wanted to discuss on their two demands of (a) judicial inquiry of *Lathi* charge on students on 24 Chaitra and (b) an immediate release of the five arrested students. As reported, the response from the concerned official was not sympathetic. Later, the students constituted an action committee and decided to go on strike with 24 demands. There were violent clashes between Bidhyarthi Mandal and other students. Tribhuvan University decided to close the campuses for a week. The guardians were notified about the strike and the university requested their co-operation for smooth running of the classes at T.U. Campuses. The university teachers also made an appeal to the students. The Vice-Chancellor issued an appeal to the students to resume the classes and assured them that T.U. is always willing to consider their reasonable academic demands. After a week, classes were reopened, but the students continued to boycott classes. Violent clash between the students and the police occurred at Amrit Campus in April, 1979 and the students were forcefully ejected from Amrit Campus hostel.

The students were notified to vacate all the hostel and the University decided to close all the T.U. Campuses of the Kathmandu valley for an indefinite period. The student strike affected campuses at Biratnagar, Pokhara, Bharatpur and other places. Campuses in Biratnagar, Pokhara and Birgunj had already been closed for an indefinite period. Most of the secondary schools in the Kathmandu Valley also had been affected by the strike.

Research Project:

The Research Project "A Study of the Nature of the Student Problems in T.U. Campuses" was initiated only in the month of Falgun. It took about a month to finalize three sets of questionnaires for campuses, teachers and the students. We have sent questionnaires to 60 campuses. But so far we have received the filled-up questionnaires from 20 campuses which is only 33 percent of the total. We have also completed interviewing the teachers and the students at Mahendra Morang Campus and Bhadrapur Campus. We have interviewed 21 teachers and 65 students at Bhadrapur and Mahendra Morang Campuses. An effort is made here to present preliminary note of our observations. This is to be treated as very tentative.

Tentative Findings:

In the list of objectives of the projects the analysis of the political division is not included and we do not have much information on this particular aspect.

1. It seems that there are a lot of academic, administrative and examination problems which, in our opinion, have not been communicated convincingly to the T.U. Central Office.

2. In response to a question regarding semester examination, it has been said that questions are occasionally out of the syllabus and frequently out of the topics not taught in the classes.
3. In reply to a question regarding curriculum it has been responded that the contents of the courses are frequently changed; the text books are not available in certain courses; and the contents of some of the courses are difficult.
4. In answer to a question regarding administration it has been responded that the changes in regulation are nor sent to the campuses in time, and the information of the change in regulation are not given well in advance to the teachers and the students.
5. More than 65 percent of the students interviewed have expressed that the teaching have been unsatisfactory. Approximately so percent of the students have opined that there are too many examinations and the preparation time given for semester examination is inadequate. About 60 percent of the students have expressed that the National Education System has given unnecessary power to the teachers.
6. More than 70 percent of the teachers interviewed have expressed that frequent changes in regulations and curriculum have caused dissatisfaction among the students. The also think that the information of the changes in T.U. regulation and the curriculum are not given to the teachers and students well in advance.
7. Approximately 60 percent of the teachers have responded that the courses are lengthy and the text books are not available in certain courses.

Observations:

On the basis of these very tentative analyses of the responses from the T.U. campuses, teachers and students, we would like to present here some of our observations.

1. It seems there are quite a number of academic, examination and administrative, problems, such as

unsatisfactory teaching, unavailability of the text books, fre2uent changes in regulation and in the content of the courses. Changes in T.U. regulation and in the content of the courses are not communicated in time to the campuses, teachers and the students.

2. Sadan-wise student organizaitons have been constituted in 12 campuses out of 20 campuses from where we have received the filled up questionnaires. These Sadan-wise student organizations regularly organize social, cultural and recreational activities. But these Sadan-wise student organizations have not done much to air the students' grievances and the general problems of the students to the concerned officials. Students in individual capacity cannot communicate to the concerned official, even their genuine grievances. In such a situation the problems tend to be accumulated and the students remain helpless and frustrated. Students' grievances should have been carefully analyzed and reviewed occasionally; and on the basis of findings, remedial measures could have solved the students' grievances to a considerable extent.
3. In the list of 24 demands there are, of course, a few genuine demands of the students, which need to be sympathetically reconsidered.
4. Rastriya Bidyarthi Mandal is not only creating problems in the T.U. campuses, but is responsible for aggravating the present student's agitation. In our opinion, some sort of controlled students' union should be permitted to be constituted in the campuses. In the absence of the students' union, it creates a vacuum and it becomes difficult to have a dialogue with the students even regarding their genuine demands. In such a situation the students are exploited by the political groups in achieving their political aims.

Source: Sorya L. Amatya, Jagadish Agrawal, Krishna P. Pradhan, A Study in the Nature of Student Problem in Tribhuvan University, Tribhuvan University, Rector's Office, Research Division, Kirtipur, 1980.

Bibliography

Primary Sources

I have made every effort to collect records and information about the activities of the past through interviews with those who had involved themselves in Nepal's democratic movements, and with those who had taken part in the movements during their student life living outside or inside the country. All the unpublished interviews are safe with the writer (the scholar myself).

Mr. Ramhari Sharma, Leader, Nepal Praja Parishad (Kathmandu, Feb., 1996); Mr. Sundar Raj Chalise, Leader Nepali Congress (Kathmandu, Feb., 1996); Mr. Yudu Nath Khanal, Intellectual (Kathmandu, Sept., 1998); Mr. Kanshi Raj Upadhyay, Leader, Nepal Praja Parishad (Kathmandu, Feb., 1997); Mr. Shree Bhadra Sharma, Leader, Nepali Congress (Kathmandu, Jan, 1997), Mr. Ram Hari Joshi, Leader, Nepali Cognress (Kathmandu, April, 1996); Mr. Govinda Prasad Upadhayay, Leader, Nepali Congress (Kathmandu: April, 1996), Mr. Chandra Shekhar Shrestha, Leader, Nepal Praja Parishad (Lalitpur, March, 1996); Mr. Diwakar Bhaju, Leader, Nepal Praja Parishad (Kathmandu, August, 1997); Mr. Bhuwan Lal Pradhan, Intellectual and Politician (Kathmandu, March, 1997); Mr. Manmohan Adhikary, Leader, Nepal Communist Party (Kathmandu, April, 1997); Mr. Jeewan Lal Satyal, Leader, Nepali Congress (Kathmandu, Oct., 1997); Mr. Chiranjivi P. Rijal, Leader, Nepali Congress (Kathmandu, Feb., 1997); Mr. Ramal Raj Regmi, Leader, Panchayat (Lalitpur, May, 1997); Mr. Rajeswor Devkota, Leader, Panchayat (Kathmandu, March, 1998); Mr. Khada Nanda Sharma, Leader, Nepali Congress (Kathmandu, Feb., 1997); Mr. Padma Shankar Adhikary, Leader, Nepali Congress (Kathmandu, Jan., 1996); Mrs. Shahana Pradhan, Leader, Nepal Communist Party (Kathmandu, July, 1998); Mrs. Shadhana Pradhan, Leader, Nepal Communist Party (Kathmandu, Feb., 1996); Mrs. Kanaklata Shrestha, Leader, Nepal Communist Party (Kathmandu, Sept., 1996); Mrs. Snehalata Shrestha, Leader, Nepal Communist Party (Lalitpur, Sept., 1997); Miss Shanta Shrestha, Leader, Nepal Communist Party (Kathmandu, Nov., 1996);

Mrs. Urmila Gurung, Student Leader, Leftist (Lalitpur, jan., 1997); Mrs. Tula Rana, Student Leader, Leftist (Kathmandu, Aug., 1996); Mrs. Kokila Vaidya, Student Leader, Leftist (Kathmandu, June, 1998); Mr. Shambhu Ram Shrestha, Leader, Nepal Communist Party (Kathmandu, Sept., 1998); Mrs. Shashi Shrestha, Leader, Nepal Communist Party (Kathmandu, Nov., 1997); Mr. Bharat Raj Joshi, Leader, Nepal Communist Party (Lalitpur, Sept., 1998); Mr. Basudev Dhungana, Student Leader, Leftist (Kathmandu, March, 1997); Mr. Ganesh Ballav Pradhan, Student Leader, Rightist (Kathmandu, Feb., 1997); Mr. Krishna Prasad Bhattarai, Leader, Nepali Congress (Kathmandu, April, 1998); Mr. Biswobandhu Thapa, Leader, Panchayat (Kathmandu, April, 1998); Mr. Parasunarayan Chaudhary, Leader, Panchayat (Kathmandu, May, 1998); Mr. Bharat Mani Sharma, Leader, Panchayat (Kathmandu, May, 1997); Mr. Dhanendra Bahadur Singh, Leader, Panchayat (June, 1997), Mr. Keshar Jang Rayamajhi, Leader, Nepal Communist Party (Kathmandu, April, 1997); Mr. Achyut Raj Regmi, Leader, Panchayat (Kathmandu, May, 1997), Mr. Govinda Prasad Lohani, Leader, Nepal Communist Party (Kathmandu, May, 1998); Mr. B.C. Malla, Leader, Nepali Congress (Kathmandu, April, 1996); Mr. Hikmat Singh Bhandary, Leader, Nepal Communist Party (Kathmandu, May, 1997); Mr. Devi Lal Shrestha, Leader, Nepal Communist Party (Kathmandu, Feb., 1997); Mr. Shree Ranga Pathak, Leader, Nepali Congress (Kathmandu, Feb., 1997); Mr. Basu Dev Risal, Leader, Nepali Congress (Lalitpur, Jan, 1996); Mr. Jaya Krishna Panthi, Student Leader, Rightist (Kathmandu, Feb., 1996); Mr. Nutan Thapaliya, Student Leader, Rightist (Kathmandu, Jan., 1996); Miss Jeewan Dangol, Student Leader, Rightist (Kathmandu, Feb., 1997); Mr. Makabul Shah, Student Leader, Leftist (Kathmandu, Aug., 1996); Mr. Marshal Julum Shakya, Student Leader, Rightist (Kathmandu, Aug., 1996); Mr. Janak Man Shrestha, Student Leader, Leftist (Kathmandu, Nov., 1997); Mr. Dambar Bir Thapa, Student Leader, Rightist (Kathmandu, Jan., 1997); Mr. Shambhu P. Acharya, Student Leader, Leftist (Lalitpur, March, 1997); Mr. Maheswor Man Shrestha, Student Leader, Leftist (Kathmandu, Jan., 1996); Mr. Harihar Raj Joshi, Student Leader, Leftist (Lalitpur, Sept., 1996); Mr. Diwakar B. Rana, Student Leader, Leftist (Kathmandu, Sept., 1998); Mr. Mahesh Kumar Upadhaya, Student Leader, Leftist (Lalitpur, Sept., 1998); Mr. Hirannya Lal Shrestha, Leader, Nepal Communist Party (Kathmandu, June, 1997),; Mr. Yagya Prasad Acharya, Student Leader, Leftist (Lalitpur, Nov., 1997); Mr. Arjun Narashing K.C., Leader, Nepali Congress (Kathmandu, July, 1997); Mr. Lila Mani Pokharel, Leader, Nepal Communist Party (Kathmandu, Oct., 1997); Mr. Sharan Bikram Malla, Student Leader, Nepal Communist Party (Kathmandu, Jan., 1996); Mr. Basu Dev Tripathi, student Leader, Sanskrit Chhatra Sang (Kathmandu, Aug., 1997); Mr. Kamal Krishna Joshi, Student Leader,

Nepal Communist Party (Lalitpur, Jan., 1997); Mr. Pradip Giri, Leader, Nepali Congress (Kathmandu, April, 1996); Mr. Kailash Karki, Student Leader, Leftist (Kathmandu, Nov., 1997); Mr. Kamal Chitrakar, Student Leader, Rightist (Kathmandu, Sept., 1998); Mr. Mohan Pokharel, Student Leader, Leftist (Kathmandu, Dec., 1997); Mr. Govinda Bhattarai, Student Leader, Rightist (Kathmandu, Jan., 1997); Mr. Kamal Chitrakar, Student Leader, Rightist (Kathmandu, Sept., 1998); Mr. Mohan Pokharel, Student Leader, Leftist (Kathmandu, Dec., 1997); Mr. Govinda Bhattarai, Student Leader, Rightist (Kathmandu, Jan., 1997); Mr. Govardhan Rana, Student Leader, Rightist (Lalitpur, March, 1997); Mr. Bhim Neupane, Student Leader, Leftist (Kathmandu, Oct., 1997); Mr. Bhim Rawal, Leader, Nepal Communist Party (Kathmandu, Oct., 1997); Mr. Tanka Karki, Leader, Nepal Communist Party (Kathmandu, Nov., 1996); Mr. Bimalendra Nidhi, Leader, Nepali Congress (Kathmandu, Dec., 1997); Mr. Surya Lal Amatya, Intellectual (Lalitpur, Jan., 1997); Mr. Sher Bahadur Deuba, Leader, Nepali Cogrgess (Kathmandu, Feb., 1997); Mr. Bipin Koirala, Leader, Nepali Congress (Kathmandu, Nov., 1997); Mr. Ram Chandra Paudel, Leader, Nepali Congress (Kathmandu, July, 1998); Mr. Bijaya Kumar Gachayadar, Leader, Nepali Cognress (Kathmandu, March, 1997); Mr. Ram Sharan Mahat, Leader, Nepali Cogrgess (Kathmandu, March, 1997); Mr. Tika Pokharel, Student Leader, Rightist (Kathmandu, Nov., 1998); Mr. Shankar Pokharel, Leader, Nepal Communist Party (Kathmandu, Aug., 1997); Mr. N.P. Saud, Leader, Nepali Congress (Kathmandu, Dec., 1997); Mr. Hiradayas Tripathi, Leader, Nepal Sadbhavana Party (Kathmandu, April, 1997); Mr. Lok Raj Baral, Student Leader, Rightist (Kathmandu, April, 1997); Mr. Janardan Acharya, Student Leader, Leftist (Kathmandu, Jan., 1997); Mr. Pitambar Dahal, Student Leader, Rightist (Kathmandu, Aug., 1997); Mr. Yogesh Bhattarai, Student Leader, Leftist (Kathmandu, Oct., 1997); Mr. Kapil Shrestha, Intellectual (Kathmandu, Oct., 1997); Mr. Padam thakurathi, Leader, Panchayat (Kathmandu, Jan, 1997); Mr. Chuda Raj Upreti, Intellectual (Kathmandu, April, 1997); Mr. Mohan Chandra Adhikari, Leader, Nepal communist Party (Kathmandu, Sept., 1997); Mr. Viswo Kanta Mainali, Student Leader, Leftist (Kathmandu, May, 1997); Mr. Mukunda B. Shrestha, Student Leader, Leftist (Kathmandu, March, 1996); Mr. Barta Raj Acharya, Student Leader, Rightist (Kathmandu, May, 1997); Mr. Nawa Raj Kattel, Student Leader, Rightist (Kathmandu, May, 1997); Mr. Arbinda Rimal, Student Leader, Leftist (Kathmandu, Aug., 1998); Mr. Shiddhi Lal Singh, Leader, Nepal Communist Party (Lalitpur, Jan., 1996); Mr. Arun Nepal, Stduent Leader, Leftist (Kathmandu, June, 1998); Mr. Gokarna Bista, Leader, Nepal Communist Party (Kathmandu, May, 1996); mr. Bachaspati Devkota, Leader, Nepal Communist Party (Kathmandu, July, 1997); Mr. Rabindra Adhikari, Student Leader, Leftist (Kathmandu,

May, 1996); Mr. Bala Bdr. K.C., Leader, Nepali Congress (Kathmandu, July, 1997); Mr. Navin Prakash Jung Shah, Student Leader, Rightist (Kathmandu, July, 1997); Mr. Prithucharan vaidya, Student Leader, Leftist (Bhaktapur, Feb., 1996); Mr. Naryan Man Bijukchhe (Rohit), Nepal Workers' and Peasants' Party (Bhaktapur, Aug., 1997); Mr. Jeet Bdr. Arjel, Leader, Panchayat (Kathmandu, Nov., 1997); Mr. Niranjan Thapa, Leader, Panchayat (Kathmandu, March, 1998); Mr. Mohamad Mohishim, Leader, Panchayat (Kathmandu, March, 1998); Mr. Bishnu Bdr. Manandhar, Leader, Nepal Communist Party (Kathmandu, Sept., 1997); Mr. Sunil Manandhar, Student Leader, Leftist (Kathmandu, Sept., 1997); Mr. Pruna man Shrestha, Student Leader, Leftist (Kathmandu, Oct., 1997); Mr. Dinesh Tripathi, Student Leader, Rightist (Lalitpur, Nov., 1998); Mr. Yagya Prasad Adhikari, Student Leader, Rightist (Kirtipur, Dec., 1998); Mr. Gyanendra Karki, Student Leader Rightist (Kathmandu, March, 1998); Mr. Kausal Raj Regmi, Student Leader, Rightist (Kathmandu, Jan., 1997); Mr. Barana Bdr. Karki, Student Leader, Leftist (Kathmandu, June, 1996); Mr. Laxman Rajbanshi, Student Leader, Leftist (Kathmandu, Jan., 1996); Mr. Iswor Baral, Student Leader, Rightist (Kathmandu, Sept., 1996); Mr. Binod Bhattarai, Student Leader, Rightist (Kathmandu, July, 1996); Mr. Devendra Raj Upadhayaya, Student Leader, Rightist (Lalitpur, Jan., 1996); Mr. Dhuswa Sayami, Writer (Kathmandu, Aug., 1997); Mr. Devi Pd. Kisan, Writer (Kathmandu, Aug., 1997); Mr. Nilambar Acharya, Leader, Nepal Communist Party (Kathmandu, Dec., 1996); Mr. Rishikesh Shah, Intellectual and Politician (Kathmandu, Feb., 1997); Mr. Daman Dhungana, Leader, Nepali Congress (Kathmandu, Feb., 1997); Mr. Nawa Raj Subedi, Leader, Panchayat (Kathmandu, March, 1997); Mr. Laxmi Bdr. Haluwai, Student Leader, Leftist (Kathmandu, Jan., 1997); Mr. Ram Narayan Shrestha, Student Leader, Rightist (Kathmandu, Feb., 1998); Mr. Chakra Pd. Bastola, Leader, Nepali Congress (Kathmandu, Nov., 1997); Mr. Kumar Mani Acharya Dixit, Leader, Nepali Congress (Kathmandu, July, 1997); Mr. Jeetendra Dev, Student Leader, Leftist (Kathmandu, Nov., 1997); Mrs. Gauri Rana, Student Leader, Rightist (Kathmandu, Dec., 1997); Mr. Dil Nath Giri, Student Leader, Leftist (Kathmandu, Aug., 1997); Miss Shama Sahi, Student Leader, Rightist (Kathmandu, Aug., 1997); Mr. Nirmal Kumar Aryal, Student Leader, Leftist (Kathmandu, Jan., 1996); Mr. Ram Nath Dhakal, Leader, nepal Communist Party (Kathmandu, Jan., 1996); Mr. Ambir Pandey, Student Leader, Rightist (Kathmandu, Sept., 1997); Mr. P.L. Singh, Leader, Nepali Congress (Kathmandu, April, 1996); Mr. Navindra Raj Joshi, Leader, Nepali Congress (Kathmandu, April, 1996); Mr. Bal Mukunda Kharel, Student Leader, Leftist (Kathmandu, Dec., 1997); Mr. Keshav Khatiwada, Student Leader, Rightist (Kathmandu, June, 1997); Mr. Chiranjeevi Wagle, Leader, Nepal Congress (Kathmandu,

April, 1998); Mr. Devendra Bahadur Nepali, Student Leader, Rightist (Kathmandu, Dec., 1998); Mr. Yog Pd. Upadya, Leader, Nepali Congress (Lalitpur, Aug., 1997); Mr. Ganesh Raj Sharma, Advocate (Katmandu, Nov., 1997); Mrs. Krishneswari Panta, Widow of Late Bhavadev Panta (Kathmandu, May, 1996); Mr. Harihar Adhikari, Student Leader, Rightist (Kathmandu, Oct., 1996); Mr. Prem Kasaju, Student Leader, Rightist (Kathmandu, Jan., 1997); Mr. Govinda Malla, Leader, Nepali Congress (Kathmandu, Jan., 1997); Mr. K.B. Gurung, Leader, Nepali Congress (Kathmandu, July, 1998); Mr. Babu Ram Bhattarai, Leader, Nepl Communist Party (Kathmandu, July, 1998); Mr. Babu Ram Bhattarai, Leader, Nepal Communist Party (Kathmandu, Aug., 1996); Mr. Trailokya Nath Uprety, Intellectual (Kathmandu, Sept., 1997); Mr. Sarbagya Bhakta Malla, Student Leader, Reightist (Kathmandu, Oct., 1997); Mr. Bhuwan Man Singh Rajbhandari, Student Leader, Leftist (Kathmandu, July, 1997); Mr. Durga Pd. Bhandari, Intellectual (Kathmandu, June, 1997); Mr. Krishna Pd. Panta, Student Leader, Rightist (Kathmandu, Feb., 1997); Mr. Bhakta Govinda Shrestha, Leader, Nepali Congress (Kathmandu, Feb.1997); Mr. Raghu Panta, Leader, Nepal Communist Party (Kathmandu, March, 1998); Mr. Abhi Subedi, Intellectual (Kathmandu, Jan., 1997); Mr. Basanta Subedi, Student Leader, Leftist (Kathmandu, Jan., 1997); Mr. Govinda Man Srhestha, Student Leader, Leftist (Kathmandu, June, 1997); Mr. Ballav Mani Dahal, Intellectual (Kathmandu, June, 1997); Mrs. Kamala Panta, Leader, Nepali Congress (Kathmandu, Jan., 1996); Mr. Tulasi Bhattarai, Student Leader, Rightist (Kathmandu, Nov., 1996); Mr. Tirtha Ratna Bajracharya, Intellectual (Kathmandu, Sept., 1996); Mr. Guna Dev Bhattarai, Intellectual (Lalitpur, Oct., 1997); Mr. Him Bdr. Chhetri, Student Leader, Leftist (Kathmandu, May, 1996); Mr. Hemanta Bdr. B.C., Leader, Nepal Communist Party (Kathmandu, March, 1996); Mr. Prabhat Dixit, Leader, Nepal Communist Party (Kathmandu, April, 1998); Mr. Bharat Lal Shrestha, Leader, Nepal Communist Party (Kathmandu, July, 1997); Mr. Jhala Nath Khanal, Leader, Nepal Communist Party (Kathmandu, Aug., 1997); Mr. Baikuntha Pd. Lakaul, Intellectual (Lalitpur, Dec., 1998); Mr. Dinesh Nath Gangol, Student Leader, Leftist (Kathmandu, Jan., 1997); Miss Narayan Devi Shrestha, Student Leader, Rightist (Kathmandu, Feb., 1997); Mr. Hari Neupane, Student Leader, Rightist (Kathmandu, March, 1998); Mr. Krishna Pd. Pradhan, Intellectual (Kathmandu, May, 1997); Mr. Jagadish Agrawal, Intellectual (Kathmandu, Oct., 1997); Mr. Gopal Regmi, Student Leader, Rightist (Kathmandu, Dec., 1996); Mrs. Sarojani Manandhar, Student Leader, Rightist (Kathmandu, March, 1997); Mrs. Prava Shrestha, Student Leader, Rightist (Kathmandu, Nov., 1998); Mr. Madan Mani Dixit, Leader, Nepal Communist Party (Kathmandu, Sept., 1998); Mr. Gauri Bhakta Pradhan, Leader, Nepal Communist Party (Kathmandu,

July, 1996); Mr. Ganesh Man Singh, Leader, Nepali Congress (Kathmandu, Jan., 1996); Mr. Chetan Nath Sharma, Leader, Nepali Congress (Kathmandu, Nov., 1996).

Secondary Sources

Books in English

Acharya, Madhu Raman, *Nepal Encyclopedia,* Kathmandu: Nepal Encyclopedia Foundation, 1994.

Adhikary, K.R., "The Fruits of Panchayat Development," *Himalayan Research Bulletin,* Vol. 15, No. 2, 1995.

Altabach, P.C. (ed.), *Turmoil and Transition: Higher Education and Student Politics in India,* Bombay: Lalvani Publishing House, 1968.

----------, *The Student Revolution: A Global Analysis,* Lalvani Publishing House, 1970 A.D.

Amatya, Soorya L. Jagadasih Agrawal & Krishna Pd. Pradhan, "A Study of Student- Problem in Tribhuvan University," *TU Journal,* Kirtipur: Rector Office, Research Division, T.U., 1980, p. 3.

Apter, David, *The Politics of Modernization,* Chicago: University of Chicago, University Press, 1965.

Baral, Lok Raj, *Nepal's Politics of Referendum,* Delhi: Vikas Publishing house, 1983.

----------, *Oppositional Politics in Nepal,* Nepal Delhi: Abhinav Publishing, 1977.

Baum, Richard, *The Road to Tiananmen: Chinese Politics in the 1980s In Roderick Mac Farquhar (ed.), The Politics of China 1949-1989,* Cambridge: Cambridge University Press, 1993.

Beer, Samuel H., *Modern Political Development,* New York: Random House, 1974.

Bhattachrajee, G.P., *India and Politics of Modern Nepal,* Calcutta: The Minerva Associates, 1970.

Black, C.E., *The Dynamaics of Modernization,* New York: Harper and Row, 1966.

Brinton, Crane, *The Anatomy of Revolution*, New York: Prentic Hill, 1952.

Chandra, Prabadh, *Student Movement in India*, Lahore: 1938.

Chhaterjee, Bhola, *A Study of Recent Nepalese Politics*, Calcutta: World Press, 1967.

----------, *Nepal's Experiments with Democracy*, New Delhi: Ankur, 1977.

----------, *Palace, People and politics*, New Delhi: Ankur, 1980.

Chaturvedi, S.K., *Nepal-Internal Politics and its Constitutions*, New Delhi: Inter-India Publication, 1993.

Chauhan, R.S., *The Political Development in Nepal, 1950-1970*, (Conflict Between Tradition and Modernity), New Delhi: Associated Publishing House, 1971.

David, Apter and Harry Eskstien, *Comparative Politics*, Surjeet Publication, 1996.

Dharam Vir, *Education and Polity in Nepal*, New Delhi: Northern Book Centre, 1988.

Dinkar Sakrikar, *A History of the Student Movement in India*, (type written Manuscript), New Delhi: 1946.

Emmerson, Doko (ed.), *Student and Politics in Developing Nations*, London: Pall Mall Press, p. 19.

Gaige, Frederick, *Regionalism and National Unity in Nepal*, Delhi: Vikash Publication, 1975.

Gupta, Anirudha, *Politics in Nepal*, Delhi: Kalinga Publications, 1993 (Re-print).

Hans Dall, *The Logical Development of the Student Movement*, Leideu, 1963.

Harry, Schumer and Robert Stanfield, *Assessment of Student Role Orientations in College*, Washington D.C.: 1966.

Hoftun, Martin, et al., *People, Politics and Ideology: Democracy and Social Change in Nepal*, Kathmandu: Mandala Book Point, 1999.

Howes, H. & C.A. Paker, *A Survey of Student Services in Indian Higher Education*, New Delhi: USEFI, 1972.

Hradagh, J., *The New French Revolution,* NY: Secber and Warburg, 1968.

Johari, J.C., *Principles of Modern Political Science,* New Delhi: 1989.

Joshi, Bhuvan L. & Leo E. Rose, *Democratic Innovations in Nepal, Berkely: University of California Press, 1966.*

K.C., Keshar Bahadur, Nepal After Revoltuion, Kathmandu: Sharada Prakashan, 1975.

Koirala, B.P., "Manifesto of the Nepali Congress, 1950," *Reproduced by Rashtra Pukar Weekly,* (Oct./Nov., 1982)

Lohani, Shreedhar, Rmeshwar Adhikary & Abhi Subedi, *The Heritage of Words,* Kathmandu: Ekta Books Distributors Pvt. Ltd., 1998.

Louise, Brown, T., *The Challenge to Democracy in Nepal: A Political History,* London: Routledge, 1996.

Mannen, G. Van, *The International Student Movement,* The Hague, 1966.

Muni, S.D., *Foreign Policy of Nepal,* Delhi: National Publishing House, 1973.

National Education Planning Commission, *Education in Nepal,* Kathmandu: College of Education, 1956.

Nickson, R. Andrew, "Democratization and the Growth of Communism in Nepal: A Peruvian Scenario in the Making?" *Journal of Commonwealth and Comparative Politics,* Vol. 30, No. 3, 1992.

Ole, Borre et al., *Nepalese Political Behaviour,* New Delhi: Aarhus University Press, 1994.

Parmananda, *The Nepali Congress Since its Inception,* Delhi: B.R. Publishing Corporation, 1982.

Peterson, Richard E., *The Scope of Organized Student Protest in 1964-65,* Princeton: 1966.

Pradhan, Bishwa, *Panchayat Democracy in Nepal,* New Delhi: Rakesh Press, 1963.

Raeper, William & Martin Hoftun, *Spring Awakening,* New Delhi: Viking, 1992.

Reddy, M. Muni, *The Student Movement in India,* Lucknow: 1947.

Regmi, D.R., *The Nepali Democratic Struggle,* Varanasi: Nepali National Congress, 1948.

----------, *A Century of Family Autocracy in Nepal,* Varanasi: Nepali National Congress, 1950.

Rose, Leo E., *Communism Under High Atmospheric Condition: The Party in Nepal, in Scalapino* (ed.), *Comparative Communism in Asia,* New York: Prentice Hall, 1965.

---------, *Nepal: Government and Politics,* New Haven: Human Relations Area Files, 1956.

--------, *England, India, Nepal, Tibet, China, 1765-1958,* Berkeley: University of California Press, 1959.

--------, *Nepal: Strategy for Survival,* Berkeley: University of California Press, 1971.

Rose, Leo E. & Fisher Margaret W., *The Politics of Nepal: Persistence and Change in an Asian Monarchy,* Ithaca: Cornell University Press, 1970.

Seale, P. & Mc. Conville, M., *French Revolution, 1968,* New York: Heinemann and Penguin Books, 1968.

Shah, Rishikesh, *Nepali Politics: Retrospect and Prospect,* 2nd ed., Delhi: Oxford University Press, 1978.

----------, *Politics in Nepal,* New Delhi: Manohar, 1993.

Shrestha, Kedar N., *Educational Experiments in Nepal,* Kathmandu: Tribhuvan University, Institution of Education, 1982.

Singhri, L.M. (ed.), *Yough Unrest: Conflict of Generations* (publish under the auspices of the Institute of Constitutional and Parliamentary Studies, New Delhi), New Delhi: 1975.

Tribhuvan Nath, *The Nepalese Dilemma,* New Delhi: Sterling Publishers, 1975.

Tuladhar, Tirtha R., *Partyless Democracy: Its Basis and Background,* Kathmandu: Royal Palace Secretariat, 1962.

Uprety, Prem R., *Nepal: A Small Nation in the Vortex of International Conflicts,* Nepal, 1984.

--------, *Political Awakening in Nepal,* New Delhi: Commonwealth Publishers, 1992.

--------, *Political Instability in Nepal: Impact on Nepali Democracy,* Chandra Bikram Budathoki (ed.), Kirtipur: Central Department of history, T.U., 1999.

Vaidya, T.R. & B.R. Bajracharya, *Nepal Government and Party Politics,* New Delhi: Anmol Publications, 1996.

Varshney, Ashutosh, *Democracy, Development and Countryside,* London: Cambridge University Press, 1996.

Verma, Yugeshwar P., *Nepal: Progress and Problems 1972-80,* Mahottary: Printibha Verma, Dhobauli, Jaleshwar, 1981.

Walker Richard, *Student, Intellectuals and the Chinese Revolution,* New York: 1963.

Articles in English

Bhatta, D.B., "An Academic and Administrative Frame of the Institutes," A working paper, presented at the national Conference of Higher Education, held in December, 1971.

Giri, M.K., "Tribhuvan University Services," Student Services Review, New Delhi: USEFI, 6:1, 1971.

Malla, K.P., "The National Education Plan: Some Problems of Implementation in Higher Education," *Vashuda,* XV:8, 1975.

Manandhar, T.B. "Man Power and Education: A Survey," in M. Mohasin and P. Kasaju (eds.), *Educational in Nepal,* Kathamdnu: National Education Committee, 1974.

Shrestha, K.N., "A Study of the Problems of Improvement of Instruction: Views of Campus Cheifs," *Education and Development,* Special issue of Higher Education, Kathmandu: National Education Committee, 1978.

Singh, G.R., "Students Problems in Nepal," *Education Quarterly,* XV: 1 and 2, 1971.

Wedge, B., "The Case Study of Students Political Violence: Brazil, 1964 and the Dominican Republic, 1965" *world Politics,* XXI, 1969.

Reports and Public Documents in English

H.M.G. of Nepal, Ministry of Education, 1971, National Education System Plan for 1971-76, Kathmandu.

Kamal P. Malla, *The Role of the Rector,* Tribhuvan University, Kathmandu: 1979 (Mimeo).

National Education Committee, 1989, Full Evaluation of NESP (Mimeo).

Pasricha, P. (ed.), 1967, *Student Service Review,* New Delhi: USEFI, 2: May and 1: 2 Nov.

---------, 1969, *Student Services Review,* New Delhi: USEFI, 3: 2 and 4: 1 Nov.

Student Service Board, University of Jedhpur, 1970, Student Advising, Proceedings of the Seminar held in Collaboration wit the USEFI, Sept, 26 to Sept. 30, 1970, Jodhpur.

The United States Education Foundation in India 1965, Student Services Manual, A Guide for Teachers Counselors and Administrators, Delhi.

Reports and Public Documents in Nepali

Tribhuvan University, 1976, T.U. Bulletin 4-5.

Tribhuvan University 1976, T.U. Niyamharu (rules and regulations) with amendment upped 1975 A.D., Kathmandu.

Tribhuvan University, n.d., Tribhuvan Bishwabidhyalaya Biniyamharoo (Tribhuvan University rules and regulations) with amendment upped 1979, Kathmandu.

Tribhuvan Multiple Campus, 1977, Alok, Special Issue, Published on the silver Jubilee University of the Campus, Palpa, Nepal.

Books in Nepali

Adhikari, Suryamani, *Nepal ma Prajatantrik Andolan ko Itihas* (Demcoratice Movement of Nepal), New Delhi: 1998.

Brihat Nepali Sabdakos (Nepali Comprehensive Dictionary), Kathmandu: Royal Nepal Academy, 1983.

Bhandari, Dhundiraj, *Nepal ko Aitihassik Vivechana* (Historical Analysis of Nepal), Banaras: 2014 V.S. (1958).

Bhattarai, Hariraj (ed.), *Chandradhar Upreti Smritee Grantha* (Memorandum of Chandradhar Upreti), Kathmandu: 2044 V.S. (1987/88).

Chalise, Pushparaj, *Nepal ko Prajantantrik Andolanma Bhaktapur ko Bhumika* (The Role of Bhaktapur in the Democratic Movement in Nepal), Kathmandu: K.L. Uday, 2051 V.S. (1994/5).

Devkota, Grishma Bahadur, *Nepal Ko Rajnaitaik Darpan: Pahilo Bhag* (Political Mirror of Nepal, Part I), 3rd ed., Kathmandu: Dhurva Bahadur Devkota, 1979.

----------, *Nepal ko Rajnaitik Darpan: Dosro Bhag, Am Nirvachan ra Tyspachi* (Political Mirror of Nepal: Part 2, The General Election on After) 2nd ed., Kathmandu: Arjun Bahadur Devkota, 1980.

---------, *Nepal ko Rajnaitik Darpan: Tesro Bhag, Panchayat Byabastha ko Pradurbhab* (Political Mirror of Nepal, Part 3, Emergence of the Panchayat System), Kathmandu: Upendra Bahadur Devkota, 1983.

---------, *Nepal ko Rajnaitik Darpan: Janmat Sangrah ra Tyspachi* (Political Mirror of Nepal: The Referendum and After), Kathmandu: Umesh Bahadur Devkota, 1983.

Dhakal, Dhanendra Purush, *Jan-Andolan: 2046* (People's Movement, 1990), Lalitpur: Bhupendra Purush Dhakal, 2049 V.S. (1992/3).

Gautam, Rajesh, *Nepal ko Prajatantrik Andolan ma Nepal Prajaparishad ko Bhumika* (The Role of Nepal Praja Parishad in the Nepalese Democratic Movement), Kathmandu: the author, 2046 V.S. (1989/90).

Giri, Pradip, *Nepali Congress ko Sankshipta Itihas* (An Abridged History of Nepali Congress), Banaras: 1974.

Joshi, Ram Hari, *Nepal ko November Kranti* (November Movement of Nepal), Kathmandu: Antarrastriya Manch, 2048 V.S. (1991/92).

Manandhar, Tri Ratna, Niranjan Sharma, *Audhnik Nepal ko Rajnitik Itihas* (Political History of Modern Nepal), Lalitpur: Research Center for Nepal and Asian Studies 2053 V.S. (1996).

Pradhan, Bhuwan Lal, *Durbar High School: Samchhipta Jhalak* (Mirror of Nepal Darbar High School) Kathmandu: Rumu Prakashan, 2052 V.S. (1995/96).

----------, *Nepal ko Jana Kranti 2007* (Democratic movement of 1950), Kathmandu: 2047 V.S. (1990/91).

Pandey, Bhim Bahadur, *Tes Bakhat ko Nepal* (The then Nepal), Vol. 1, Lalitpur: Research Center for Nepal and Asian Studies, 2039 91982).

Paudel, Bhupahari, *Aitihasik Makai Parba* (Historical Meizan Massacre), Kathmandu: 2040 V.S. (1993/94).

---------, *Sanskrit Chhatrabas ko Itihasik Samargi* (Historical Matters of the Sanskrit Student Hostel), Kathmandu; 2048 B.S. (1991).

Paudel, Ram Chandra, *Ne Wi Sang Ko Itihas* (History of NSU), Kathmandu: 2040 V.S. (1983/84).

Rana, Gobardhan, *Prajatantrik Andolan ma Nepal Bidhyarthi Sangha* (The Nepal Students' Federation in the Democratic Movement), Kathmandu: Nepal Students' Federation Western Zones Coordination Committee, 1994.

Rawal, Bhim, *Nepal ma Samyabadi Andolan- Pdbav ra Bikas* (The Communist Movement in Nepal- Rise and Development), Kathmandu: Pairavi Prakashan, 2047 V.S. (1990/91).

Shivakothi, Narayan Prasad, *Jan-Andolan ra Sahidharu* (The People's Movement and the Martyrs), Kathmandu: Bhishma Kariya, 2047 V.S. (1990/91).

Sharma, Jeevaraj, *Nepal ko Rajanitik Chahalpahal* (Nepal's Political Discuss), Gyaneswor: Nepal, 2048 V.S. (1991/92).

Shahid (Martyar), *Published by Madan Asrit Smriti Pratistahan*, (Kuleswor, Kathmandu: 2052 V.S. (1991/92).

Sharma, Shree Bhadra, *Jayatu Sanskritum Andolan: Ak Smaran* (A Memoir of Jayatu Sanskritium), Kathamdnu: 2054 V.S. (1997/1998).

Subedi, Jhalak P., *Nepali Vidyarthi Andolon ko Addha Satabadhi 1997-2047 V.S.* (Half Century of Nepal's Student Movement, 1940-1990), Pokhara: 2048 V.S. (191-92).

Sharma, Balchandra, *Nepal ko Aitihasik Ruprekha* (An Outline of the Hisotyr of Nepal), Banaras: 2012 V.S. (1951).

Sharma, Ramhari (ed.), *Swarna Jayanti Smarika Nepal Praja Parishad* (Golden Jubilee Memorandum of Nepal Praja Parishad), Kathmandu: 2043 V.S. (1986/87).

Tanka Prasad Acharya Smriti Grantha (Memorandum Vol. of Tanka Prasad Acharya), published by Tanka Prasad Acharya Smiriti Partisthan, Kathmandu: 2054 V.S. (1997/98).

Upadhaya, Govinda Prasad, *Nepal ko Prajatantrik Itihas Sandharva* (Context of Nepal's Democratic Movement), Kathmandu: Ratna Pustak Bhandar, 2054 V.S. (1997/98).

Bulletins, Magazines and Others Documents Published by the Student unions in Nepal

ANNFSU (5th), mouth piece

A.N.N.F.S.U. (6th), fourth piece Sangin, 1996, Pokhara.

Arunodaya, Nepali Literature 1963-1990, published by Tindhara Sanskrita Chhatrabas, Kathmandu.

Bulletins, published by Nepal Krantikari Vidyarthi Snag-

Bulletins of Nepal Rastriya Vidyarthi Federation, issue No. 5, 6, 11, 13, 14, 17, 19, 21, 24 and 25.

(i) Documents passed by the 5th National Convention

(ii) Sangharasaka 35 years (1950-85)

(iii) Introduction of Nepal Rastriya Vidyarthi Federation, 1997.

Chatra, published by Nepali Chhatra Sang, Annual Magazines from 1950-60, Banaras.

Chhatra Bani, a Magazine published by Akhil Banaras Nepali Chhatra Sang 1952-59, Annual.

Chhatra Dut, published by Nepali Sanskrit Chhatra Parishad, Baranasi, Annual 1950-60.

Chhatra and Chhatra Batu, published by Sanskrit Pathashala, date not mention.

Daurali, published by the TU Student Union, 1962-69.

Himanchal, published by Himanchal Chhatra Sang, Annual Magazines from 1994-95, Calcutta.

Jayatu Sanskritam, Monthly Magazine, published by Sanskrit Chhatra Sang, Nepal Prakashan, 1960-64.

Mulprabaha, mouth piece of Nepal Prajatishil Vidyarthi Union, issue No. 5-8, no year mentioned.

(i) *Vidyarthi Samachar*, issue No. 11, 16, 17, 18, 19, 20, 21, 22, 24, 25.

(ii) *Vidyarthi Awaj*, issue No. 8, 9, 10, 11, 12, 15.

(iii) *Appeal*, issued by 8th National Conference Preparatory Committee, report and resolutions adopted by 9thy National Conference.

(iv) *Vidyarthi Jagaran*, 1991.

Nepali Chhatra Sang, Annual Magazines, published by Kanshi Hindu University, Nepalese Student, 1950-58a.

(i) *Vidyarthi Bulletins, 1968-90.*

(ii) *Larko*, 1980

(iii) *Dunduvi* (issue No. 1 and 2) 1982-85.

(iv) *Mirmire*, 1983, Minbhawan Campus Unit Committee.

(v) *Awaj*, special issue 1990 4th National Conference preparatory Committee.

Nepali Vidyarthi Andolan Tatha A.N.N.F.S.U. (6th) Sanchhipta Itihas, published by A.N.N.F.S.U. (6th) March, 1997, Kathmandu.

N.S.U.S. mouth piece of Gandaki Chhatra Samiti, all the issues.

Reports and Statues of Different Student Unions in Nepali

Constitutions and Reprot-1990, adopted by 13th National Conference of ANNFSU (6th), 1996 A.D.

Constitution with amendment and adopted by 7th National Conference of Nepal Revolutionary Student Union, 1990 A.D.

Constitution with amendment and adoted by 7th National Conference of Nepal Nationalist Student Federation 1986 A.D.

Different documents and papers published by different TU campus student unions.

Demand papers and manifestos.

Nepal Vidyarthi Sang, 1970, Amended Constitution 1991 A.D.

Other different papers published by different student organization.

Nepali and English News Papers and Magazines

Gorkhapatra Daily, 1901-1990 A.D.

Nepal Press Digest, 1957-1990 A.D.

Nepal Press Report, 1957-1990 A.D.

Kantipur Daily, 1993-1997 A.D.

Matribhumi, Dainik Nepal, Nepal Smachar, Naya Samaj, Samishya, Nepal Gazette, Samaya, Samaj, Nepal Times, Majdur Monthly, Swotantra Samachar, Dainik Nirnaya, New Herald, Nawin Khabar, Asiali Awaj, Pratidwoni Weekly, Nepal Rajapatra, Nepal Bhumi, Hindu, Rising Nepal- 1958-1990 A.D., *Inap Newari Weekly.*

'Tarun' all issues, published by Nepal Tarun Dal, Banaras, India. 'Tarun' papers issues 1 to 9.

The Commonner, 1957-1990 A.D.

The Motherland, 1957-1990 A.D.

Foreign Papers

Aryabarta, Hindi Daily, India, Patna

Dharmayug, Hindi Monthly, New Delhi

Eastern World, Monthly, London

International Studies, Weekly, New Delhi

Janata, Hindi Weekly, India, Patna

Newsweek, Washington D.C.

Nawa Bharat Times, Hindi Daily

Statesman Daily, New Delhi

Times of India, Weekly, New Delhi

Time, Washington D.C.

Other Papers

Garima, Nepali Monthly, Kathmandu

Nawayug, fortnightly, mouth piece of C.P.N. (UML)

Purnima, Nepali quarterly, Kathmandu

Rolamba, Nepali quarterly, Lalitpur

Voice of History, Annual, Kirtipur

Yugbani, Nepali monthly, Banaras

Unpublished Essays and Articles

Arjyal, Nirmal Kumar, "Those Dangerous Days of Student Movement," 1994.

Rimarl, Arbinda Nath, "Historical Aspects of Student Movement," 1995.

Unpublished Dissertation (English)

Budathoki, Chandar Bikram, History of Democratic Movement in Nepal: 1931-1953, unpublished Ph.D. Dissertation, Patna University, 1974 A.D.

M.A. Dissertation (Nepali)

Gautam, Rajesh, "Nepal's a Mission of Rana Period," unpublished Master's Degree Dissertation, History Department, T.U. Nepal, 2037 B.S. (1980).

K.C. Surendra, Nepalma Samyabadi Andolan ko Itihas, 2006-2019 V.S. (The Communist Movement in Nepal, 1949-1962 A.D.), unpublished Ph.D. Dissertation, History Department, T.U., Nepal, 2052 B.S. (1995).

Mahato, Soma Raj, "R ole of Chitwan of the People's Movement of 1990," T.U. Department of history (unpublished), Nepal 2048 B.S. (1992).